D1432605

# Shattered Lives

## Jeff Ingber
## with Joe Connor

*For Alex Berger, Frank Connor, Jim Gezork,*
*Steve Schlag, Harold Sherbourne, and all other*
*victims of terrorism as well as those who protect us*

*History says, Don't hope*
*On this side of the grave,*
*But then, once in a lifetime*
*The longed-for-tidal wave*
*Of justice can rise up*
*And hope and history rhyme.*
                    —Seamus Heaney

# CONTENTS

# Contents

*Tom, Joe, Frank, and Mary Connor circa 1972*

# PREFACE
## *January 2017*

*When they talk of the first terrorism in New York, people*
*often mention the bombing of the World Trade Center in*
*1993. No one says anything about Fraunces Tavern. It's*
*as if it never happened.*

—Mary Connor Tully

IN THE FADING TWILIGHT of his years in office, and
following a tradition whose origins reach back to the
Anglo-Saxon monarchs of the Middle Ages, President
Barack Obama and his Justice Department invoked the
most unfettered of executive powers—the granting of
clemency. The Obama administration would exercise
this prerogative, in the form of a full pardon or, more
simply, a commutation of sentence, for the benefit of
close to two thousand convicted criminals.

Only two grants would be the subject of widespread
criticism. One was the clemency bestowed on Oscar
López Rivera, who had celebrated his seventy-fourth

birthday in January 2017 while serving his thirty-sixth year of incarceration. López Rivera had been labeled by sympathizers as Puerto Rico's most prominent freedom fighter, and compared to Nelson Mandela. The impassioned calls for his release were reflected in parades, demonstrations, and concerts, T-shirts emblazoned with words of support worn by thousands of Puerto Rican youth, various web and Facebook sites, and dozens of petitions containing more than a hundred thousand collective signatories. Those joining in the crusade for López Rivera included the Governor, Governor-elect of Puerto Rico, and Mayor of San Juan, as well as high-ranking U.S. and global politicians and leaders, the United Nation's Special Committee on Decolonization, Nobel laureates, Broadway and Hollywood celebrities, widely-read columnists and editorialists, and noted human rights organizations.

Why then, for years, had one man, supported by a cadre of law enforcement agents, waged a campaign of opposition to the grant of clemency for López Rivera? The answer lies in the past. In the evolution of the United States as a colonial power. The emergence of Fidel Castro's Cuba as a revolutionary force in the Americas. The timeless societal struggles that continue to set fire to our world. And the actions of a group claiming support for Puerto Rican independence known as the "Fuerzas Armadas de Liberación Nacional Puertorriqueña" (Armed Forces of Puerto Rican National Liberation, or "FALN")—the most active domestic terrorist organization in American history.

# CHAPTER 1
## *A Client Lunch*

*I had been to the Tavern many times and thought the food was just mediocre. But I knew that it was a special place for out-of-towners.*

—Bill Newhall

ON FRIDAY, JANUARY 24, 1975, six men sat at a table reviewing several international trade financing transactions in a plush conference room in a four-story corner Italian Renaissance-style building with an impressive marble facade. Located at 23 Wall Street, in the heart of Manhattan's Financial District, the building was so well known as the headquarters of Morgan Guaranty Trust Company that it was deemed unnecessary to mark the exterior with the Morgan name.

One of the attendees was Frank Connor, an Assistant Vice President at Morgan. Thirty-three years old, broad-faced, and stocky, he appeared younger, except for his receding auburn hairline. Seated next to him were his colleagues Bill Newhall and Charlie Murray. Across the table from Frank was Alex Berger of Rohm and Haas, a specialty chemicals manufacturing company based in Philadelphia. The other two Morgan clients were Dave Erskine and his boss, James Gezork, who worked for Scott Paper, also headquartered in Philadelphia and, at the time, the world's largest manufacturer and marketer of sanitary tissue products, with operations in twenty-two countries.

The group was scheduled to have lunch in the Morgan Guaranty dining room. "It had the best food, service, and ambiance in the Wall Street area," recalls Murray. "But Bill Newhall and I screwed up, each thinking that the other had made a reservation. When we finally called upstairs, they didn't have an open table for six."

Around noontime, Murray's secretary hurriedly telephoned nearby restaurants to find one able to accommodate them. She hit pay dirt with Fraunces Tavern, and Murray suggested the men take a quick walk there for lunch. Newhall stayed behind for a few minutes to finish paperwork. "I considered skipping the lunch," he recalls, "but decided that would have been rude."

When the men arrived at the tavern, they were led to a table for five in a corner area of the restaurant's 101 Broad Street annex. Murray informed the host they were a party of six, and the group was moved to an oval table in the back of the restaurant overlooking Broad Street, close to the southwest stairway, which led to the "Anglers Club" on the second floor. That private club, to which luminaries such as Presidents Harding, Hoover, and Eisenhower once belonged, was for "gentlemen anglers," who paid $125 per year for the privilege of reserving tables where they could tell tall fishing tales over lunch. When Newhall finally arrived, he found that his colleagues had saved him a seat at the east end of the table.

Around 1:20 p.m., a man whose shabby trench coat and nervous demeanor suggested that he didn't belong entered the crowded restaurant carrying a gray rectangular duffle bag with black straps that had been carefully packed with ten pounds of dynamite, propane tanks, shrapnel, and a watch altered to serve as a timer. He planned to leave it in the restaurant's first-floor Bissell Room, a large space overseen by a mural painting of colonial Manhattan spread across an entire wall. Chased away by a waiter, the man instead placed the bag in the southwest stairway landing, behind a thin wooden emergency exit door. The bag's side packed with shrapnel faced the dining room.

A member of the Anglers Club noticed the bag as he walked up the stairs. Thinking that someone had carelessly left the bag where it could easily be tripped over, he pushed it aside with his foot, shifting the bomb's impact away from the greater part of the dining room, but into the direction of Frank Connor's table, only eight feet away. This casual act saved the lives of many while irreversibly changing the fate of others, rewriting the history of generations.

# CHAPTER 2
## *Fraunces Tavern*

*Scarce a broadside was ended 'till another began again,*
*By Jove! It was nothing but Fire away Flanagan!*
*Till he drove a round shot through the roof of Sam Francis.*

—Philip Freneau

FRAUNCES TAVERN, AN OPULENT, three-story red-and-yellow brick building located at the southeast corner of Broad and Pearl Streets, was targeted because of its symbolic significance. Much of the early history of New York and the nation revolves around the building, the oldest one in Manhattan. Built in 1719–20 on Manhattan's first landfill as a mansion home, it was purchased in 1762 at auction by Samuel Fraunces and converted into the "Queen's Head" Tavern.

Fraunces was a remarkable figure—patriot, spy, and one of the first restauranteurs on the continent. Believed to have been of mixed race and born in the West Indies, he became a close friend of George Washington and served as Chief Steward for three of Washington's residences.

The Queen's Head Tavern, soon commonly referred to as "Fraunces' Tavern," became a bastion of New York social, economic, and political life. It was there that travelers and locals mingled over ale and spirits, ship cargo was auctioned, letters were exchanged, and clubs like the newly formed New York Chamber of Commerce held meetings. Despite being named for England's Queen Charlotte, the tavern became the favorite secret meeting place of the New York chapter of the Sons of Liberty, a clandestine group that roused popular support for the nascent revolution.

Fraunces Tavern was where the "New York Tea Party" of April 1774 was planned. Angry New Yorkers boarded the British ship HMS *London* and dumped its tea into the harbor. They brought the eighteen emptied chests that held the tea back to the city, where they were used to ignite bonfires in the streets.

In August of the following year, under cover of darkness, a group of American rebels, including twenty-year-old Alexander Hamilton, a student at King's College (now Columbia University), dismantled the British cannons from the artillery on "The Battery" at the tip of lower Manhattan. The patriots then fired on the British warship HMS *Asia*, which retaliated by bombarding the area for hours with cannon fire. The first of its eighteen-pound cannon balls blasted through the roof of Fraunces Tavern.

During the Revolutionary War, New York City was occupied by the British Army. At the Battle of Monmouth, Samuel Fraunces was captured by the British and forced into servitude as a general's cook. At great risk, he took the opportunity to both smuggle food to starving American prisoners of war and to pass on information on British troop movements and strategies overheard while serving dinner. At the end of the war, former slaves congregated at his tavern. If they could prove their military service to the British, they were recorded in the "Book of Negroes" and received certificates of freedom and safe passage.

After the British evacuated Manhattan in November 1783, Washington led a parade of his triumphant troops back into the city and chose the tavern to serve as his headquarters and residence. Most notably, on December 4, 1783, its "Long Room" was the site of Washington's farewell to his military officers over lunch, when he famously uttered, "With a heart full of love and gratitude, I now take leave of you." By 1787, three departments of the new American government—Foreign Affairs, Treasury and War—had leased rooms in the building, where they remained until December 1790, when the new American government moved to Philadelphia.

Fraunces Tavern had served as a focal point during the American battle for independence. Two centuries later, it would become a flash point for a markedly different kind of struggle.

# CHAPTER 3
## *Carnage*

*The person who walked into Fraunces Tavern knew that
when the bomb went off, it was going to kill a lot of people.
Fraunces Tavern was a bustling restaurant in the middle
of Wall Street. That is why he went there. He didn't go
there to protest Puerto Rican independence. He put the
bomb down to kill people. That is all he came there to do.*

—Don Wofford, FBI

SIX MEN SAT AT A TABLE soaking in the ambiance and
camaraderie. None was older than thirty-three. Each was
smart, talented, and successful. Each had an impressive
past and a bright future. Each loved and was loved.

By 1:27 p.m., with the business conversation winding
down, Bill Newhall asked their waitress for the check.
As he reviewed it, Charlie Murray leaned over to Dave
Erskine to bum a cigarette. The speed of a shock wave
is faster than the speed of sound. They never heard the
explosion.

The bomb blast shattered the double-hung windows in the dining room, collapsing the concrete and marble stairway, punching a hole in the hallway floor, and blowing through a wall and out the ceiling. It made missiles of every object in the second-floor dining room, which *The New York Post* described as, "a black chaos of bodies, torn limbs, and demolished furniture." One of the second-floor diners years later testified to Congress that his luncheon companion "literally flew over the table in front of me, and I did what felt like a back flip as my chair flew up in the air … I crawled along the floor to the light I could see through the blown-out windows, hearing the screams of terror and pleas for help … I saw firsthand what dynamite does to human flesh." Edythe Brous, a secretary being treated to a birthday lunch by her boss, Michael Snead, witnessed shrapnel ripping into Snead's throat and nose and his legs being torn open. Joseph Cotogno, a transportation executive, was finishing dessert with a business associate when their table "flew up and hit the ceiling, and bodies started flying over our heads." Robert Morden, the proprietor of Fraunces Tavern, was in the kitchen overseeing the baking of spice bread, a restaurant specialty, when he felt a shockwave and heard a muffled "whoomph," followed a split second later by a blast that sounded "as if the skies were opening."

The entire building rocked, though diners in the Bissell Room were shielded from the worst effects of the blast by thick walls. Deafened and concussed survivors formed a human chain and staggered outside. Others were carried outdoors, only to see equally stunned pass-ersby in whose skins were buried razor-sharp shards of glass. One of the first firemen to arrive, Charles Anderson, was sickened by the sight of blood- and plaster dust-covered men and women writhing in agony, shrieking under piles of rubble, mumbling in shock, or wandering about with blank stares, several with body parts torn off. A motorized ladder known as a "cherry picker" was used to remove several victims from the second floor. As for those lying on the street, firemen initially weren't sure if they were pedestrians or had been blown out of the building.

The blast could be heard throughout lower Manhattan. Its force shattered heavy plate glass doors and windows in a New York Telephone Company building across the street. Next to the telephone company building was a windowless data center, in which Richard Shadick was repairing a mainframe. "All of a sudden, the entire build-ing shook. I had no idea what it was, but the last thing on my mind was terrorism. I assumed it was something like a boiler or gas line exploding."

Hundreds of policemen ultimately would make their way to the scene through the crowded, twisting streets of lower Manhattan, sent in part to help control the thou-sands of voyeurs. The first cops to reach the Tavern were George Toth and Henry Petersen, who had been patrol-ling near City Hall. They were about to grab lunch when the call came over the First Division radio. "Want car for a report of an explosion at Broad Street and Pearl Street in the First Precinct." The dispatcher's voice betrayed urgency. The cops flipped on their emergency lights and siren, with its wail echoing off the buildings. As they drove, their radio was filled with static as multiple calls flooded the frequency. Upon arriving, Petersen shouted into his radio to notify "Citywide" of the carnage. Within minutes, cops and medical personnel swarmed the area.

Of the six men finishing lunch at a table in Fraunces Tavern, one was looking forward to dinner with his family to celebrate his two young boys' birthdays. Another anticipated meeting his pregnant wife at his parents' new apartment in Queens. The lives of those two men ended in a flash, along with two others. More than sixty were injured, with several being forever maimed. All those in and near the restaurant that afternoon would carry the trauma for the rest of their lives.

Later that day, an FALN communiqué announced that the bombing had been committed in the name of the fight for Puerto Rican independence. How could that be? What connection was there between Fraunces Tavern and a tropical island sixteen hundred miles away? The explanation began a half-millennium earlier.

# CHAPTER 4
## *The Occupation of Puerto Rico*

*The American flag has not been planted on foreign soil to acquire more territory, but for humanity's sake.*

—President William McKinley

IN NOVEMBER 1493, on his second voyage to the New World to claim lands for Spain, Christopher Columbus sailed to a verdant, mountainous island located at the crossroads of the Atlantic Ocean and Caribbean Sea, and two continents. Columbus named the island "San Juan Bautista," but it was known to the native Taínos as "Borikén," and to this day, Puerto Ricans refer to each other as "Boricuas."

One of Columbus' lieutenants was Juan Ponce de León, who later established and cruelly ruled the initial Spanish settlement. De León eventually was appointed by the Spanish crown as the first Governor of what he renamed in a baptism ceremony, inclusive of the two smaller islands of Vieques and Culebra, as "Porto Rico."

The native Taínos, who adorned their clothing and bodies with gold found in the island's rivers and streams, were enslaved, plagued with smallpox brought by the Spaniards, and gradually extinguished. They were replaced by slaves from West Africa. During the 17th century, Spain successfully fought off numerous attempts by the Dutch, English, and French to take control of its prized colony that was the most essential military outpost in the New World. Spain's colonization of Puerto Rico would continue for four hundred years.

During the nineteenth century, inspired by liberation movements in Latin America, Puerto Ricans began to push for independence from a weakened Spanish crown. The most significant action, known as "El Grito de Lares (The Cry of Lares)," took place on the night of September 23, 1868. Over a thousand Puerto Ricans traveled to Lares, a small city in the western highland ornamented with Spanish-era style churches, to protest for an independent republic. Brutal suppression by Spanish forces led to more than five hundred arrests and eighty-eight deaths, most of which occurred in prison. A principal leader of El Grito de Lares was Dr. Ramón Emeterio Betances, who had established an alliance with the Cuban Revolutionary Party and built a network of pro-independence supporters within Puerto Rico. Betances also helped develop an abolitionist movement in Puerto Rico, and one of the goals of the uprising was the elimination of slavery, influencing dozens of slaves to join the Lares demonstration alongside their owners.

In the autumn of 1897, in the wake of military defeats during Cuba's war for independence, Spain's Prime Minister issued three decrees, known as the "Carta Autonómica (Charter of Autonomy)," ceding limited independence to the governments of Cuba and Puerto Rico. Pursuant to the Charter, in February 1898, a new government was inaugurated in Puerto Rico with the power to draft laws, establish an independent currency, issue postage stamps, regulate customs and trade, and offer town councils autonomy in local matters. General elections for the new legislature were held the following month.

But progress toward independence halted when the Spanish-American War broke out in late April of that year. The American objective was to seize all Spanish colonies, including its possessions in the Pacific—the Philippines and Guam. By July, the destruction of Spain's Caribbean fleet at the Battle of Santiago de Cuba had secured American control of the Caribbean waterways. General Nelson Miles, Commander of the U.S. Army, received orders to sail for Puerto Rico. A week later, he landed at Guánica on its southwest coast. Miles gave assurances that the U.S. military "did not come to make war upon the people of a country that for centuries has been oppressed but, on the contrary, to bring you protection, not only to yourselves, but to your property, to promote your prosperity, and to bestow upon you the immunities and blessings of the liberal institutions of our Government."

By the middle of August, after meeting with little resistance and many welcoming Puerto Ricans, the island came under American control. On December 10, 1898, the Treaty of Paris was signed. Spain renounced all claims to Cuba and transferred sovereignty over Puerto Rico and its other colonies to the U.S. In turn, it was compensated $20,000,000.

Spain's world empire ended, while America's emerged. After an initial military occupation, the U.S. allowed Cuba conditional independence, including that it be granted a perpetual lease on land that became the naval base at Guantánamo Bay. But because of Puerto Rico's strategic location—it was thought to be critical to the protection of the planned future canal through Central America—the U.S. determined to maintain control over the island. Over the decades, and particularly during World War II, the U.S. developed several military installations in Puerto Rico, among which were the controversial Atlantic Fleet Weapons Training Facility on Vieques Island and the Roosevelt Roads Naval Station in Ceiba, once one of the largest naval facilities in the world.

Puerto Ricans now faced a new overseer, one that they might have expected to be benevolent considering its distinctive democratic tradition and constitutional protections. A country that achieved self-determination only after its own bloody battle for independence.

# CHAPTER 5
## *Colonialism*

*Tax-incentive schemes ... showered U.S. corporations with*
*tax abatements in exchange for low-wage "job creation."*
*These corporations repatriated their profits to the U.S.;*
*none invested in Puerto Rican infrastructure. And when*
*the abatements expired, the corporations abandoned the*
*island, creating a deepening cycle of unemployment and*
*economic dependency.*

—Nelson Denis

SINCE ACQUIRING PUERTO RICO from Spain, the
U.S. has continuously struggled with the type of status to bestow on it. In April 1900, President William
McKinley signed into law the Foraker Act, which established a civilian government but left little room for
true self-rule. The governor, members of the Supreme
Court, and upper house of a bicameral legislature all
were Presidential appointees, and the governor pos-
sessed a right of veto over any law approved by the

legislature. In 1901, Puerto Rico, like the Philippines, was granted a "Resident Commissioner" who was permitted to propose bills and participate in U.S. Congressional debates, but not vote. At first, the Puerto Rican Resident Commissioner was not even allowed on the floor of the House of Representatives. Three years passed before the House ceded to the Commissioner the right to speak to Congress and serve on committees.

This treatment of Puerto Rico differed from Congress' handling of other territories, such as Arizona, Hawaii, New Mexico, and Oklahoma, which were permitted autonomous legislatures. American officials viewed Puerto Ricans as racially inferior and dishonored Puerto Rico's deep-rooted Spanish heritage and distinctive cultural identity by imposing an "Americanization" of the island and its institutions. Puerto Rican Spanish was considered an unintelligible "patois." During the first half of the 20th century, various attempts were made to mandate English as the language of school instruction, even though few teachers on the island themselves spoke English. Rafael Cancel Miranda of Mayagüez, who would later become a famous *independista,* recounts how "in high school [in the 1940s], when they tried to make us all speak English in class, we organized a student strike in defense of our language ... they kicked me out of school for a year."

President McKinley believed in the munificence of American rule. But he blundered in his choice for the first civilian governor of Puerto Rico. Charles Herbert Allen, a former congressman and Assistant Secretary of the Navy (succeeding Theodore Roosevelt), arrived in San Juan in April 1900. Dressed in military regalia, he was announced by a cannon salute and accompanied by the 11th U.S. Infantry Band and a division of armed soldiers. Allen quickly imposed ruinous taxes on farmers, raided the island's treasury, issued no-bid contracts to friendly U.S. businessmen, and created a government bureaucracy staffed largely by American officials.

Allen, who learned the basics of business at an early age while working in his father's Massachusetts lumber company, was particularly focused on the lucrative potential of sugar. Known as "white gold," sugar was insatiably desired by Europeans and Americans in a time when alternatives were not available. Columbus had brought to the New World sugar cane plants from the Canary Islands, and over the centuries, sugar cane plantations sprang up in Puerto Rico, Cuba, and throughout the New World. They were brutal enterprises run like factories because sugar cane must be processed quickly. The cutting of the cane was a backbreaking job performed over long hours under an intense sun and fierce pressure to be productive. After the abolition of slavery in Puerto Rico in 1873, the pay received by plantation workers was minimal and impoverishing.

Allen wrote to McKinley of Puerto Rico's lush soil and available labor pool, and proposed that, "A large acreage of lands, which are now devoted to pasturage, be devoted to the culture of sugar cane." After seventeen months in office and McKinley's assassination, Allen resigned his governorship to join J.P. Morgan & Co., the prominent merchant bank that traced its roots back to John Pierpont Morgan and the banking partnership he formed in 1871 with Philadelphia banker Anthony Drexel. J.P. Morgan was integral to many of the largest global transactions of the time, including, in 1904, the financing of the Panama Canal. Its raising of capital, typically from European investors, for U.S. Steel Corporation, General Electric, International Harvester, and various railroads and seaports helped to transform the United States into an industrial power and New York into the world's leading capital market.

After joining J.P. Morgan, Allen used his dozens of political appointees in Puerto Rico to provide favorable land grants, tax subsidies, water rights, railroad easements, and tariffs for the benefit of a sugar syndicate he would become president of—the American Sugar Refining Company. Later renamed Domino Sugar, it became the largest sugar producer in the world. Sugar came to dominate Puerto Rico's economy, at the expense of native crops such as fruits, vegetables, tobacco, and coffee. (Puerto Rico's beans were widely considered to be among the best in the world, and when the U.S. assumed control of Puerto Rico in 1898, coffee was its principal export.) The plantations were combined into enormous *centrales*, which were held by the American companies that also owned the coastal railroad and San Juan international seaport. Puerto Ricans were forced to import many food items, progressively displacing local farmers.

The influence of American finance on Puerto Rico would be deeply felt for many decades and cast a shadow on debates about independence because, without a sustainable economic life, political standing matters little. Ensuring lasting American economic dominance was the U.S. Merchant Marine Act of 1920, which effectively required all foreign merchandise headed for Puerto Rico first to be off-loaded from the original carrier and reloaded onto a U.S. vessel, greatly increasing American shipping income while inflating costs for Puerto Rican consumers. (The *Wall Street Journal* later labeled the law a "legally sanctioned shakedown for U.S. shipping interests") In July 2016, when the Puerto Rican government defaulted for the first time on its constitutionally guaranteed debt, its Governor, Alejandro Garcia Padilla, declared that the days of Puerto Rico being "a colony of Wall Street" were over. "We are starting the process of putting [Puerto Rico] back in the hands of Puerto Ricans."

After Spain ceded Puerto Rico to the United States, many influential Puerto Ricans believed the American occupation to be a positive development and assumed that Puerto Ricans would become full American citizens. Those who initially held that view included José de Diego, a statesman and politician referred to at the turn of the century by his peers as "The Father of the Puerto Rican Independence Movement." But Allen fought granting U.S. citizenship to Puerto Ricans, and the issue became hotly debated, in part because citizenship enables unfettered entry into the U.S. In 1902, the Treasury Department issued immigration guidelines denying Puerto Ricans the right to immigrate to the U.S. Those guidelines were challenged in the Supreme Court, which in 1904 determined that Puerto Ricans were not "aliens" and could not be denied entry. The court, however, declined to proactively determine that Puerto Ricans were U.S. citizens.

These developments inspired Teddy Roosevelt (who believed that the "white man's burden" applied to Puerto Rico) and other prominent Americans to publicize their support for Puerto Rican citizenship, which arrived in 1917 via the Jones-Shafroth Act, along with Prohibition—*The New York Times* article on the enactment of the statute was entitled, "Porto Rico Bill Signed: Gives Citizenship to Natives and Makes the Dependency 'Dry.'" The law also changed Puerto Rico's status to an organized, but unincorporated, territory. But over the years, it became clear that the citizenship right established by Jones-Shafroth was not intended to be a full grant—which is hugely significant because citizenship means the acquisition of certain rights even above and beyond due process, equal protection, and others provided in the Constitution, such as being able to apply for federal employment and to receive a variety of federal benefits. Rather, it was more of a revocable legislative acknowledgment that Puerto Ricans can freely live anywhere within the U.S. Critics claimed that citizenship was granted primarily to provide the U.S. with an increased conscription pool for World War I. More than 20,000 Puerto Ricans would serve in the U.S. armed forces during that war.

Jones-Shafroth reshaped Puerto Rico's government. It created a bill of rights, which extended many but not all U.S. constitutional rights to Puerto Rico. The statute also authorized the popular election of the Resident Commissioner, previously a Presidential appointee, and the upper legislative house, and granted Puerto Rican bonds triple tax exemption (Puerto Rico's debt is triple-exempt no matter where the purchasing American lives). A century later, this last feature would help lead to an explosion of Puerto Rican debt and a fiscal crisis, the resolution of which is complicated by Puerto Rico not being able to seek either federal bankruptcy protection or aid from the International Monetary Fund as could an independent country.

Another aspect of citizenship is the right to vote. However, under Jones-Shafroth, Puerto Ricans continued to be barred from voting in presidential elections, a state of affairs that remains today, although Puerto Ricans do participate in the Presidential primaries. The flip side of this restriction is that Puerto Ricans generally are exempt from federal personal income tax for work performed on the island—to do otherwise would violate the dearly held American principle of no taxation without representation.

With the legal barriers to migration to the mainland eliminated, including any visa requirement, the Puerto Rican government, during the following decades, encouraged immigration as an antidote to unemployment and poverty. Another impetus, albeit inadvertent, was "Operation Bootstrap," initiated by the U.S. government in 1942. Using direct investment as well as tax exemptions, tariff incentives and the lure of cheap labor, the program was designed to shift the Puerto Rican economy from agrarian-based to industrial. But for various reasons, including cheaper labor in Asia and Latin America and the expiration of tax credits, Operation Bootstrap ultimately failed, as new jobs created in manufacturing did not fully compensate for jobs lost in agriculture.

Hundreds of thousands of Puerto Ricans resettled to urban centers in the continental U.S. The pervasive Puerto Rican influence on New York would become widely memorialized, most notably in *West Side Story*. In the song "America" from that play, and later movie, the difficulty of life in Puerto Rico is teasingly mocked by Puerto Rican girls: "Puerto Rico, my heart's devotion. Let it slip back in the ocean. Always the hurricanes blowing. Always the population growing." (The comedian Freddie Prinze, half Puerto Rican, who grew up in Washington Heights, joked that *West Side Story* "set us back a hundred years … it made people think that all we did was stand in the streets whistling and dancing.")

Two Puerto Ricans who arrived on the mainland separately in 1944 were Juan Sotomayor and Celina Báez. Báez had grown up in a wooden shack in the middle of sugar fields. Her entry into the U.S. came via the Woman's Army Corps during World War II. After Juan and Celina met and married, they lived in a South Bronx housing project, where their first child, Sonia, was born. She would go on to become an Associate Justice of the Supreme Court, and would write in her autobiography, "The Latina in me is an ember that blazes forever."

Millions of others, of course, immigrated to America and nourished it with pride in both their ethnic heritage and adopted country. One was a woman who would live close to a full century, enduring great heartache while keeping her faith in church, family, and America's gifts. She would be among the many profoundly tied to the horror that was the Fraunces Tavern bombing.

# CHAPTER 6
## *Frank Connor*

*Frank was not a family name, nor was it Francis like other
Irish-American children. My father was just Frank. When
she was in her mid-90s, I finally asked Grandma, 'Was
my dad named after Sinatra?' With a sly grin, she replied,
'Now maybe he was.' I wonder if my father even knew that.*

—Joe Connor

MARGARET MARY MALONEY was born in December
1903, during the week the Wright Brothers would demonstrate to the world powered, heavier-than-air flight. Her
family knew nothing of such news, living in remote Leahive
Creggs, a village in County Galway, Ireland. Margaret
grew up in a time and place where the seasons dominated
economic life and the Catholic Church was intertwined
into the fabric of society. She would live long enough to
recount to her grandchildren memories of the Irish War of
Independence, which Margaret would refer to as "gossip."

In October 1924, after processing in Ellis Island,
Margaret arrived in New York City aboard the ship

*Celtic* in search of a "better life," which meant, as she put it, "getting a job." A decade later, Margaret married English-born Thomas Connor, an elevator operator at Radio City two years younger than his bride. Margaret and Tom settled in a fifth-floor apartment in the north Manhattan neighborhood of Washington Heights, on West 171st Street near the newly opened George Washington Bridge and the apartment of her sister Della, brother-in-law Johnny Schlag, and their son, Donald.

At age thirty-seven, Margaret gave birth to her only child, whom she named Frank Thomas. Frank was an unexpected gift, inspiring Margaret to swear that she would never have another unhappy day in her life.

*Margaret (left) and Della Maloney, circa 1925*

*Margaret, Thomas, and Frank Connor, 1945*

*Donald Schlag & Frank Connor, 1948*

Frank, widely described as "happy-go-lucky," was a
son of New York who immersed himself in neighborhood
life and rooted for both the football and baseball Giants,
his dad's favorite teams, who each played at the Polo
Grounds at nearby Coogan's Bluff. Margaret encouraged
his explorations and experiments. Frank and his friends

built zip guns with barrels made from car antennas, rode their English Racer bikes across the GW Bridge and a dozen miles through heavily trafficked roads to Paramus, New Jersey, to swim in its town pool, and even embarked on an impromptu road trip to Daytona Beach, Florida, in a red convertible, a difficult venture in a time before Interstate 95 existed. On Friday nights, Frank's group would walk to the banks of the Hudson River north of the red lighthouse in Fort Washington Park to drink and fish in the dark. As Edward (Buddy) Howe, one of Frank's friends, tells it:

> We were all under eighteen and weren't supposed to be able to buy beer. But we would go to Nat's Grocery on Audubon Avenue, and Paddy Ward, who worked there, would sell us a case of beer for four dollars. He'd leave the case by the back door leading to the basement. Half the time we never even paid for it.

Cousin Donald recounts another story: "Frank must have been about fifteen when he and some other guys bought this boat they kept at the Dyckman Street boat yard on the Harlem River. One day, they let me drive it. Of course, the minute I took the wheel, it locked up, and we were headed straight for the 'Shit Line,' which was a strip of garbage, oil, plastic, and probably bodies in the middle of the river. They saw that the cable from the wheel to the motor was kinked. Someone snapped the cable and killed the motor; then they started it up again and steered it by hand back to the shore in a strong current. Those kids didn't have life jackets or boat licenses, but they were self-sufficient and fearless."

During his years at Bishop Dubois High School, Frank was less than a serious student, with his only strong subject being religion. At his graduation ceremony in June 1959, Frank turned to his cousin and said, "I really didn't think I would ever get a diploma." A day later, Frank found himself on an unexpected track. He became a mail clerk, but not at any ordinary place. Frank Connor's employer was Morgan Guaranty Trust Company, which had been formed that year through the merger of J.P.Morgan & Co. with the Guaranty Trust Company of New York. It was the most prestigious bank in the world.

Frank Connor's mail-clerk position at Morgan Guaranty had been arranged for him by his mother, who worked nights at the bank in the Facilities Department. She was pleased at the arrangement. "Unlike so many of Frank's friends who went into riskier work, my son reached executive status. And so I thought he would be safe from the dangers those other professions brought." Many evenings, Frank would spot his mom arriving for work as he was leaving, and shout out to her. Margaret would make sure to tell her son what was waiting in the stove for him, often a "chop."

Soon after Frank began his first full-time job, he enrolled in night classes at tuition-free City College, located in a striking Gothic Revival-style Harlem campus.

*Frank at his high school graduation*

By the late 1960s, eager for career advancement in an environment in which an Ivy League pedigree was common, Frank dropped out of City College to enroll at Fairleigh Dickinson University in Teaneck, New Jersey. Frank judged that school to be more prestigious, although he soon would refer to it as "Fairly Ridiculous University." But his prime focus remained on work. Frank had morphed into a young man filled with ambition. A colleague, Tom

Mullany, recalls that when Frank would deliver mail to where the officers sat, an area with fine furniture, plush carpeting, elegant chandeliers, and a library-like hush, "he made perfectly clear to the rest of us that's where he eventually would be working." Frank orchestrated his move to the bank's Import Documentation group, which set his career path.

One Saturday night in 1960, Frank and his friends rode the subway to midtown, intending to see an off-Broadway show. Finding that it had been cancelled, they headed to City Center, a dance hall on Manhattan's 55th Street popular with young Irish immigrants. While standing in a circle with his friends, drinking beer and checking out the crowd, Frank spotted a petite, dark-haired woman wearing spiked heels and a tight red dress. He asked her to dance.

Mary Anne Lynch was pleased. "I had noticed Frank earlier. He was so clean looking, nicely dressed in a suit and neatly groomed. Even though he had his back to me, I knew that he would be good looking." By the end of the evening, Frank was smitten. Recounting to his sons his early days of wooing their mom, Frank would say, "She was pretty and didn't talk so much but was a good listener, unlike the B.I.C.s [Bronx Irish Catholics] I was accustomed to being with."

Like Frank's mother, Mary had grown up in rural Ireland—in her case, a farm in County Cavan. "My parents toiled day and night. My dad was always tinkering and fixing his machinery, and he believed that if he cursed long and loud, his old tractor might start." One of ten children, Mary remembers that, "feeding the chickens, gathering eggs, bringing up the cows for milking, and washing pots at the pump that sat outside the front door were only some of our chores." For Mary and her siblings, attending school required a walk of several miles, carrying a "sod" of turf to heat the pot-bellied stove in each of the three classrooms. When not in school or working, the Lynch children roamed the fields and rivers with their dogs, poaching rabbits and fishing in rivers and lakes.

The Church was central to the social lives of the Lynch family. "We both feared it and loved it," remembers Mary, who was a Lynch on both sides. "Going to confession and telling of silly things, like stealing sugar. Fearing going to hell if we were bad, like eating meat on a Friday. On the other hand, it was an escape when we got to go to the 'Stations of the Cross' and to Mass, where we met up with our friends and got to wear our best outfits."

Historians refer to the 1950s in Ireland as the decade of "doom and gloom." Work was scarce for young people, causing hundreds of thousands to flee. Two of them were Mary and her twin brother, Harry. "It took about a year to prepare to leave home," Mary recalls. "Having health checks, going to the American Consulate, forever filling in forms, and waiting."

At age nineteen, Mary and Harry boarded a plane for the first time at Shannon Airport. "I was terrified," Mary remembers. "I prayed and held on to the rosary beads for the entire trip, until we arrived at Idlewild [now JFK Airport] in Queens." Picking them up was their father's sister Julia, whom had never met. Julia had written that she would wear a red rose in her hair. "But we didn't need to see the rose to know she was our aunt. She looked just like a Lynch." Julia drove Mary and Harry to her brick Cape Cod house in Maywood, New Jersey, where they would live. "Not only was I amazed by New York City," recalls Mary, "but also that my aunt was driving the car. We went through the Lincoln Tunnel, and I refused to believe that it was under the Hudson."

Frank was Mary's first "real boyfriend." "To me, he was everything I dreamed of—handsome, kind, and courteous. Even though I knew he was no saint, as he did his share of drinking and fighting and staying away from church, Frank was the most mature guy I ever met for his age. He was sure of himself and what he wanted out of life." Mary also was impressed by Frank's line of work. "I loved the fact that he was a banker, as no way did I want to get involved with a farmer or blue-collar worker. I had seen too much hardship on the farm." But the clincher for Mary was Frank's love for his mother and her for him. "It was honest and true."

While dating Frank, Mary became increasingly comfortable with life in her adopted country. It was the opposite for Harry, who could not adjust to the educational system in the States and soon returned to Ireland. Mary declined her mother's subsequent request to come back. "I had found myself a boyfriend, and I could safely say I was 'in love.' Frank Connor made all the other boys I knew seem puny in comparison."

A year after meeting at City Center, Frank proposed to Mary. "He gave me a pearl ring for an engagement ring. It cost a hundred dollars, which was a lot of money then." They wed in September 1962 in St. Anastasia's Church in Teaneck. Mary was twenty-four years old, which made her three years older than Frank. Wearing a tiara securely attached to her thick, dark hair and a radiant smile "as big as County Cavan," she walked down the aisle in an $80 dress from Rose's Bridal Store, holding on dearly to her uncle, Michael McNamara. "That dress made me feel like Scarlett O'Hara. And I wanted to look beautiful in the pictures I would send to Ireland to my family."

For Mary, it was a bittersweet day, as she had none of her immediate family in attendance. They couldn't afford the trip. "However, we did resolve this by November, during our belated honeymoon to Ireland. My family loved Frank and he them. My father took Frank hunting and told him that if our marriage failed, it would be because of me, as I was a 'wicked little thing.'"

The couple settled down in Mary's "cozy" one-bedroom rental apartment in Teaneck. Frank kept close with his Washington Heights buddies, hosting parties for them on weekends that, Donald Schlag recounts, "inevitably turned into an orgy of beer drinking and furious babble." Even though, through his smarts and

*Mary and Frank on their wedding day*

drive, it became apparent that Frank's path would be far different from theirs, "he never lost touch with the old gang," recalls Donald. "Because, when dealing with others, he always led with his heart."

Mary gave birth to Thomas Martin Connor in January 1964 during a blizzard. Two Januarys later, Joseph Francis, was born. By then, Frank and Mary had purchased a modest Cape Cod brick house in middle-class Fair Lawn, New Jersey, near where Donald Schlag, his wife Pat, and their children Steven, Jean and by 1966, Ellen, lived. Mary was "the happiest girl in the world. There was a euphoria that surrounded me, as if I were a drug addict on a high. But, somehow, I knew that this bliss was not going to last."

Heartache first struck in November 1967, when Grandpop Tom, sixty years old, checked into Columbia Presbyterian Hospital suffering from back pain. Margaret and Frank visited every night. Tom's health began to unravel from decades of chain smoking and hard drinking. He never left the hospital.

Soon after, Mary and Frank's newborn son Martin died from complications from the "RH blood factor." The presence or absence of the blood protein Rh, named for the rhesus monkey in which it was discovered, can lead to severe immune reactions in Rh-positive babies born to Rh-negative mothers. It was not until the late 1960s that a drug treatment for the disease was developed. Until then, the Rh blood factor was a grave health issue, implicated in the deaths or severe disabilities of thousands of babies annually.

*Jean Schlag, Steve Schlag, Joe Connor,*
*Ellen Schlag, and Tom Connor, Catskills, 1970*

Reflecting on the day of Martin's birth, Mary recalls, "Everything happened so fast. I remember seeing his face and thinking he looked just like Tom and Joe. I heard a wheezing sound, and that was the last I remember until I woke up and he was nowhere in sight." One month after losing his father, Frank travelled again to St. Raymond's Cemetery in the Bronx—this time to open his father's grave and bury his baby son beside him.

"For months after Martin died," Mary recalls, "I lay in bed tired or sick, suffering from guilt that somehow God was punishing me." Mary secretly sought the help of a mental health counselor, not even telling Frank. "It was the one dark period in my marriage. I felt I had to deal with it by myself, or I might have been seen as having mental problems, and that was not acceptable. No one, not even Frank, could understand what I was going through." Frank struggled with how to help his wife. "Frank started to take me for rides out in the country," Mary recounts, "and that was the perfect medicine." Meanwhile, Frank kept the family together. "My husband wasn't afforded the luxury of grief. He dutifully went each day to work to pay the bills."

Decades later, Mary wrote a letter to Martin. "Life never turns out like we would like it to, and not having you around has been one of the hardest things to bear. But I can't be greedy and should not complain. For after all, your granddad needed company in Heaven, and what better way to cheer him up than with a grandson!"

Tom and Joe were raised in a neighborhood filled with playgrounds, parks, bike paths, and athletic fields, all of which Frank played and rode with them in. His parenting style was a blend of humor, sarcasm, and directness. "Dad was not a disciplinarian," says Joe, "but he didn't baby us either. He wanted us to know him and what he expected of us. When we were a pain in the ass, he would tell us to go play on Route 4." Frank regaled his sons with stories of his life in Washington Heights. Although he grew up in a blue-collar, white neighborhood during times of racial hostilities, his sons never heard him utter an ethnic slur, except self-deprecating ones. "He always taught us to treat everyone equally," recounts Tom.

Joe and Tom, two years apart, played, fought, and competed with intensity. "I would tag along with Tom and his friends, and often came home crying." Joe remembers. "But he was a good brother, someone I always looked to for approval, even when my dad was alive." After Tom's first communion, Frank brought his sons to Morsan, a local sporting goods store, using Tom's communion money to buy a tent and sleeping bags. While browsing, Joe swooned over a Spalding baseball glove signed by his favorite Met, Tom Seaver. "I kept it on my hand while we were in the store, talked about it all the way home in the car, and continued to do so during the following week. My dad was not one to spend frivolously and, despite my lobbying, he did not give in to me."

One day, Tom showed up at the park where Joe was playing with friends to tell him that his dad wanted to see him right away. "That was never a good thing," Joe says. "It usually meant I had forgotten to do something, like feed the dog or make my bed. My dad wouldn't do those things for us. He made us do what we were responsible to do." Joe nervously rode his bike home. "When I saw my dad, he smiled and pulled the Seaver glove out of a bag. Years later, while watching the end of *Field of Dreams*, I imagined having a catch with my dad using that mitt."

Every year in the early 1970s, Frank and Mary brought their young sons to Morgan's famed employee Christmas Party. "It was the best day of the year," Joe recalls. "We got to go to our dad's office. They would put on a show. I remember one with Mr. Jiggs, the chimp. Then you would go meet Santa Claus, and get a really nice gift."

Belying his "American Dream" life, Frank Connor didn't plan long-term. "He would say to me," says Mary, "'I will be a long time pushing up daisies before you come.' I believe that, subconsciously, he was preparing me." Regarding anything that might occur years in the future, Frank told his sons that he would be "gone by then." Tom recalls, "I once said that I wished it was Saturday, and Dad told me, 'Don't wish your life away. Enjoy every day.' Those words have stayed with me."

In the autumn of 1971, the year prior to his graduation from Fairleigh Dickinson with a degree in Business Administration, Frank was recommended for appointment to officer status, which was, by all accounts, "a very big deal." But he was passed over, in favor of an Ivy League graduate with less experience and a lower performance rating. After considering quitting the bank, Frank was rewarded the following year with a promotion to Assistant Treasurer. In his 1972 performance appraisal, his boss wrote, "Connor's performance this year has really been outstanding. Connor has come into his own and is a most important part of the Export Group." The following year, Frank was described as "an integral part of this group."

Again, he was promoted, this time to Assistant Vice President, despite it being uncommon to receive a promotion in consecutive years at Morgan Guaranty. Frank's career was progressing so well that he and Mary were considering moving to a larger house in either Wyckoff or Ramsey, which were "swankier neighborhoods."

In the summer of 1974, the Connor family traveled to Florida. Two days were spent in Disney World, which had opened only three years earlier. "What sticks in my memory," recounts Joe, "is the Mr. Toad's Wild Ride and that we had to split into pairs. I got to be with my dad. More than loving the ride, I loved sitting with him." It was their last vacation together.

As 1975 dawned, Frank had become, as Margaret put it, with a grin, a "bigshot." Frederick Moseley, the Executive Vice President of Morgan Guaranty in charge of Personnel, would write to Mary after Frank's death, "He accomplished in a few years what most men do not accomplish in a lifetime, and his future had great promise."

January 19, 1975, a Sunday and the day before Joe's ninth birthday, was unusually balmy. Frank brought his family to a place he frequented as a youth—the banks of the Hudson River in the shadow of the majestic Palisades cliffs. "It was a day that seemed to last forever," Joe recalls. "The four of us and our beagle Bonnie played along the river. We laughed, talked, and threw rocks. It is the final clear memory I have of my father."

*Joe and Frank*

# CHAPTER 7
## Rise of the Puerto Rican Nationalist Movement

*If it was true that the American flag represented freedom
and democracy in the world, here in Puerto Rico, it
represented colonialism and plunder.*

—Pedro Albizu Campos

IN 1922, THE "Partido Nacionalista de Puerto Rico
(Puerto Rican Nationalist Party)," was formed through the
combination of three existing pro-independence groups
to oppose continued American rule of the island and the
dispossession and impoverishment of its working class.
The party came to be led by Pedro Albizu Campos, who
broadened the Party's membership and appeal beyond
professionals and intellectuals to common folk.

Albizu Campos was born in Ponce, known as the
"Ciudad Señorial (Majestic or Noble City)" because of
its hundreds of beautiful, multi-colored neoclassical
buildings and facades. Olive-skinned, he was of Basque

heritage on his father's side. Albizu Campos' mother, a laundry worker and a *mestiza* (of mixed racial ancestry) was the daughter of slaves. As a seven-year-old, he stood with her watching General Nelson Miles' American troops march through that city's streets. Among Albizu Campos' many accomplishments was being the first Puerto Rican to graduate from Harvard College and Harvard Law School, the latter as class valedictorian.

While in college, Albizu Campos developed an interest in global liberation groups after meeting in person with the Indian poet Rabindranath Tagore, a follower of Gandhi's passive resistance movement who was on tour speaking out in support of independence for India. At Harvard, Albizu Campos also met Éamon de Valera, the Irish Republican who was one of the leaders in the failed 1916 Easter Uprising and later became the president of Sinn Féin, a nationalist party, about which Mary's mother, Kathleen Lynch, would regale her grandsons Tom and Joe with stories of. The two men conversed at length about the oppression both felt their home islands were subject to.

When the United States entered World War I, Albizu Campos joined the Army's infantry branch and was commissioned as a second lieutenant. The Army assigned him to the 375th Infantry Regiment—an "all-Negro" regiment. Albizu Campos came to bitterly resent the Army's rampant racism, which was the beginning of his turning "anti-Yanqui." Albizu Campos believed that Puerto Rico had enjoyed sovereignty since the Spanish grant of authority in 1897, and it was the United States' obligation to free the island. "The Treaty of Paris, imposed by force on Spain by the United States ... is null and void as it pertains to Puerto Rico." His worldly views led him to denounce British rule over India, Japan's invasion of China, Italy's occupation of Ethiopia, and Germany's persecution of its Jews.

Albizu Campos was slender, with bushy hair, prominent cheekbones, and a trimmed mustache. Standing only five feet, four inches tall, he habitually wore a black suit, white shirt, and black bow tie—the attire of a Harvard law student. From a distance, he presented a frail, modest, and mild-mannered persona, but Albizu Campos was a brilliant organizer and fiery, compelling orator.

The Nationalist Party failed repeatedly to perform well in island elections. For example, in 1932, the Party won only two percent of the vote, a lack of support that was attributable in part to efforts by insular officials to curb the separatists but, also, reflected the widespread belief that independence would harm the island's fragile economy. But, under Albizu Campos' determined leadership, the Nationalist Party became a militant grassroots organization present in every municipality.

Among the injustices that Albizu Campos fought was the "imposition of American culture, which destroys our own culture and language." He also railed against the succumbing of a "legion of proprietors" to American capitalism. In a speech to the Associated Press, Albizu

Campos said, "The United States controls our economy, our commerce … The result is exploitation and abuses perpetrated at will, resulting in poverty for our people."

In 1934, Albizu Campos organized an island-wide agricultural strike that brought the economy to a standstill, ending only when the sugarcane workers' wages rose to $1.50 per day—more than double what they'd been receiving. Fearing ongoing social unrest, Franklin Roosevelt appointed recently retired U.S. Army Judge Advocate-General Blanton Winship—a Spanish-American war veteran whom *Nation* magazine described as having "an inbred sense of the superiority of the United States and its institutions and a kindly contempt for 'backward and underprivileged people'"—as governor of Puerto Rico. Winship was given the mission of restoring order on the island. Winship brought with him Naval Intelligence Officer Francis Riggs as Puerto Rico's new chief of police. Riggs had spent the previous several years advising Nicaraguan dictator Anastasio Somoza on how to set up a secret police unit and use violence, torture, and terror to suppress opposition.

Winship and Riggs militarized the island's police department and made clear they would proactively apply force against the Nationalists. Riggs used secret Spanish-speaking police agents, fabricated criminal charges, and brutality to identify, arrest, and strike fear into those who spoke out in favor of independence.

The subsequent years were filled with violent confrontations. A notable one was the October 1935 "Massacre of Río Piedras," during which local police officers gunned down four Nationalist Party supporters near the University of Puerto Rico campus. Albizu Campos demanded the biblical "eye for an eye," which arrived the following February when two Party members murdered Riggs, who had ordered the prior killings, after he had attended Mass at a San Juan cathedral. The two Nationalists were taken to the San Juan police precinct and summarily executed.

In March 1936, Albizu Campos and six other Nationalist leaders were arrested and charged with conspiracy to overthrow the island's government. Albizu Campos, using his legal training, represented himself and his cohorts, arguing that the numerous killings were not part of the Nationalist program but only "incidental outbreaks" between the police and individuals. After a mistrial caused by a hung jury followed by a rejiggering of the second jury's composition to majority Anglo, the defendants were convicted upon retrial. During his sentencing of Albizu Campos to lengthy imprisonment, the judge admonished, "The blood of some of your own faithful followers is on your hands."

In March 1937, a peaceful Nationalist Party-led protest in support of Albizu Campos was organized to take place on Palm Sunday in Ponce. After hearing of the planned demonstration, Governor Winship ordered police units from across the island to gather there. They carried the latest riot control equipment, including tear gas bombs, rifles, and submachine guns. As the marchers assembled, more than two hundred policemen positioned themselves in front of the protestors, forcing a standoff.

At three p.m., a crowd, which included not only Nationalist Party members but, also, city residents and visitors, was gathered behind a four-cadet color guard bearing the symbols of Puerto Rico and the Nationalist Party. A small musical band began playing the original, 1868 revolutionary version of "La Borinqueña," Puerto Rico's national song. Its lyrics begin with:

> Arise, boricua!
> The call to arms has sounded!
> Awake from the slumber,
> It is time to fight!

The demonstrators started marching toward Our Lady of Guadalupe Cathedral in the city's main square. And the police, who stood on each side of the intersection, began firing. Members of the crowd ran for their lives, but escape was difficult. The gunfire went on for several minutes. Men, women, and children were struck in the back. Some were chased by police and shot or clubbed at the entrance of their houses or a nearby church, while others were dragged from their hiding places and killed. Many nonparticipants were shot in the face while peering out a window or doorway. In the end, twenty-one died and more than two hundred were injured, many horribly.

After an attempted cover-up by Winship and other Puerto Rican officials, an independent investigation was ordered by the United States Commission on Civil Rights, led by Arthur Garfield Hayes, co-founder of the American Civil Liberties Union. The "Hayes Commission" concluded "the facts showed that the affair of March 21 in Ponce was a MASSACRE (original emphasis)." Congressman Vito Marcantonio, who represented East Harlem and was the nation's most prominent supporter of the Puerto Rican community and of independence for Puerto Rico, would later characterize Winship, in his five years as Governor, as having "destroyed the last vestige of civil rights in Puerto Rico. Patriots were framed in the very executive mansion and railroaded to prison. Men, women, and children were massacred in the streets of the island simply because they dared to express their opinion or attempted to meet in free assemblage."

Albizu Campos was confined to an Atlanta penitentiary until July 1943, when he became seriously ill from mistreatment during his incarceration. Marcantonio gained Albizu Campos' admission to New York's Columbus Hospital. Albizu Campos remained hospitalized there for two years. Marcantonio visited frequently. In 1944, upon being informed that the FBI was listening in on Albizu Campos' telephone conversations, Marcantonio ripped out the microphone and threatened to produce it on the floor of the House of Representatives.

During his imprisonment, Albizu Campos was re-elected as president of the Nationalist Party, which began to organize within the growing Puerto Rican communities in New York and Chicago. When he returned to Puerto

Rico in December 1947, Albizu Campos was greeted by thousands of supporters at the dock. At a mass rally in Sixto Escobar Stadium in San Juan, filled with more than fourteen thousand tumultuous admirers, he declared, "It is up to us to confront this despotism." After condemning the U.S. Navy's occupation of much of Vieques and the teaching of English in Puerto Rican public schools, Albizu Campos proclaimed, "You are my people, and this is our island."

After World War II, the Philippines, along with India and many other colonies, gained their independence. Puerto Rico did not, although in May 1947, Congress authorized the first popular election for governor of Puerto Rico. The ability to elect their chief executive was celebrated by most Puerto Ricans, but the Nationalist Party repudiated this development as a sham not offering the option of complete independence or even statehood.

In January 1949, Luis Muñoz Marín of the Popular Democratic Party assumed the governorship. Although Muñoz Marín was the son of a prominent Puerto Rican politician who had been a major figure in the struggle for autonomy at the turn of the century, he became a fierce opponent of the independence cause and the Nationalist Party. Muñoz Marín favored status for Puerto Rico as a "free associated state," a balance between achieving autonomy and maintaining a close, favorable relationship with the U.S.

In 1948, in a further effort to suppress the Nationalist movement, the Puerto Rican government passed "La Ley de la Mordaza," aka, the "Gag Law," which was loosely modeled after the Alien Registration Act of 1940 that set criminal penalties for advocating the overthrow of the U.S. government and required all non-citizen adult residents to register with the government. (Prosecutions under the Alien Registration Act continued until a series of United States Supreme Court decisions in 1957 reversed convictions under it as unconstitutional.) The Gag Law prohibited, and provided lengthy prison terms for, the display of the Puerto Rican flag, the singing of patriotic songs, and any discussion of Puerto Rican independence. The statute clearly violated the First Amendment of the U.S. Constitution, but the U.S. Supreme Court had declared decades earlier that because Puerto Rico was a territory not incorporated into the Union, the U.S. constitution did not apply to its residents. And although the law also violated a similar freedom-of-speech provision in the Puerto Rican Bill of Rights, it would remain in force for nine years until repealed.

Tensions further escalated as the local police, actively supported by the J. Edgar Hoover-led FBI, began a campaign of arresting, imprisoning, torturing, and murdering Nationalists. In reaction to that and the upcoming registration effort for a vote on a new constitution, a series of armed protests spread throughout Puerto Rico in late October 1950. They included an attack on La Fortaleza, the governor's mansion in San Juan, in an attempt to kill Muñoz Marín. The revolt was suppressed by the U.S. military, working with the Puerto Rican National Guard, with dozens of Nationalists being killed.

The bloodiest day was October 30, when Nationalists staged actions in various towns focused on taking over local police stations and seizing weaponry. In the Villa Palmeras section of San Juan, as told by the noted Puerto Rican author, Esmeralda Santiago, this led to forty policemen and National Guardsmen surrounding a barbershop owned by the Nationalist leader Vidal Santiago Diaz:

> The windows of the shop were shuttered, but every once in a while, gunfire erupted through the slats and was returned ... with pistols, machine guns, rifles, and tear gas. The siege lasted more than four hours. When the police were finally able to ax their way into the shop, they found a man slumped in a corner, his torso ripped by a grenade ...

Remembrance of the Nationalist insurgency would have a profound effect on future generations. As recalled by Elizam Escobar, an FALN member who grew up in Ponce:

> My initiation into politics was as a direct observer in 1950, as a young child, during the Nationalist insurrection. My mother's brother was killed in a police confrontation with the Nationalists in *El Barrio* Macana in Peñuelas [a municipality west

of Ponce] ... My father took me into his arms as the police were shooting into a house ... I used to have a recurring dream where I saw people who had been shot dead, lying in the gutters.

In one town, Utuado, located in Puerto Rico's central mountain range, nine unarmed Nationalists who had surrendered were taken behind police headquarters and machine-gunned, an incident that became known as the "Utuado Massacre." But it was another deadly clash occurring that day, which took place only fifteen miles away, that would change the course of the Nationalist movement and bring the fight to the "belly of the beast."

# CHAPTER 8
## *The Death of True Nationalism*

*Puerto Ricans must understand that we're the best thing that ever happened to them, that they'd be lost without our justice, our government, and our laws, that they haven't matured enough to stand by themselves.*

—Franklin Delano Roosevelt

NAMED AFTER A TAÍNO CHIEF who fought the Spanish conquistadors, the municipality of Jayuya is tucked into a lush valley in the island's highest mountains, accessible only via a treacherous winding road. Albizu Campos often visited Jayuya and ordered a cache of weapons to be stored in Nationalist family houses there.

On October 30, 1950, armed Nationalist Party members gathered in Jayuya, led by Blanca Canales, who had organized the "Daughters of Freedom," the female-only wing of the "Cadets of the Republic," the quasi-military youth branch of the Nationalist Party. One of her key assistants was fellow-Jayuyan and cousin, Elio Torresola.

The group attempted to occupy the police station after first issuing a demand for the police inside to surrender. In the ensuing gunfight, one officer was killed, three were wounded, and the other officers surrendered. The Nationalists then occupied the post office and cut the phone lines leading to the telephone station. Canales led the group to the town plaza, raised the Puerto Rican Flag (which was outlawed by the Gag Law), and declared Puerto Rico a free republic.

In response, the town was savagely attacked by police and Puerto Rican National Guard members using U.S. fighter planes (Republic P-47 Thunderbolts used in World War II), artillery, mortar fire, and grenades. Over three days, much of Jayuya was destroyed, arguably a level of devastation from armed conflict not seen on U.S. soil since the Civil War.

In the aftermath of the uprising, among the many Nationalists arrested were Elio and his sister, Doris, who was wounded by a bullet that perforated her throat. A third Torresola sibling, Griselio, was living in Manhattan at the time. A former bodyguard for Albizu Campos, Griselio was now his secret revolutionary representative in the U.S. Torresola was a member of the New York branch of the Nationalist Party, led by Oscar Collazo, a native Puerto Rican who'd been raised in Jayuya by his older brother. After the family farm was sold to avoid repossession by an American loan company, Collazo immigrated to the Bronx.

After learning of the failed insurrection and Albizu Campos' arrest for his leadership role, Torresola and Collazo boarded a train to Washington, intent on bringing world attention to the Puerto Rican independence movement. Two days later, they attempted to force their way into the Blair House, the President's guest residence, to assassinate President Truman, who was staying there while the White House was undergoing renovation. Torresola approached a guard booth and shot three Secret Service agents, including one, Leslie Coffelt, point blank in the chest and abdomen. As he lay dying, Coffelt, an Army veteran and expert marksman, killed Torresola with a bullet to the head. On Torresola's body, Secret Service agents found letters from Albizu Campos authorizing him to assume leadership of the movement in the United States and to use Nationalist Party funds for further actions.

Meanwhile, Collazo, a diminutive man who was as inept a gunman as Torresola was skilled, approached the Blair House from the opposite direction. His first shot was aimed at the back of the head of Donald Birdzell, a large, muscular, and formidable officer. But, fortunately, Collazo had forgotten to remove his pistol's safety pin. After doing so, Collazo unleashed a wild flurry of shots, with one striking Birdzell in the knee. In the return fire, Collazo was hit with a non-fatal shot to the chest.

President Truman had watched the gunfire exchanges from his bedroom in the Blair House, before one of the agents yelled at him to move away from the window. Truman revealed in his book *Where the Buck Stops: The Personal and Private Writings of Harry S. Truman* that he felt Collazo and Torresola "were misguided fanatics and not really killers at heart." After trial, Collazo received a death sentence, but Truman commuted it to life imprisonment.

Puerto Rico's Governor, Luis Muñoz Marín, quickly issued a condemnation:

> The people of Puerto Rico are profoundly indignant at the attempt made at Blair House, in which two Puerto Rican nationalists were involved. We would feel ashamed of calling ourselves Puerto Ricans if it were not for the fact that the nationalist gangsters are less than 500 in number, among the more than two million decent, democracy-loving American citizens that make up our community.

In prison, Collazo was asked why he had targeted Truman, who was in favor of self-determination for Puerto Rico, stating during a 1948 visit to San Juan that "the Puerto Rican people should have the right to determine for themselves Puerto Rico's political relationship to the United States." Collazo replied that he had nothing against Truman personally, but that he was "a symbol … You don't attack the man, you attack the system."

Collazo and Torresola had acted on direct orders from Albizu Campos. After the attack, Albizu Campos was imprisoned in the horrific dungeons of the San Juan District Jail, commonly known as "La Princesa," next to the governor's mansion, before being convicted of sedition and sentenced to eighty years imprisonment. Years later, the U.S. District Court in Puerto Rico would rule that the conditions in La Princesa constituted cruel and unusual punishment in violation of the Eighth Amendment, citing the prison's overcrowded condition, failures to provide adequate beds, clothing, facilities and equipment for personal hygiene, the insufficient number of guards, the admission of mentally deranged persons "or those with known dangerous propensities," and the gross lack of medical services.

In July 1952, pursuant to legislation signed by Truman and a popular vote, a new Constitution of Puerto Rico created a semi-autonomous "commonwealth." This ambiguous label was abstrusely defined by the Office of Insular Affairs as "an organized United States insular area, which has established with the Federal Government, a more highly developed relationship, usually embodied in a written mutual agreement." Chief Justice Earl Warren called Puerto Rico's commonwealth standing "perhaps the most notable of American governmental experiments in our lifetime." This revised status, something between statehood and a mere territory, was expected to lead to greater social and political autonomy for the island while preserving the economic benefits of Puerto Rico's relationship with the U.S. The odd sovereign status of Puerto Rico remained, one vestige being that Puerto Rico fields its own Olympic team, separate from the U.S. team.

The Nationalist Party was unappeased. Albizu Campos asked a Party member living in New York, Lolita Lebrón, to lead an armed protest that would "draw the world's attention to the truth about Puerto Rico." Born in 1919 in Lares, Lebrón won as a teenager the municipality's annual "Queen of the Flowers of May" beauty contest. In 1937, after the Ponce Massacre, she became an independence activist. In 1940, by then a single mother, Lebrón left her newborn daughter in the care of her family and sailed to New York, where she found work in a garment shop as a sewing machine operator. Soon after, Lebrón became a union leader and eventually joined the Puerto Rican Nationalist movement. One of her Nationalist colleagues was Rafael Cancel Miranda, a press operator in a shoe factory, whose political views also had begun to take shape in 1937, when he was six years old. His parents participated in the Ponce rally that turned violent. "My mother went to Ponce dressed in white and returned dressed in red, covered in the blood of the dead, whose bodies she had to crawl over as the bullets flew overhead."

On March 1, 1954, the Puerto Rican independence movement assumed global center stage when Lebrón, Miranda, Andrés Figueroa Cordero, and Irvin Flores Rodríguez recited the Lord's Prayer before unfurling a Puerto Rican flag in the Ladies' Gallery, a visitors balcony, in the House of Representatives, during a debate over an immigration bill. They then, with semi-automatic weapons, rained down dozens of shots at the Congressmen, wounding five. One, Representative Alvin Bentley, was hit in the chest below the heart. Lebrón, stylishly dressed and wearing bright lipstick, emptied the chambers of her Luger pistol but, unlike the others, aimed only at the ceiling. She then threw it down and screamed, "Viva Puerto Rico!" A note inside Lebrón's purse read: "Before God and my world, my blood claims for the independence of Puerto Rico. My life I give for the freedom of my country. This is a cry for victory for our struggle for independence. The United States of America is betraying the sacred principles of mankind in their continuous subjugation of my country."

The next day, on the front page of *The New York Times* was a photo of Lebrón wrapped in the revolutionary flag of Puerto Rico, her left fist raised high. The four were tried and convicted in federal court of various charges related to the gun attack, including seditious conspiracy. (Seditious conspiracy is committed when two or more persons knowingly collude to forcibly destroy or overthrow the U.S. government or its property. It differs from treason, the most serious federal crime and one punishable by death, in that it does not require the defendant to "owe allegiance to the United States," does not contemplate the presence of an enemy foreign state or an actual war, and necessitates at least two persons to commit.) Lebrón, acquitted of the charge of assault with the intent to kill, received a sentence of sixteen years and eight months to fifty years in prison. The three men each received a term of twenty-five to seventy-five years.

Lebrón would become a larger-than-life but distant figure to her family. On March 1, 1977, the twenty-third anniversary of the attack on Congress, Lebrón's daughter Gladys, who had seen her mother only four times in her entire life, committed suicide in Puerto Rico in front of her eight-year-old daughter, Irene, by jumping out of a moving car. Irene would undergo her own troubles— including multiple abortions and suicide attempts—before becoming an editor, literary agent, and author of several books. Of her mother, Irene Vilar would say, "There was nothing she could do to be truly original. Unless, of course, you count her suicide, and I do."

The Nationalists' lengthy imprisonments would become a focal point of protest by future Puerto Rican independence groups, including the FALN, which in one of its communiqués stated, "Puerto Rico suffers the highest degree of exploitation and oppression of any country in the western hemisphere. A classic example of this is the imprisonment of our five nationalist patriots [that number includes Oscar Collazo] whose only crime was a desire and commitment to see our country free."

The goal of the small but passionate movement that Albizu Campos led was not to overthrow the U.S. government but, rather, to call attention to the cause of Puerto Rican independence. The Nationalist Party's violence was politically inspired, as all terrorism may be said to be, but it largely attacked symbols of authority and sought to minimize harm to the public at large. Before the October 1950 rebellious actions began throughout Puerto Rico, Albizu Campos gave strict orders that policemen were to be given the chance to surrender to prevent bloodshed, and that no harm to civilians would be countenanced. With notable exceptions—including the assassination attempt on President Truman that led to the murder of White House Police Officer Leslie Coffelt, and the 1954 shootings of five Congressmen—the Party did not purport to engage in violence as a form of communication.

Albizu Campos was a devout Catholic who believed that Catholicism had "destroyed every deep racial division." He disliked socialist systems, with their anti-religious tendencies. His free market economic vision for Puerto Rico promoted both industrialization and the return to a country of independent, self-sufficient farmers and producers.

But many within the Party were sympathetic to socialism. One was the imprisoned Rafael Cancel Miranda. "I believe in socialism as much as I believe in independence for my country. I wouldn't want a free country … so that two or three parasites could take over the lives of our people and enrich themselves at the expense of our people."

The 1954 assault on Congress was followed by two decades of relative inaction on the part of *independistas*. In 1956, while in prison, Albizu Campos suffered a stroke and became partially paralyzed and unable to speak. By then, the Party, desperate and in disrepair, had sought help from two Puerto Rican organizations with socialist, if not communist, foundations—The Federation of University Students for Independence and the Pro-Independence movement. This alliance would presage the beginning of the end of the Nationalist Party, which disbanded after Pedro Albizu Campos' death in 1965 (a year after he was pardoned by the Puerto Rican Governor). Nationalism as represented by Albizu Campos and his movement was reincarnated, but into a corrupted form within the shadow of radical leftist ideology. Going forward, the Puerto Rican independence cause would mask a devotion to Marxist–Leninist principles and Castro's revolutionary ideals. With its moral fabric torn apart, the movement would evidence a penchant for the kind of senseless violence that had wracked the world throughout the century.

# CHAPTER 9
## *Alex Berger*

*Alex was the whole package. An incredibly special person,*
*who everyone loved. On our first date, I knew he was the*
*one. I couldn't believe that he was interested in me.*

—Deenie Berger Ettenson

OF THE MILLIONS OF European Jews vulnerable to
the horrors of Nazism, one was teen-aged Joséf Berger
of Czechoslovakia. Following the *Anschluss* (forced
union) of Austria with Nazi Germany in March 1938,
it became clear to Joséf's parents that the conquest of
their country was inevitable. They were correct. On
September 29, 1938, Germany, Italy, Great Britain, and
France signed the Munich Agreement, which forced the
Czechoslovak Republic to cede to Germany its western
and northern regions, known as the "Sudetenland." In
reaction, Winston Churchill, in a speech to the House of
Commons, famously said, "This is only the beginning of

the reckoning. This is only the first sip, the first foretaste of a bitter cup ..."

In March 1939, the German Army marched into Czechoslovakia, and the Gestapo arrested thousands of Jews and other Czechs suspected of being anti-Nazi, sending them to concentration camps. Fortunately, by then, the Berger family had fled, leaving behind a substantial business.

Until the outbreak of war in September 1939, Uruguay remained one of the few countries issuing entry visas to Eastern European Jews. The Bergers ultimately would make their way to Montevideo. There, Joséf met, courted, and married another Jewish refugee, Cecilia Blum. Cecilia, known as "Cilly," was born and raised in Vienna. Her father was a rabbi, and both her parents worked in the family business—a company that manufactured shirts sold throughout Europe.

The Blums lived for a year under Nazi oppression. In November 1938, they endured *Kristallnacht* (Night of Broken Glass), a widespread wave of violence that resulted in dozens of murders, the imprisonment of thousands of Austrian Jews, and massive property destruction including the burning of hundreds of synagogues. After struggling to obtain passports and Uruguayan visas, the Blums left Vienna in January 1939, headed to Genoa, Italy, via Budapest. Their trip on the ship *The Augustus* to Montevideo took seventeen days. As Cilly recalls, "On board ship, we had to pretend we were on a fun vacation because there were Gestapo on the boat watching the passengers." Cilly would carry throughout her life vivid memories of being taunted on the streets, expelled from school, her family's factory confiscated, and seeing her father taken in for questioning by the Gestapo.

Joséf and Cilly sought to set the horrors of their early years behind them and build a new life in Uruguay. In 1946, Cilly gave birth to a son, Alejandro, nicknamed "Alex." Cilly would develop medical problems that left Alex as their only child, and the light of their lives.

Uruguay, democratic and for a time the most economically prosperous nation in Latin America, initially was a paradise for the Bergers. Alex grew up distinguishing himself academically and athletically, particularly in soccer. But, by 1963, increasing anti-Semitism drove the Bergers to move to Israel. Alex finished high school in Tel Aviv before opting to attend college in the United States. Blond-haired and blue-eyed, Alex had grown into a handsome, witty, warm, and affable adult who spoke six languages and was "scary smart"—he had graduated valedictorian of his class at the Philadelphia College of Textiles and Science.

After graduating fourth in his class from The Wharton School of Business at the University of Pennsylvania, Alex joined the International Division of Rohm and Haas. By then, he had married Philadelphia-born-and-raised Diana Greenberg, known as "Deenie," a pretty, petite, physical therapist. The two had been introduced to each other in 1969 by a mutual friend and, after a whirlwind romance, were married less than six months later.

*Deenie and Alex Berger, 1974*

Alex was assigned to the Brazilian office of a subsidiary of Rohm and Haas, from where he would represent the company's South American interests. He and Deenie set up house in São Paulo. But in the early 1970s, South America was rife with guerrilla wars and terrorism, and Uruguay became ruled by a military dictatorship that maintained power through human rights violations, torture, and random abductions of its citizens. Alex feared for his safety carrying a Uruguayan passport. At Alex's request, Rohm and Haas moved him back to the United States to enable him to fulfill the residency requirement to obtain U.S. citizenship.

Deenie became pregnant in the fall of 1974. Upon learning the news, Joséf and Cilly decided to move to the

U.S. They found an apartment in Queens, a two-hour drive from Alex and Deenie. The bliss of grandparenthood approached.

Joséf, Cilly, and Alex Berger would struggle their entire lives to shield themselves from violence, only to have it find them in the unlikeliest of places.

# CHAPTER 10
## *Cuba's Proxy*

*I remember when I was a university student. I belonged to
the Puerto Rico Pro-Independence Committee. One day,
in front of the U.S. Consulate in Old Havana, the police
beat me because I was participating in a demonstration to
support the independence of Puerto Rico.*

—Fidel Castro

IN JANUARY 1959, WHEN many Puerto Ricans were
celebrating the success of Fidel Castro's guerilla campaign, the Movimiento Pro Independencia de Puerto Rico
(M.P.I.) arose on the island as an heir to the declining
Nationalist Party. The M.P.I.'s ideals were greatly influenced by the Cuban Revolution, linking Cuba and the
Puerto Rican independence movement from the moment
of Castro's ascension to power. Fidel believed Puerto Rico
to be central to his global liberation agenda, calling Cuba
and Puerto Rico "two daughters of the same history, with

a common language and culture and association with Latin American, not Anglo-Saxon, countries."

Pedro Albizu Campos had been a hero to Castro since childhood. After the failed Bay of Pigs invasion, Fidel unsuccessfully demanded, as he negotiated the return of those captured, that Albizu Campos be released from prison. In the early 1960s, Castro granted Cuban citizenship to Albizu Campos' Peruvian wife, Laura Meneses, who met Albizu Campos when he was at Harvard and she at Radcliff College, and their three children. Castro then appointed Meneses as first secretary of the Cuban mission to the United Nations. Thereafter, Cuba consistently led efforts in the United Nations to place Puerto Rico's status on the General Assembly's agenda.

In January 1965, the first "Tricontinental Conference of African, Asian, and Latin American Peoples," a pro-Communist, anti-American forum, was convened in Havana. One of the delegates from Puerto Rico, Narciso Rabell Martinez, declared, "The independence movement is continuously being organized among the Puerto Rican people so that we may unflinchingly confront U.S. imperialism. It is a fight waged from within the very heart of the monster." Fidel Castro closed the conference with one of his typically prolonged speeches, during which he proclaimed that what unites the people of the world "is the struggle against imperialism, the struggle against colonialism and neocolonialism, the struggle against racism ... whose center, axis, and principal support is Yankee imperialism."

Cuba supplied arms to M.P.I. and other Puerto Rican *independistas*. In May 1964, Puerto Rican law enforcement authorities presented proof that Cuba was sending weapons into Puerto Rico through the Ponce airport. Over several decades, dozens of leaders of subversive Puerto Rican groups traveled to Cuba for indoctrination and training in guerilla war tactics, preparation of explosives, and sophisticated methods of sabotage. As stated by South Carolina Senator Strom Thurmond in 1975 after Congressional hearings on the Cuba-Puerto Rico link, "Cuba has been the fountainhead of revolution in Puerto Rico since Castro took over."

At its Eighth General Assembly in November 1971, the M.P.I. transformed into the Puerto Rican Socialist Party (P.R.S.P.), an organization committed to Marxist-Leninist principles. Under the leadership of its founder, Juan Mari Brás, whom FBI agents determined had been recruited as a Cuban intelligence agent as early as 1963, the P.R.S.P. denounced colonial rule in Puerto Rico, launched campaigns against U.S. military bases on the island, and, in the tradition of Albizu Campos, held massive rallies where it was declared that independence would result from the revolutionary organization of the people. The P.R.S.P. also developed *Claridad*, a newspaper created by the M.P.I., into a daily publication that highlighted past stages of the independence movement and the resistance of the native Taínos and black slaves.

During the same era, in the United States, a revitalized independence movement was mirrored in the rise of the Young Lords, which began as a gang in Chicago's Lincoln Park neighborhood and soon expanded to New York. As explained by Pablo Guzmán, one of the Young Lords' leaders, "Our people have been taught to believe that when they rounded up Albizu Campos and two thousand members of the Nationalist party, they broke the back of the party. But now the people can think about Albizu and all of a sudden it seems like the Nationalist party has just been going through different kinds of changes for twenty years."

Inspired by the Black Panthers, the Young Lords used conferences, marches, and more confrontational tactics not only to support independence for Puerto Rico but, also, to promote civil rights and neighborhood empowerment. The group's lawyer was none other than Geraldo Rivera, who recalled, "The reason they were so unique is they were the first Puerto Rican activist group whose focus was not primarily on the status of the commonwealth of Puerto Rico ... but rather the social condition of the people living in Spanish Harlem and the Lower East Side and the South Bronx." The Young Lords became a target of the FBI's COINTELPRO program (COINTELPRO is a portmanteau derived from COunter INTELligences PROgram), aimed at surveilling, infiltrating, and disrupting any domestic organization deemed subversive, effectively reducing its influence after the early 1970s. (In May 2000, FBI Director Louis Freeh admitted to the House Appropriations Committee that "there had been egregious illegal action, maybe criminal

action, over decades by the FBI in Puerto Rico," and the
FBI released a massive amount of classified documents,
including ones on the COINTELPRO program.)

The Young Lords' legacy in the U.S. and the P.R.S.P.
militancy in Puerto Rico inspired the spawning of the
FALN in a Cuban incubator during a time when the Cold
War was raging, and both Cuba and the Soviet Union
were backing "national liberation" movements throughout
the Americas. (Mark Rudd, a leader of the Students for
a Democratic Society (S.D.S.), a 1960s student activist
movement in the U.S. that represented the "New Left,"
describes in his book *Underground: My Life with SDS and
the Weathermen* a three-week meeting of twenty S.D.S.
members in February 1968 in Havana, remarking, "All
my beliefs that at home seemed so radical, outrageous,
and even illicit were the norm here.") Consistent with
P.R.S.P. principles, the FALN's founder, Filiberto Ojeda
Ríos, stated, "The struggles for social justice and equality … have been tendencies that have determined human
progress and, therefore, have been an integral part of
the Marxist methodology of analysis." The P.R.S.P. and
Ojeda Ríos would influence future FALN members such
as Elizam Escobar, who spoke of his coming into contact,
"before the militancy … with the literature of the Cuban
Revolution, the guerrilla movements in Latin America,
and Black Power in the United States, but especially
Marxist literature from China."

Filiberto Ojeda Ríos, who the FBI considered the
"kingpin" of Puerto Rican terrorism, was born in 1933

in Rio Blanco, a small agricultural and fishing community in eastern Puerto Rico known as "the town of the drenched" because of its numerous rivers and brooks fed by the constant rain. Ojeda Ríos' grandparents on both sides were farmers who lost their land to American sugar companies and became "macheteros," (sugar cane cutters) whose wages left them impoverished. Ojeda Ríos' father was a member of the Cadets of the Republic, the quasi-military youth branch of the Nationalist Party.

When Ojeda Ríos was eleven, he immigrated with his mother to New York City, attending schools in Manhattan and Brooklyn. "It was then," he recalled, "I was confronted, for the first time in my life, with all the elements of racism, social discrimination, and social oppression that characterized the life of Puerto Rican migrants." During the 1950s, Ojeda Ríos worked in various factories, played the trumpet in orchestras and bands that were precursors to the salsa wave, and participated in political activities supportive of the Puerto Rican independence movement.

Ojeda Ríos married and, in 1961, moved his family to Cuba, where he became a member of M.P.I. While studying political science at the University of Havana, Ojeda Ríos joined the Cuban intelligence service, volunteering to work to infiltrate U.S. military bases in Puerto Rico. He became friendly with Cuban leaders such as Che Guevara, who presented him with a specially made Cuban-Puerto Rican flag. (The Cuban and Puerto Rico flags have the same design and red, white, and blue colors, but those colors are reversed. The Puerto Rico flag resembles the Cuban flag because in December 1895, a group of Puerto Ricans gathered in Manhattan and organized a political group, which they associated with the Cuban Revolutionary Party.) Later, Fidel Castro met with Ojeda Ríos and encouraged him to form a Puerto Rican armed resistance group, which Cuba would help train. Ojeda Ríos returned to Puerto Rico in 1969 to organize and lead the first of Puerto Rico's new militant political groups, the Movimiento Independentista Revolutionary Armando, aka "M.I.R.A." After dozens of successful guerilla actions in Puerto Rico and New York City, MIRA was disbanded by police in the early 1970s based on information provided by an informant who had infiltrated the group.

In 1974, Ojeda Ríos was arrested, but after being granted bond in Puerto Rico, he fled to New York, where he worked in the Cuban mission to the U.N. While immersed in that supposed peace-promoting environment, Ojeda Ríos established the FALN along with former M.I.R.A. members, supported logistically by Cuban intelligence services.

In contrast to groups such as the Young Lords, which had a public face, the FALN began as and remained a clandestine organization with an overriding goal—to promote armed conflict with the "colonial forces of the United States." Many FALN members were born and raised in the continental United States, and the FALN chose to stage its actions there for maximum effect.

By the 1960s, the Puerto Rican independence movement had become interwoven with struggles for "liberation" and equality by African-Americans, Chicanos, women, and other groups. In particular, the FALN courted the Chicano (Mexican-American) movement, as both shared a common culture and language. To a greater extent than other Puerto Rican *independistas*, the FALN developed links to domestic terrorist groups, which were facilitated by Cuba.

The FALN partnered with and was greatly influenced by the militant, left-wing Weathermen group (also known as the "Weather Underground"), which took its name from a Bob Dylan lyric, "You don't need a weatherman to know which way the wind blows." FALN members were acquainted with the book *Prairie Fire: The Politics of Revolutionary Anti-Imperialism,* written and published covertly in 1974 by Bill Ayers, Bernardine Dohrn, and others, which functioned as the Weathermen's ideological manifesto and vision for the impending world revolution. (Ayers, a key member of the WU's Central Committee, later became a University of Illinois professor whose political relationship with then-candidate Barack Obama became publicized during the 2008 presidential campaign.) The use of the term "prairie fire" is taken from a Chairman Mao quote—"Even one small spark can start a prairie fire"—and the manifesto was written "to all sisters and brothers who are engaged in armed struggle against the enemy." The book is rife with references to imperialism, capitalism, and revolution to overthrow the American government—concepts the FALN would latch onto in their own communications.

The Weather Underground's intensive experience in the crafting and planting of bombs was shared with FALN members. It also educated the FALN on the prominent symbols of American "imperialism," of which none was greater than Morgan Guaranty Trust Company.

# CHAPTER 11
## *Morgan Men*

*I wasn't sure which offer to take, so I asked my old boss at Huntington Bank for advice. He told me there's no better bank than Morgan Guaranty.*

—Charlie Murray

ONE OF MORGAN GUARANTY'S specialties was trade or export finance, a specialized type of commercial lending. For products sold and shipped overseas, it bridges the gap between buyers, who prefer to delay payment until they receive and resell the goods, which may take weeks or months, and sellers, who want to be paid as quickly as possible. Designing financing for a specific trade deal is a complex process that weighs a number of risks and financial considerations. Its availability at favorable terms can be a make-or-break proposition. As a large multinational bank, Morgan Guaranty typically would provide its trade financing service only for major clients, and require high transaction minimums.

It is a testimony to Frank Connor not only that he rose steadily through the ranks of blue-blooded Morgan Guaranty Trust but, also, that in March 1970 he was assigned to the bank's Export Finance Group. There, he focused on deals involving financing and guarantees from the Federal Government's Export-Import Bank for the benefit of American businesses and their customers in foreign markets. Frank impressed some of Morgan's largest clients, including Texas Instruments, Scott Paper, and U.S. Steel.

One of Frank's colleagues was Charlie Murray. Unlike Frank, Murray was from the American heartland, having been born in Evanston, Illinois. In the summers, Murray would visit Mackinaw Island in upper Michigan and work various odd jobs in a family-owned hotel, an experience that would serve him well in later life. After graduating from Bowling Green State University in Ohio with an M.B.A. degree, he took a position with Huntington National Bank in Columbus, Ohio. Murray decided to make a career in the international side of the banking industry. "To do that, I felt I needed to move to New York City, where we wanted to live anyway."

Murray, along with his wife, Elaine, and growing family, which would come to include three daughters, settled in Brooklyn Heights, an upcoming neighborhood of picturesque row houses and mansions. He enrolled in the American Institute for Foreign Trade (now the Thunderbird School of Global Management), which focused on international management and was the first graduate school to train students in global business. While studying at the Institute, Murray interviewed with many New York banks and received several offers. He chose Morgan Guaranty.

Murray's work on international transactions led him to meet Frank Connor. "He was the spokesman for the Export Group. I always admired Frank because he spoke so well and obviously knew his stuff." The two men bonded during a business trip to the Midwest to line up banks to share the financing risk of an upcoming export deal. "We'd go out for a couple of pops each night and review the day's meetings. Frank always would have me on the floor. He had a devastating sense of humor."

Murray and Connor were the same age, married, and the father of young kids. Not surprisingly, they became friends. Each also was smart, personable, and gregarious, ideal characteristics for facing off against key clients.

Newer to Morgan Guaranty was Bill Newhall, twenty-six years old, who joined the bank in March 1974 after graduating from Wharton. Newhall, tall, distinguished-looking, and with a commanding voice, was from rural Connecticut. He grew up with a love of sports, playing football, skiing, and competing in track. After studying history as a Princeton undergraduate, Newhall coveted an acting career (which he would pursue much later in life, appearing in the soap opera, "One Life to Live"), but decided to make his livelihood in business. He lived with his wife in a Manhattan apartment.

As was required of new hires, Newhall completed Morgan Guaranty's rigorous and prestigious training program, with emphasis on accounting and corporate research and analysis. He then worked briefly on special real estate projects before being transferred to the International Financing group, where he would meet Frank Connor and Charlie Murray. Newhall was overjoyed with that assignment, unaware that it would soon propel him toward a seminal event in his life.

# CHAPTER 12
## *Emergence of the FALN*

*It was an act of God's grace that no one, not a night worker, a cleaning lady, a police officer, whoever, walked by one of those bombs and got blown up.*

—Don Wofford, FBI

THE LATE 1960s AND following decade was a period of fervent anti-Vietnam War protest, social unrest, and militant advocacy of a myriad of racial, national, and religious interests. Dissent was taken to the next level by the Weathermen and numerous other radical groups such as the anti-Castro Cubans, Black Panthers, Black Liberation Army, New World Liberation Front, and the Symbionese Liberation Army, which set off hundreds of bombs across the country. Terrorist acts became a part of American life.

The deadliest incident occurred in December 1975 at LaGuardia Airport when a blast that detonated near the TWA baggage terminal killed eleven and injured seventy four. The bomb, equivalent to twenty-five sticks of dynamite, had been placed in a coin-operated locker in the baggage claim area of the central terminal. As described by *Observer Magazine*:

> When it detonated just after 6:30 pm, the explosion shredded a wall of lockers, creating a wave of shrapnel that scythed down everyone in its path. Bodies were shattered, limbs were severed ... Blood, mixed with thousands of gallons of water pumped by firemen, spilled all over the terminal and into the taxi stands outside. The bodies of the 11 dead were mangled, some unrecognizable, while many of the dozens of injured were close to death.

No one claimed responsibility, and that bombing was never solved, although investigators and historians suspect that nationalists within the "Fighters for Free Croatia" group were the most likely perpetrators. In response, *The New York Times*, in an editorial, prophetically observed that, "In an age of violence such as we are now experiencing, efforts to respect civil rights and individual privacy sometimes result in the creation of massive security gaps that make every public place a potential human deathtrap."

The FALN evolved within the battlegrounds that were America's major cities. Its first public action was not particularly noteworthy. In late September 1974, a bomb was detonated outside police headquarters in Newark, New Jersey, with no resultant injuries. That summer,

Newark had been the site of what came to be known as the "1974 Puerto Rican Riots," which started when county police tried to break up what one officer believed was an illegal dice game taking place during a Puerto Rican festival. The situation escalated after an officer's horse knocked over a gaming table. City police were called in for backup. Full-scale rioting ensued, which lasted nearly three days, during which a young girl was trampled by a horse and a man was fatally clubbed by a police officer, who later was acquitted of murder charges.

On October 27, 1974, a massive pro-Puerto Rican-independence rally was held in Madison Square Garden that included speeches by Juan Mari Brás, Angela Davis (a prominent counterculture activist and leader of the American Communist Party), actress Jane Fonda, the Cuban ambassador to the U.N., and Pedro Albizu Campos' son, Pedro Jr. The rally was timed to coincide with hearings on the status of Puerto Rico by the U.N. Special Committee on Decolonization. (In 1977, that Committee, pushed by Cuba, reaffirmed "the inalienable right of the people of Puerto Rico to self-determination and independence.")

In the early morning hours of the previous day, five FALN bombs exploded in downtown Manhattan. Each explosive device was concealed in a blue airline shoulder bag containing propane tanks, dynamite, a detonator, a wrist watch timer, and a battery. One, planted in a car parked in the back of the Marine Midland Building at 140 Broadway, blew a crater in the street. It tore the car in half, sending its rear end flying more than 150 feet over a retaining wall and into the Chase Manhattan Bank Plaza across the street. The blast shattered windows in as high as the twenty-first floor of the bank's tower and in surrounding buildings such as the Federal Reserve Bank of New York's neo-Florentine fortress, littering the area with broken glass. The FALN had left the bombs laying on the sidewalk, without taking any measures to ensure that passersby wouldn't be injured or killed.

Afterward, a woman with a Hispanic accent, who identified herself as a member of the FALN, which no one then knew of, called the Associated Press. She directed reporters to a telephone booth on Broadway where they found the first FALN communiqué, typewritten, three pages long, and bearing a logo in the masthead comprised of a five-point star emblazoned with shadowed capital letters "FALN" and the words "Fuerzas Armadas de Liberación Nacional—Puertorriqueño." The statement demanded unconditional and immediate independence for Puerto Rico, asserting that "mayor Yanki corporations" had been attacked because they were "an integral part of Yanki monopoly capitalism" and were to be considered "responsible for the murderous policies of the Yanki government in Puerto Rico." It contained references to Marx and a Revolutionary People's Army, and ended with, "LONG LIVE FREE PUERTO RICO. LONG LIVE THE UNITY OF ALL PEOPLE IN A STRUGGLE AGAINST IMPERIALISM. FALN CENTRAL COMMAND."

In the wake of those bombings, a sizeable New York Police Department contingent began working on the case, and the NYPD's intelligence branch put a score of informants out on the streets. Also, the FBI assigned close to twenty agents to investigate. Most were seasoned veterans, some of whom participated in the probes of the attacks on the Blair House and House of Representatives in the early 1950s. But two—Don Wofford and Lou Vizi—were brand new to the Bureau and had only arrived in New York that month.

Vizi, who grew up in Philadelphia, was tall and angular, with a brooding look. He had considered becoming a priest before dropping out of Jesuit school and joining the Air Force. Wofford was short, mustached, bespectacled, smoked incessantly, and spoke without coming up for air with a southern accent, having been born and raised in Wilmington, North Carolina. "While he doesn't look like him," Joe Connor observed, "Don makes me think of Dennis Weaver in the 'McCloud' TV show, a fearless cowboy marshal riding around the Big Apple."

Vizi and Wofford, each a Vietnam vet, met for the first time at the start of the FALN investigation and would go on to work together for over forty years, the first eight years "hand in glove." "Every night," Wofford recalls, "we'd go over the details of the FALN case and what we had learned that day while trying to find out who could drink the most Budweisers. Lou saw things from an urban street smarts background that I didn't have." After Vivi's death from leukemia in 2016, Wofford confessed, "I'll never have another friend like Lou."

Wofford and Vizi were assigned to cover leads and interview suspects. But they were unable to develop useful information. Many on the FBI team suspected there was no separate Puerto Rican terrorist group and that the bombs had been planted by a splinter group of the Weathermen that had recruited some Puerto Rican members. Wofford was asked to read up on and learn about the Puerto Rican independence movement, which he "had no clue about before then."

Close to midnight on December 11, 1974, a female with a "Nuyorican" (a New York-born Puerto Rican) Hispanic accent—one that police old-timers correctly pegged as belonging to someone who'd grown up in Spanish Harlem—called 911 to report a dead body in an abandoned five-story tenement building in East Harlem, known as "El Barrio" for its large Puerto Rican population. A radio car from the 23rd Precinct was dispatched, driven by Angel Poggi, a twenty-two-year-old father of two who was ending an eight-hour shift on his first day on patrol. In the seat next to Poggi was his training officer, Detective Ray Flynn.

Upon arriving at 336 East 110th Street, Flynn headed for an exterior doorway leading to the cellar. Poggi walked up the stoop to the main entrance double doors, directly underneath a fire escape. He tried to open a door, but it barely budged. Using his flashlight to peer inside, Poggi saw that part of the foyer wall had fallen in.

Poggi was unable to see that secured to the inside of the door was a flight bag filled with propane tanks, a lantern battery, and a pipe nipple containing dynamite. When he tried again to open the door, a clothespin-styled firing device detonated the bomb. The explosion shattered the door into shards and drove Poggi back onto the sidewalk, his face, neck, and chest riddled with fragments of the bomb and door. Blown off the door was a sheet of tin on which was a crudely drawn hammer and sickle containing the words, "The W.A.S.P.S. own this country and we the minorities must change it."

The FALN subsequent communication made clear the group's intention to harm cops. It also cited a revenge motive—"the response of the Puerto Rican people to the brutal murder of Martin (Tito) Perez by the sadistic animals of the 25th Precinct on Sunday, December 1, 1974." Perez was a teenage Puerto Rican arrested for playing conga drums in a subway train. Hours later, he hanged himself with his own belt in a cell. An East Harlem neighborhood committee was formed to protest Perez's death, claiming that he "never wore a belt" and that "he was murdered, left to hang on the bars of his cell to create the appearance of a suicide."

After a month-long grand jury investigation, during which eighteen witnesses were interrogated, it was determined that Perez had committed suicide. The police officer who failed to remove Perez's belt while he was in custody was suspended for thirty days. Wofford and Vizi visited the 25th Precinct, in East Harlem, and read through the files. "We also interviewed several officers, the district attorney's investigators, and even some prisoners who were in the same cell block at the time," recounted Wofford. "Bottom line is that, like the grand jury concluded, it was just a screw-up. Although in the streets of Spanish Harlem, everyone was convinced that the police had killed Perez."

Officer Poggi was disfigured and lost his right eye as well as partial vision in his left eye, and the use of his right hand was impaired. Given the city's severe fiscal crisis, Poggi had been one of three hundred officers scheduled to be laid off in February 1975. But spurred by this attack, the New York City Council worked with the New York State legislature to pass legislation to exempt any civil servant from dismissal for up to one year if he was hospitalized because of injuries sustained in the performance of his duties and judged medically unfit to return to work. Poggi would remain on the NYPD force in a clerical position until 1982, when he retired. NYPD detective Elmer Toro, who investigated the bombing, later said that "Poggi became part of the living dead. Emotionally, he was gone."

Poggi was Puerto Rican-born, making the first human casualty of the FALN a Boricua landsman. He was typical of the Puerto Rican policemen who would come to hate the FALN and the *independista* movement, which they viewed as the opposite path for themselves and their families to a better life.

Poggi easily could have been killed, and it would take only to the next month for the FALN to assume a murderous label.

# CHAPTER 13
## *Consequences*

*My father's incident with terrorism continues to haunt me, and I continue to mourn him. He is not the same person, and we are not the same family. For myself and my sisters, it was much more than a glance at the violence on television. Violence had entered our home and hearts.*

—Kelley Murray

ON JANUARY 24, 1975, during lunch hour in Fraunces Tavern, Bill Newhall, Charlie Murray, and Dave Erskine had been seated on the side of the table opposite the bomb. Their lives were spared because the blast, as it came through the wall, raised the thick wooden table into the air milliseconds before it impacted the men, providing a partial shield. But each suffered massive wounds, many of them from shrapnel, glass, and flying silverware that lodged in their torsos.

Erskine, short, slender, athletic, and with a slim face whose eyes burned with intensity, was blown across the room, ending up face down on the floor. "I was so disoriented at first that I thought I was dead. There was stuff piled on top of me that I managed to throw off. When I got to my feet, I saw dust everywhere." Erskine stumbled to a window. "A large black man stood outside. He reached up, grabbed me, lifted me out, and put me down gently across the street leaned up against a building." As Erskine sat battered and shivering, waiting for help, a woman hurried over. "She was wearing a camel hair coat, which she took off and laid it on me. The blood oozing from me must have ruined her coat. For the rest of my life, I will always remember the kindness of those two persons." An EMT medic spotted Erskine and examined him. At first, the medic thought that bones were sticking out of Erskine's legs, but then realized they were pieces of a table. "You won't dance for a while," he told Erskine, "but you'll live."

Murray, after regaining consciousness, noticed that a beam had fallen on his right side, and that "the body of my good friend Frank lay dead at my feet." Alex Berger also died at the scene, while Jim Gezork, a married father of two girls who had his leg blown off, passed away hours later on a hospital operating table. Gezork had joined Scott Paper out of college in 1964 as a shift floor manager. His career quickly progressed, and, by December 1974, after receiving an M.B.A. in Finance from Wharton, he had risen to become an Assistant Treasurer. Gezork was a "great guy," recalls Erskine. "He was big, gangly, and quite an athlete. We both had been sprinters in college. In fact,

Jim was captain of the Swarthmore track team. We joked that we would settle who was fastest with a race down the road behind Scott Paper. We never got to do that, and I suspect that, if we had, Jim would have whooped me." Gezork's wife, Cynthia, had known him since nursery school. "She was utterly devastated," remembers Erskine.

Newhall was found outside, lying on a sidewalk grate. He woke up in the emergency room of nearby Beekman-Downtown Hospital, which was overwhelmed with casualties, asking why he was there. At his side was his wife, who had heard the explosion from a building in the Wall Street area, where she worked. "Someone brought me a hand mirror and showed me what I looked

*Sidewalk victims*

*Damage inside*

like," remembers Newhall. "I could only see out of one eye. It was as if I had sat on a stool and let Muhammed Ali and Joe Frazier pummel my face. I had no idea it was that bad." Newhall's boss visited, witnessed Newhall, and promptly rushed out into the hall to throw up.

Yet Newhall was among the lucky ones. As he stated twenty-five years later while giving testimony before the Senate Judiciary Committee, "Jim, Alex, and Frank died terrible deaths." The Medical Examiner's Office described their bodies as mangled "almost beyond recognition."

Alex Berger (not immediately known to be Jewish) and Frank Connor were given last rites by The Reverend Daniel Rooney of the nearby Our Lady of the Rosary

Church, along with the fourth fatality, Harold "Chic" Sherbourne. Sherbourne was a sixty-six-year-old Navy veteran, Anglers Club member, and prominent investment banker whose career on Wall Street spanned four decades. Known as a "perfect gentleman," Sherbourne was yet another of the victims with a tie to Wharton, serving as chairman of the board of trustees of the school's Securities Industry Institute. Part of a flying door smashed through his skull while he sat having lunch with friends at his favorite restaurant. Sherbourne had planned to leave moments later for a skiing weekend in Vermont.

Deenie Berger, twenty-seven years old and six months pregnant, was driving from her home from Cherry Hill, New Jersey to Queens to meet her husband at his parents' apartment when she heard on the radio about a "pretty serious" bombing in the Wall Street area. Deenie kept ruminating over the story. By the time she reached Queens, Deenie was deeply worried that it involved Alex and that "it wasn't good."

As soon as Deenie arrived at Alex's parents' apartment, she asked if they had heard from him. "When they said no, I knew for sure, because Alex would certainly have telephoned to reassure them." Deenie repeatedly called police stations, hospitals, and news stations, to no avail. Finally, she called her parents, who had been told of Alex's death by his boss. "My mother answered, heard my voice, and began crying hysterically. My dad took the phone from her. I said, 'Do you have any information about Alex?' He hesitated. 'He was injured.' 'How badly?'

I responded. He hesitated again before admitting, 'He's in the morgue.'"

Deenie's family struggled to locate the morgue that Alex's body had been taken to. They forbade her from going there to identify Alex, out of fear that the trauma might cause a miscarriage. It was Deenie's brother, Gary, who identified Alex's body and claimed Alex's possessions, which included a wristwatch stopped at the exact time of the detonation.

Forced to accept that she was a widow, Deenie had to compose herself enough to convey to Cilly and Joséf Berger that their beloved son had been murdered. The following Sunday, at the funeral home, Deenie led her father-in-law to Alex's open casket. "He had a hard time believing it was Alex," Deenie recalls. "It was his face. Alex always had a smile on his face. Now the expression was ... different."

When Frank Connor left for work that Friday morning, as was his usual custom, he called upstairs to his sons, "Love you guys." They didn't answer, an omission that ordinarily would have meant nothing. Upon returning from school, Joe helped his mother layer the meat, cheese, and pasta for the highly anticipated lasagna dinner to celebrate his birthday and Tom's. "Mom was a good cook," Connor recounts, "and made great Italian food for an Irish woman."

When she first heard of a bombing at a place she knew Frank occasioned to dine with clients, Mary wasn't worried. "Frank always wore one of his best suits when he had clients in town to entertain, and he hadn't done so on that day." Nonetheless, Mary dialed Frank's office, and when someone answered his direct line, she responded, "Frank! It's you! Thank God you're alright!" But it was the voice of one of Frank's colleagues. "He was there, wasn't he?" Though it would be hours before his death was confirmed, Mary knew that instant. "All I wanted to do at that moment was run out the door, and keep running."

The news traveled quickly. Mary's niece, Jean Schlag Nebbia, twelve years old, remembers her father Donald being told of Frank's death over their kitchen phone. "He stumbled back and grabbed onto the wall. We all got quiet. He told us kids that Uncle Frank had been killed by a bomb, and then he rushed out." Joe Quinn, a friend of Joe's whose family was close with the Connors, recalls, "It was the only time I remember hearing my dad cry."

Tom and Joe, playing in a field across from their house, were summoned home by their mother. As darkness settled, the house grew smaller as it began to fill with relatives, friends, neighbors, and a knot of men in dark suits who were Frank's bank colleagues. One of them was Tom Mullany. "We were all in shock. Most of Frank's friends were no older than in their early thirties. Death was a faraway notion."

Joe tried to console his mother by insisting that his father hurt his leg and was trapped under wood and bricks, waiting for the firemen to rescue him. "I can still see the hopeful image I had in my head that day. An injured Frank Connor struggling, pushing away debris, trying to free his trapped legs." Finally, Joe and Tom were told that their daddy "was gone." Recalls Joe, "The man who said that to me picked me up. I reached over his shoulder and punched him in the back with all my strength. It was the moment our lives ended."

Donald Schlag took on the responsibility of going to Margaret Connor's apartment to convey the news and bring her to the Connor house. "She was speechless. Numb. Her son was the love of her life."

That night, Tom and Joe huddled in their mom's bed. In tears, Joe asked if Grandma Connor was still his grandmother. "Mom looked at me very assuredly and answered, 'Of course, she will always be your grandmother.' That meant everything to me at that point, because I knew that Mom and Grandma would keep the family together."

A few days after the bombing, Joe dreamt of his family walking along the Hudson River. "We were once again a complete family. Happy, loving, and all together. While I was euphoric that my dad was back, there was this nagging feeling that it could not last. Right before the dream ended, I asked my father, 'Why did you leave us, Daddy?' I can still sense his warmth, and even his smell, as he looked at me and replied, 'I didn't want to, but I had to.'"

# CHAPTER 14
## *The FBI Mobilizes*

*In answer to the bombing of Fraunces, the FBI threw away the book with respect to resource economy. Not only because it was so heinous but because the FBI had a point to make. That they could solve this type of crime, quickly and efficiently.*

—Rick Hahn, FBI

THE FRAUNCES TAVERN BOMBING was striking in its savagery. Evil strode onto the U.S. stage and revealed itself, the kind we are more acquainted with today. Despite it occurring during an era plagued with violence, Americans were not yet imbued with the sense of being on the front line, carrying the unease of potential victimhood.

The FALN never articulated a coherent vision of what Puerto Rican independence would mean. Rather, they sought to garner media attention, show the government as unable to protect its citizenry, goad law enforcement to over-react, and polarize Puerto Ricans and Americans generally. A description by author and journalist Rick Perlstein of radicals generally is aptly applied to the FALN: "They are narcissists detached from reality, certain that their spark would ignite the great silent masses who share the same sense of futility and frustration."

Within fifteen minutes of the detonation, the Associated Press received a phone call from a male with a Spanish accent boasting that the action was the handiwork of the FALN. He directed police to a nearby phone booth, which contained a note stating, "We, FALN, take full responsibility for the especially [sic] detonated bomb that exploded today at Fraunces Tavern, with reactionary corporate executives inside." The FALN communiqué ended with the admonition, "You have unleashed a storm from which you comfortable Yankis cannot escape."

The language "We, FALN, take full responsibility" was significant, as no individual would ever be conclusively identified as the bomber. Those words made clear that the bombing was a group effort, with every member bearing responsibility for it.

The note claimed that the violence was retaliation for a "CIA ordered bomb" that went off two weeks earlier in a restaurant in the main plaza of Mayagüez, one of Puerto Rico's largest cities. A bomb, placed by an unidentified and presumably right-wing group, did explode in a Mayagüez restaurant on January 11, 1975 during a celebration of the birthday of Eugenio María de Hostos, a nineteenth-century Puerto Rican educator, philosopher, and independence advocate. Two persons were killed, and ten others were injured. The event had been organized by the Puerto Rican Socialist Party, and its leader, Juan Mari Brás, was the main speaker.

The reference to the Mayagüez incident, and the deaths of two Puerto Ricans, helped explain why the Fraunces Tavern bombing, designed to kill on a large scale, deviated from the FALN's previous focus on symbolism and damaging property. (Over four decades later, FALN leader Oscar López Rivera would refer to the Mayagüez violence in answering a question posed to him in a Minneapolis community forum about his role in the Fraunces Tavern bombing.) As observed by Louise Richardson, an Irish political scientist and author whose field of study is terrorism, "The most powerful theme in any conversation with terrorists past or present ... is revenge." To which may be added Mahatma Gandhi's view that, "The old law of an eye for an eye leaves everybody blind."

The headline of *The New York Post* the next day correctly blared out, "Massive Hunt for Terrorists." The FBI is the U.S.' lead law enforcement agency for investigating and preventing acts of terrorism. At that time, its New York field office was headed by John Malone, who by then was the longest-serving field division head in FBI history. Malone's office had launched inquiries into the early 1970s attacks on New York police and others by domestic terrorist groups, airplane hijackings, major East Bloc spies operating in and around New York, and violent bank robbers such as the ones portrayed in the movie "Dog Day Afternoon." By 1975, the FBI also had the benefit of new legislative tools, particularly Title III wiretap authority and the Racketeer Influenced and Corrupt Organizations Act, which offered the Bureau additional ways to address organized criminal groups as a whole rather than piecemeal.

Given the complexity of the search, the concurrent jurisdiction of the local police, and the NYPD's potential invaluable assistance (none of the FBI agents on the case were from New York), at Malone's invitation, the NYPD assigned a half dozen more of its own officers to the FBI's forty-agent operation. The enhanced squad was provided by senior FBI officials with a myriad of highly sought-after vehicles, surveillance aircraft, and technological equipment.

Don Wofford was appointed to lead the FALN task force, which would become the forerunner of future joint terrorist task forces the FBI would form. Wofford and Vizi had first learned of an explosion at Fraunces Tavern while riding on the FDR Drive listening to their car's AM radio. "They said on the news something to the effect of 'Fraunces Tavern has been blown up,'" Wofford recalls. "But not being a true New Yorker, I had no idea what Fraunces Tavern was." Soon Wofford was radioed by an FBI office supervisor and told that the explosion had been caused by a gas leak and that he and Vizi didn't need to go to the site. "So, of course, we went down there anyway."

When Wofford and Vizi arrived, NYPD Bomb Squad members took them inside. "The hole in the concrete floor, and the overall destruction caused by what appeared to be a high-intensity explosive device, made me guess that dozens of people must have been killed," remembers Wofford. Years later, Wofford would testify that the bombing was the "most unbelievable one he'd ever seen. And that includes my time in Vietnam." The assignment given Wofford and Vizi would become an obsession for them.

Vizi was tagged as the liaison to the entire NYPD, including their Bomb and Arson Squads, and helped ensure that one law enforcement agency wouldn't be surveilling the other inadvertently. Another agent on the task force was Rick Hahn, a forensic explosives expert who would become the greatest expert on the FALN and go on to assist in solving the 1993 World Trade Center, Lockerbie (Pan Am Flight 103), Avianca Airlines Flight 203, and Oklahoma City bombings. At the time, Hahn also was relatively new to the FBI, having become an agent the previous fall. Born and raised in Chicago, after Hahn graduated high school, an agent in his church congregation helped Hahn land a clerical position with the FBI. He worked at the agency while attending DePaul University, where he obtained a degree in English literature.

After completing six years of military service, Hahn "didn't know what I wanted to go into. The young agents in Chicago talked me into joining the FBI. And so, I went to the FBI Academy in Quantico for sixteen weeks and then went on active duty in the Bureau." Tall, thin, and fit from a daily regimen of running and weightlifting,

Hahn has been described as having "the eyes, the look of an agent—he sees into you." Joe Connor observed of Rick, "He looks like he could have lived in the old West."

Hahn arrived at the Fraunces Tavern site in the late afternoon and stood in the crowd watching the Bomb Squad members inside. "It was just bizarre ... like some sort of macabre pantomime. You couldn't hear much because the generators that were keeping the lights on were running. But you could see these guys moving around in the inside, knee-deep in kindling of chairs and ceiling, and cables and whatnot, trying to make sense of things."

Soon, word spread among the FBI agents that Jim Ingram, the FBI Special Agent in Charge of Foreign Intelligence and Internal Security in New York, was holding a conference across the street. "So, we all went," Hahn recalls. "Standing in front of a building, he said we're going to form a new squad and solve this case and anyone that wants to volunteer for it let me know and we'll put the squad together. Of course, I volunteered."

At the start of the FALN bombing investigation in October 1974, Wofford and Vizi were taken aside by Al Saviola, a veteran FBI agent. "Whoever did this didn't just pop out of thin air and decide to lay down some bombs," Saviola told them. "They've probably been out participating in Puerto Rican causes, demonstrations, and rallies. Writing menacing letters. Making angry threats. Just go to the files. The answers will be there."

The task force searched their files and those of the NYPD for individuals known to be active in the Puerto Rican independence movement. To that list were added names derived from numerous other sources. Some came from photographs the police had taken of the persons present at a pro-independence demonstration at City Hall that preceded the bombing which injured Angel Poggi. Others resulted from information provided by informants. The FBI placed agents on rooftops in Spanish Harlem to take photos of places where known Puerto Rican independence promoters congregated. "We also used agents who were part of the FBI's surveillance squad," Wofford recounts. "Quite a few females and minorities. They'd dress down to the point that they almost looked homeless, walk the streets or drive cabs, surveil suspects, and otherwise keep their ears open." There turned out to be no shortage of suspects to interview and track—the problem was that each one potentially required laborious and futile inquiry.

The Fraunces Tavern bombing was, as termed that day by Puerto Rico's Governor Rafael Hernandez Colon, "a tragic and senseless act which is alien to everything the Puerto Rican people believe and cherish ... an act of cowardice and ideological savagery." Its investigation would be forcefully pursued by the well-equipped task force on numerous fronts for years. Although marked by courage, perseverance, and determination, its effort would be tainted with failure.

# CHAPTER 15
## *Learning to Cope*

*One night, when my son Frank was ten months old, he was particularly cranky. I picked him up to calm him. When I looked into his eyes, I was frozen, feeling that I was holding not him but that he was my father holding me, as if my dad needed to hold his little boy just one more time.*

—Joe Connor

A COMMON SORROW EMANATING from personal tragedy is the realization that the world keeps spinning and the precious gift of time moves inexorably forward. With Frank not there to slay life's monsters, the Connor family carried on. "What gave me the strength to continue," Mary recalls "was that Frank loved me and his boys and would know and expect that I would take care of them. I could not afford to be depressed." Grandma Connor was Mary's rock. "When I would fret unnecessarily," Mary recalls, "she would half joke to me, 'You are doing okay if neither of the boys is locked up.'"

The family received an outpouring of support from family, friends, and neighbors. In a time well before the concept of a victim's compensation fund such as the one established by Congress after 9/11, the years that followed brought financial stress to the Connors. "We received only a modest insurance life insurance payment for my dad's death," Joe recalls. "My mom had to be careful and smart. I had A&P sneakers while my friends wore Pumas." Many of Frank Connor's friends and business associates contributed to a trust established for the educations of Tom and Joe.

The summer after Frank's murder, Mary brought her sons to visit her family in Ireland. Granny Lynch and other family members urged Mary and her boys to remain. While Mary would never have abandoned her mother-in-law, it was eleven-year-old Tom who responded, "I love Ireland and my Granny and Granddad, but I am American, and I want to go home."

While mourning gradually lost its dominion, Margaret, Mary, Joe, and Tom were left with, as Joe says, "the forever image of our hero murdered." Margaret was outwardly stoic. Mary recalls that the first time she saw her mother-in-law break down was years after the bombing when Margaret finally could bring herself to visit her son's grave. "I could better accept this," Margaret cried, "if he had died of cancer or was killed in an accident."

For months afterward, Mary would prepare dinner and set the dining room table for four. "Each night, I could still hear his car coming down the driveway."

During difficult moments, Mary would talk to Frank. "I would complain and then scream at him that he has it easy now. And then I would punch the door."

Well-meaning friends and family often would make wounding remarks to Mary, like "Now you have two kids and an angel in heaven watching over you." One day, a priest came to the house to console Mary, saying to her, "It was God's will." Mary was angered. "How could I tell my kids that it was God's will that their father be killed, and at the same time tell them to love God and do the right thing? Better to just tell them that Frank was at the wrong place at the wrong time."

One way in which Mary instilled in the boys the will to succeed was by having them focus on sports, wrestling in particular. "Tom and I took to it with a passion," Joe recalls. "We always had in mind our dad, who would have been disappointed with anything less than our best.

Mary Connor ultimately would find solace with another priest. Gerry Tully had immigrated to America from Ireland as a young man and tended to parishioners throughout New Jersey. One day, Frank's cousin, also a priest, invited Gerry to join his congregation in attending a play in Manhattan. There, Gerry and Mary met. Gerry helped Mary release her anger and bitterness, and to "love God more than fear Him." In 1979, after Gerry, disenchanted as a priest, received papal dispensation from Pope John Paul II, he left the clergy, a decision he later described as like going through a divorce, to pursue a career in psychotherapy.

Soon after, he and Mary married. In Mary's eyes, Gerry had been sent from God to the Connor family. But as for Joe, "I flipped out. Who was this guy who thought he could take my dad's place?" At Mary and Gerry's wedding, when Joe was thirteen, he was by his own admission, "such a little bastard. I ripped at my boutonniere so that it hung from my tuxedo jacket. I had my transistor radio and was listening to the Mets game during the entire ceremony. And afterword, I snidely told my Mom that you could see the price tag on the heel of her shoe when she knelt. But she understood. And Gerry, too."

Over the years, Gerry found many ways to honor Frank Connor. "One," explains Joe, "is simply how good he was to my mom and her family, especially Grandma Connor. Gerry treated her like she was his own mother, from repairing and painting her apartment to driving her to her appointments to visiting her all the time she was in assisted living and a nursing home." There is a plaque in a Bergen County park honoring Frank Connor, and Gerry has taken on the role of caring for it. "He brings a brush, cleaning materials, and fresh paint and cleans the plaque and repaints the name. Who else would do that? Jeez, I haven't even done that. And the irony of it is, I suspect that my dad, who grew up as a street guy, would have been amused at Gerry being so caring."

\*

Three months after Alex Berger's death, Deenie gave birth to a boy, Adrian, whose expressions and mannerisms were reminiscent of his father. "From an early age," Deenie recounts, "I introduced Adrian to Alex. So, he grew up with Alex being very much a part of our family." Deenie did not experience financial hardship. "Rohm and Haas was terrific to me. But I did have to endure being discriminated against as a single mother." Deenie had difficulty obtaining a credit card or buying a car. "Everyone expected a husband to co-sign." One day, a man from a remodeling company arrived at Deenie's house. "I asked him to give me an estimate for re-doing the bathroom. He refused to talk to me unless my husband was present and signed off. I told him to get out. The situation I was in changed my personality. I had been an extremely quiet and shy person. But now I had to fight for everything."

*

Of the dozens of people at Fraunces who were injured, some were permanently maimed, while others suffered from a variety of bodily damages, including disfigurement. The doctors' greatest initial concern for Bill Newhall was the condition of his legs, which had drains and were covered in shrapnel wounds. At first, Newhall had no sensation in them. When it returned, he was left with excruciating pain for days. Newhall came close to losing his right leg, which had a large hole in its ankle and its nerves severed. Surgery saved it.

Among Newhall's many other injuries was a punctured left ear drum, which over the years continually led to ear infections and other health problems. Newhall would develop hearing loss whenever he had a cold. In 2011, a particularly bad cold left him completely deaf in his left ear. A CAT scan revealed a hole the size of a quarter in the base of the left side of Newhall's skull, caused by the bombing. "As a result, part of my brain had pierced its lining and was protruding through the hole. Also, brain fluid was leaking out through the same hole." Because of the risk of meningitis, which could prove fatal, Newhall's doctor recommended surgery involving opening his skull above the left ear, removing the brain matter that was "sticking down into the hole," and sealing the brain lining and hole with muscle and bone from elsewhere in his body. Newhall asked the surgeon, "Do I need that part of the brain?" He replied, 'Well, we won't know until it's excised.'"

To this day, shrapnel remains embedded in Newhall's legs and head. "The doctors thought it might cause too much damage to try to dig out every piece," he recalls. "My right foot always feels on fire, particularly at night, and whenever possible I keep it elevated. At times, the pain is unbearable."

Newhall's hospital roommate was Charlie Murray. In the afternoon of January 24, Murray's daughter Kelley, eleven years old at the time, was watching the five o'clock news. She stared at the footage of the devastated restaurant and the injured. "Panic swept over me. I felt compelled to call my father's office at 23 Wall Street.

Unable to reach him, I paced in circles, breaking my path only to stare at the clock."

Hours later, Kelley's mom came home carrying a large brown shopping bag. As Kelley recounts:

> She sat down on the sofa and slowly, speechlessly sorted the contents. She pulled out his suit, covered with blood, dirt, and the powerful stench of gunpowder. From the breast pocket of the suit she extracted his blood-soaked checkbook. Such familiar pieces of my father appeared to me then distant and horrifying.

Among the possessions of Frank Connor given Mary was his wallet, of which she later would write, "Cuts, burns, and scratches were evident throughout the inside and outside of the three-inch piece of leather, with stripes of soot also visible. It looked like it was in a fight, one that was lost and, with it, the owner of the wallet."

When Kelley, along with her mom, was first able to visit her father, she witnessed a man "bruised, beaten up, and wrapped in gauze. I wanted him to laugh, but I knew that he would not. I felt ripped apart. I could not stand how fragile he looked and sounded."

Newhall and Murray each spent weeks in the hospital. During that time, several prominent Puerto Rican leaders, including Herman Badillo, the first Puerto Rican-born Congressman, stopped by to assure Newhall that New York's Puerto Rican community was opposed to the FALN's cause and found its methods abhorrent. One day, a lawyer visited Newhall and Murray to talk them into suing Fraunces Tavern. They threw him out (So did Mary Connor, separately).

When Charlie Murray returned home, his family gathered around him in the living room. Kelley remembers her sister Sarah, only three, "having her tiny hands all over his tired face. She was animated in a way we had never seen before." Murray was described by his daughter as, "a traumatized man, permanently deaf in one ear and blind in one eye, picking shrapnel from his body for months to follow. A wooden splinter had severed the tendon in his right hand, which was in a cast. When he slept, he did so sitting up to drain the blood behind his eyes." The sight in Murray's right eye did return. "But, ten years later," Murray recounts, "the retina became detached. And there was so much scar tissue that the eyesight never came back."

Kelley and her family received enormous support from their Brooklyn Heights community. "People prayed for my father in school, and he was mentioned every day at Mass. It was in church that I cried the hardest, drowned out by the hymns."

As for Newhall, it was months before he could walk and, even then, only with the use of a cane. After Newhall and Murray returned to work, their first out-of-town assignment together was a client meeting in Pittsburgh. Murray had developed severe agoraphobia, an anxiety disorder. He became hesitant to go outside and was easily startled by loud noises. Being too nervous to fly, Murray insisted on taking the train. It turned out that Newhall felt uncomfortable on his flight out to Pittsburgh, so he and Murray rented a car for the drive home.

Not long afterward, Murray quit Morgan Guaranty. "I loved my job at Morgan. I didn't want to work anywhere else. To me, it was the center of the universe. But I couldn't handle the mental rigors of the position anymore." Years later, Murray began to have "terrifying dreams in which I was lost and couldn't get home. I talked to a therapist, who told me that I was suffering from post-traumatic stress disorder. They didn't even have that diagnosis back in 1975."

Murray and his family moved out of Brooklyn Heights. "People thought we left because we were afraid of staying in New York City. That wasn't the case at all. We all loved living in the Heights. Particularly the kids. Our car was full of tears the day we left. It was so painful for me to put them through that." The Murrays resettled in southern Vermont, where they bought an inn that they operated for decades.

*

Dave Erskine woke up after the blast to find himself lying naked on a table in the trauma unit of Bellevue Hospital on First Avenue in the Kips Bay neighborhood of Manhattan. "I heard the doctor telling my parents, who lived on a farm outside of Allentown, Pennsylvania, that he didn't know if I would live or not. They had to struggle with that for a few hours until someone reassured them I would make it."

Erskine's injuries ran across his body. "I felt a sharp pain in my groin and suddenly I had this terrifying notion that I had lost something there. But it was just a catheter." Both of Erskine's eardrums were blown out. "I had four operations to put grafts in to close the eardrums. With only limited success." Erskine has endured severe hearing problems over the decades since the bombing, despite the improvement in hearing aids. "The worst part is how isolated you feel when you can't hear what's going on around you."

\*

Reminders of his father would weigh on Joe's heart through the years. "Dad was a sports fan and, above all, a Giants football fan. He made it to a few games, but for most of his life, the Giants were horrible." In January 1987, the Giants finally reached the Super Bowl. "While my Villanova University friends partied, not wanting to miss a play, I watched the game against Denver by myself on a black-and-white TV in my dorm room. As the game ended, I cried thinking of him and how happy he would be to see his Giants win the big one." (Decades later, Connor would bring his own son to Super Bowl 42 in Phoenix, where the underdog Giants beat the then-undefeated New England Patriots. "The emotions of being there with my Frank, who is so much like the grandfather he would never know, ran deep.")

Later in 1987, while out drinking with college buddies in Manhattan, Connor walked into Fraunces Tavern impromptu. "I had always been spooked by the thought of going there. I sat at the bar and struck up a conversation with the bartender. It turned out that he had been in the restaurant during the bombing and began describing what happened. I left and couldn't bring myself to go back for the longest time."

After graduating from Villanova in 1988, Connor, who had grown into the image of his father, joined J.P. Morgan Bank. "One year, the department I was working in scheduled its holiday party at Fraunces Tavern. Only days before it was to take place, someone in senior management had the venue moved because of me, although I hadn't asked for it. I was struck by the total unawareness of everyone in my area of the bombing that had happened there."

In the spring of 1990, Connor joined college buddies on a Carnival cruise of the Caribbean leaving from Puerto Rico. "Going to that island never bothered me," Connor explains, "as I knew the vast majority of the Puerto Rican people didn't support the FALN, nor would they have condoned my dad's death." On their last day out, during a ship party, he met Danielle Metz, a nineteen-year-old college student from Long Island. Once Connor began dating light-haired, only slightly Irish Danielle, he would laugh to himself recalling the advice his dad blurted out to his sons one day when Mary was on his case about something: "Bring home a blonde,

*Joe and Danielle Connor with Grandma Connor*

never marry a donkey"—"donkey" being a reference stemming from an old saying, "It's cheaper to hire an Irishman than a donkey."

Joe and Danielle wed in October 1994. Their first child, a son, was named after Connor's dad. He was followed two years later by Kathleen, the first female born into the Connor family in almost a century. As Connor's children matured, he would find the right time to tell each of them of that fateful day in January 1975. To leap back through the decades to a time when an immigrant's son held all the world's promise, before it shattered.

# CHAPTER 16
## Ascendance of the FALN

*We had a lot of scientific data and bomb scene evidence,
but for two years we really didn't know who those FALN
people were.*

—Jeremy Margolis

THE FRAUNCES TAVERN ATTACK was followed by an
onslaught of FALN explosive and incendiary attacks
in New York, with targets such as Gimbel's and Macy's
Department Stores, a Blimpie Restaurant, a Hilton Hotel,
the General Motors building, and a sculptured fountain
near one of the famous lions at the entrance of the New
York Public Library. Incendiary devices, often hidden in
cigarette packs, were used primarily for diversionary purposes—they would be detonated in stores and buildings
to start fires and draw police and Bomb Squad officers
away from the primary area to be attacked. Members of
the New York Arson Squad, in pursuit of clues, would

sift through over a dozen bins of rubble gathered from bombing sites.

In April 1975, a grand jury was impaneled in the Southern District of New York, which covers lower Manhattan, to investigate the Fraunces Tavern bombing as well as other FALN actions. During that same month, four more New York City buildings were bombed by the FALN. Its communiqué referred to Fraunces Tavern and sought to rationalize the blood on its hands:

> The bombing of the Anglers Club: an exclusive millionaires club that boasts of members like the Rockefellers, was a retaliatory attack against the sector of the North American ruling-class which is directly responsible for the actions of the CIA and for the wave of repression which is being murderously implemented in Puerto Rico ... Our attack on January 24, 1975 was not in any way directed against working-class people or innocent North Americans. The targets were bankers, stock brokers, and important corporate executives of monopolies and multi-national corporations. These are not friends of the working people but the enemies of humanity everywhere.

This message made clear that the FALN held many rigid beliefs regarding each person dining in Fraunces Tavern, including that they worked on Wall Street, as opposed to being, for example, tourists who decided to enjoy lunch in a famous location; were millionaire members of the Anglers Club; were part of the American "ruling class"; were not "working class people," were not innocent: and were directly responsible for U.S. policy toward Puerto Rico. In effect, the FALN profiled victims, which is entirely consistent with a tenet of terrorism as described by Louise Richardson that "the victim of the violence and the audience the terrorists are trying to reach are not the same."

The drumbeat of FALN bombings, along with an inability by authorities to prevent or solve them, soon could be heard in other cities, particularly Chicago. The Puerto Rican community in Chicago began to develop in the 1930s, with the initial migration coming not from the island but from New York City. After World War II, many Puerto Ricans were recruited by Castle Barton Associates, a private employment agency, as low-wage non-union foundry and domestic workers. By the 1960s, their community was centered in West Town and Humboldt Park on the Northwest Side and in Lincoln Park on the North Side.

The FALN first made its presence known in Chicago in June 1975 when it detonated bombs in the downtown Loop neighborhood at two bank targets. One of the bombs, contained in a camera bag, had been picked up by a man and tossed into the back seat of his car. He was saved from serious injury, if not death, when he opened the bag and discovered the bomb before it exploded.

On October 27, 1975, a series of coordinated attacks targeted federal, bank, and corporate offices in Chicago,

New York, and Washington DC. One of the explosions in Chicago, at the Continental Bank building, could be heard and felt by FBI agents in their office two blocks away. Another bomb, hidden in a bouquet of roses wrapped in green florist's paper, was gingerly defused by a Chicago Police bomb technician using wire cutters to sever the blasting cap from its triggering circuit, a delicate procedure that could have killed the officer had the slightest jarring movement occurred. In its communiqué related to those attacks, the FALN acknowledged the "moral support" given it by Fidel Castro in a speech made the previous August, in which he declared that the Cuban government "would do all it could to support the FALN."

On June 7, 1976, while bombs detonated at several corporate sites, an unexploded bomb was found in a trash container outside Chicago Police Headquarters. The area was cleared before it detonated. Had the device not been found, it likely would have injured or killed officers passing in and out of the building during the 11:00 p.m. shift change.

Over the next four years, the FALN claimed credit for twenty-five bombing and incendiary attacks in Chicago, including at two military recruiting offices and the Naval Armory. The group's focus on Chicago was spurred by continued unrest in that city as typified by the second "Division Street" riots of June 1977. They erupted after two men were shot to death by a policeman during a disturbance at a Puerto Rican Day festival. The first

Chicago Puerto Rican People's Parade was held in 1978 in response to these shootings, and a stated purpose of the parade organizers was to bring attention to the issue of self-determination for Puerto Rico.

Nor was Gotham spared further FALN blood lust, adding to the misery New Yorkers were suffering during the 1970s. Many neighborhoods were crime-ridden, its subway system was graffiti-laden, unsafe, and unreliable, prostitutes, pimps, and homeless people populated the streets, parks were feared as sites of muggings and rapes, and drug dealers occupied boarded-up and abandoned buildings. Jim McLaughlin, a beat cop in Hell's Kitchen in the early '70s, recalls, "On a daily basis, I encountered almost every crime imaginable, and some I couldn't have imagined having grown up in a sheltered environment." In 1975, the city came ever so close to bankruptcy— prompting the famous *Daily News* headline: "FORD TO CITY: DROP DEAD"—before being bailed out by a large federal loan. But the city's financial crisis would linger for years.

The nadir of New York's troubles came during 1977. On the stiflingly hot evening of July 13, lightning knocked out high-voltage power lines in Westchester, killing electrical power to most of the city for more than twenty-five hours. Subways and commuter trains halted, the skyline turned dark, streetlights, elevators, air conditioners, and water and gas pumps stopped working, food rotted in refrigerators and freezers, and airports shut down. Mayor Abe Beame held his crisis council by candlelight, while in poor neighborhoods across the city, looting and arson erupted.

As if that weren't enough, it was a summer during which David Berkowitz, better known as the "Son of Sam," a serial killer who prowled the nighttime streets, terrified New Yorkers. On July 31, Stacy Moskowitz and Robert Violante, both twenty, were necking in Violante's car in Bath Beach, Brooklyn when Berkowitz approached and shot each in the head. Moskowitz died several hours later. Violante survived, but lost an eye. The two would be the last of thirteen victims of the Son of Sam, although that wouldn't be known for another ten days, when Berkowitz was arrested.

On August 3, 1977, FALN bomb threats forced more than 100,000 people, including everyone in both World Trade Center towers, to vacate their offices. Then two bombs detonated in separate mid-town Manhattan office buildings. The first exploded on the twenty-first floor of 342 Madison Ave., which housed U.S. Defense Department security personnel. Before the blast, an employee noticed a woman's handbag left on a windowsill behind the Venetian blinds, and brought it to a colleague, Thomas Sweeney, an ex-New York cop. Struggling to open the bag, whose zipper had been glued shut, he spotted the face of a clock and wires, and alerted his co-workers, who fled the office. Seconds later, the bomb exploded, blowing out windows and cratering a concrete wall. As *The New York Times* reported, "Sweeney saved eight people from certain serious injury and perhaps death."

The second detonation resulted from sticks of dynamite concealed in an umbrella hung in a coat rack in a crowded ground floor employment office in the Mobil Oil building on East 42nd Street, a building in which Joe Connor would work many years later. Charles Steinberg, twenty-six years old, was standing nearby. The rear of his head was blown off. Steinberg, from East Rockaway on Long Island, fun-loving and jovial, was an accomplished electric bass and keyboard player who entered the temporary employment business after graduating from the University of Albany. Within a few years, he co-founded what became a successful agency with many significant corporate clients. Steinberg and his business partner,

*Charles (on left) and Bruce Steinberg, 1977*

Ivan Gerson, had stopped by the Mobil Oil employment office to find out if there were any open positions for his firm's applicants. Gerson was seriously injured by the bomb, suffering internal injuries and facial lacerations, as were six others. Bruce Steinberg flew to New York from Florida the next day to retrieve his older brother's personal belongings. "When I got there, they still were sweeping up glass on the street in front of the building."

Steinberg left behind a devastated family that included his college sweetheart and wife, Robin, as well as his parents and two brothers. Forty years later, Steven Steinberg would write in an article published by *The Daily News*, "Not a day goes by that I don't think about my younger brother ... My 95-year-old mom constantly dreams about Charles and what could have been ..."

An FALN note was wedged into a crevice at the base of the Central Park statue of José Martí. Martí, who founded the Cuban Revolutionary Party in 1892, drew much of his early inspiration from the 19th-century Puerto Rican independence advocate Ramón Emeterio Betances. Martí proclaimed as part of his party's mission the fomenting and supporting of Puerto Rican independence, famously stating that Cuba and Puerto Rico should stand together as "two wings of the same dove."

The communiqué described the explosions as a warning to multinational corporations that are "part of Yanki imperialism." It also referenced that Puerto Rico's status was slated to be discussed in the United Nations. Mayor Beame visited the site of the Mobil Oil blast later in the day and called for the resumption of the death penalty under New York law as a deterrent to terrorism. (It was not until 1994 that Congress enacted death penalty procedures and extended them to more than forty federal crimes. New York was without a death penalty until 1995.)

The pressure on the FBI to end the FALN's reign of terror mounted, with much of it coming from the Puerto Rican communities in New York and Chicago, who felt stained by them. But bombings are particularly difficult crimes to solve. And the FALN was more sophisticated than law enforcement initially appreciated. Its clandestine nature remained a formidable barrier.

For two years, law enforcement lacked solid leads and hard information. When a portion of the FALN's membership finally was unmasked, it was triggered not by law enforcement investigation but through serendipity.

# CHAPTER 17
## *The Unmasking*

*I had a wife and two little kids, and I got concerned.*
*After one of the bombings and communiqués, for a while,*
*the police put a cordon around the building on Riverside*
*Drive where we lived. It was scary, but it also was*
*confirmation that we had hit pay dirt.*

—Tom Engel

IN NOVEMBER 1976, Chicago Police discovered a safe-house on West Haddon Avenue in the city's northwest side, in one of many neighborhood buildings being refurbished with government grants. A drug addict had seen two men carrying giftwrapped packages into an apartment. Upon breaking in, he found hundreds of sticks of dynamite, along with ammonium nitrate, weapons, ammunition, wigs, and a professional makeup kit.

The intruder attempted to sell the dynamite on the street to a buyer who was a police informant. Chicago police, led back to the apartment by the junkie, searched it as well as a locked storage area on the building's first floor, finding a manual on waging guerrilla warfare plus extensive bomb-making paraphernalia, photographs of potential Chicago building targets, and maps of the city. The most critical evidence found were blank FALN stationery imprinted with the group's logo, a five-pointed star with the letters imposed over it. These were identified as being made on the same machine, using the same stencil, as FALN communiques dating to the first bombing.

The owner of the building was Carlos Alberto Torres, the son of Reverend José "El Viejo" Torres, who headed the First Congregational Church of Chicago. That church was a member of the United Church of Christ organization, a national Christian denomination. Torres' church was in Humboldt Park, a neighborhood so predominantly Puerto Rican that its main artery, Division Street, is known as *"Paseo Boricua* (Puerto Rican Walk)." *Chicago Magazine* described a Saturday night walk down Division Street at that time as, "full of Puerto Ricans packing the patios at restaurants...drinking rum cocktails and picking at roasted chicken, tostones, and black beans. The sound of traditional *bomba* and *plena* music echoes across the wide street ..." José Torres and his church were long active in Puerto Rico's independence movement.

Carlos Torres was born in September 1952 in Ponce, where the Ponce Massacre is commemorated annually in political and cultural events, and a consciousness of the suppression of the Nationalist movement runs deep. As a youth, Carlos moved with his parents from Ponce to

New York and later Chicago. He studied sociology at the University of Illinois before serving in Vietnam. After ending his active duty, Torres became a community organizer. An unassuming, soft-spoken man only five feet, five inches tall, he wore wide-rimmed glasses and sported a thick mustache. Torres had served on the First Congregational Church's theological task force and had helped to write a hymnal and book of religious texts in Spanish.

Torres became the first person to be positively identified as an FALN member. A warrant was issued for his arrest, and a manhunt began, with Chicago and New York police appealing to members of the Puerto Rican community for information. The search was intense enough that one man, Albert Torres of Long Island City, who resembled Carlos Alberto Torres, was arrested and released twice. Albert took the matter in stride, stating to the *New York Post*, "As far as I'm concerned, that guy is sick."

Interviews with residents, fingerprints, and information gleaned from documents found in his apartment led to the uncovering of three other FALN members—Carlos' wife Haydée Marie Beltran-Torres, then pregnant, Ida Luz (Lucy) Rodriguez, and her common-law husband, Oscar López Rivera, who managed the building along with Carlos Torres. Residents told FBI agents that nothing happened in the building that Torres and López Rivera didn't know about.

López Rivera, who along with Rodriguez escaped capture when they evacuated a nearby apartment they

*Oscar López Rivera*

rented, was the brother of José López, a Puerto Rican community leader in Humboldt Park. None of the four had criminal records, and each avoided arrest by vanishing, ending the double lives they had been leading. Rodriguez was working in a government department—the Environmental Protection Agency—when the bomb factory was uncovered.

Another piece of evidence recovered from the safehouse was a letter from a priest at an Episcopal Church in San Antonio to the National Commission on Hispanic Affairs (N.C.H.A.) of the Protestant Episcopal Church in New York, requesting funding of a church project. N.C.H.A.'s ostensible purpose was to aid self-help projects through grants involving refugees, education, and small businesses. Investigators learned that Carlos Torres was a member of the N.C.H.A. board and that other suspected FALN conspirators had been members of the Commission or associated with it, including López Rivera and Puerto Rican independence activist Julio Rosado, whose brother, Luis, was a consultant to the N.C.H.A.

There also was a link between N.C.H.A. and the FALN communiqués, as the N.C.H.A. had purchased the same type of Gestetner copier used by the FALN to produce their logo stationery. (Gestetners, in those pre-photocopier-days, were state-of-the-art duplicating machines that produced copies from stencils.) Records obtained by the FBI demonstrated that N.C.H.A. members traveled extensively in the United States and to Puerto Rico between 1971 and 1976.

N.C.H.A., which had several FALN members on its payroll and paid for their travel expenses between New York and Chicago, was quickly disbanded after exposure as a front group. In January 1977, after the expiration of the first Manhattan grand jury's term, a second federal grand jury was convened in the Southern District of New York to continue the investigation of the FALN. That grand jury issued subpoenas for financial and travel records, samples from typewriters and copying machines, voice and handwriting exemplars, and to compel testimony.

The inquiry exposed a deep schism with the Episcopal Church. It initially focused on two senior executives of the Church's national center—Presiding Bishop John Allin and his assistant, Suffragan Bishop Milton Wood. Wood, born and raised in Alabama, had been a prominent civil rights advocate going back to the 1950s. As rector of All Saint's Church in Atlanta, Georgia, he was integral to organizing hundreds of clergy there to prevent the governor of Georgia and the State Legislature from closing all public schools rather than integrate them. Allin and Wood cooperated with the grand jury, allowing the FBI into the Episcopal Church's office to review the Hispanic commission's files.

Subsequently, subpoenas were served on two female lay ministers of the church who worked for N.C.H.A. and had consulted with Torres in their office a week before the raid on his Chicago apartment. One was Maria Cueto, thirty-three, born to Russian émigré parents, who was the commission's staff director and the recipient of the San Antonio priest's letter. Given her position, Cueto knew best how members were chosen for the commission. Law enforcement's suspicions regarding Cueto were heightened when a dog trained to detect explosives was taken to her apartment and signaled that it smelled traces of dynamite. The other woman was Cueto's secretary, Raisa Nemikin, twenty-seven, who was born in Caracas, Venezuela of Russian emigre parents.

Tom Engel, the assistant U.S. attorney handling the N.C.H.A. case, recalls, "As soon as we served the subpoenas, well-known lawyers who routinely represented radicals began to show up and raise hell. So, we knew we were on to something." The lawyers for Cueto and

Nemikin argued several constitutional defenses, including violation of the separation of church and state and right of free association. Paul Moore Jr., the Episcopal Bishop of New York, whom *The New York Times* described at the time as "the most formidable liberal Christian voice in the city," publicly supported the women's efforts to avoid testifying. Also speaking out on behalf of Cueto and Nemikin was Pennsylvania Bishop Robert DeWitte, who wrote in the monthly magazine, *The Witness*, that "the essence of [the women's] concern is the gospel, which requires that we place ourselves clearly on the side of the poor, the oppressed. When the church does not take that stance, it is not the church."

Their publicly stated views were in defiance of the hands-off position of the church's national center headed by Allin, who said that the church would let the women's consciences guide them, but that it would not support their refusal to testify. Ironically, Engel, who was born and raised as a Quaker, married an Episcopalian woman and, in the fall of 1977, was baptized and confirmed as an Episcopalian in the Cathedral Church of St. John the Divine, the seat of Moore's diocese.

The reluctant witnesses' motions to quash the subpoenas were heard initially by the Federal District Judge Lawrence Pierce, a jurist who for many years was listed by *Ebony* magazine as one of the most influential African-Americans in the United States. Pierce denied each of the defense motions, including rejecting their argument that a priest-penitent privilege applied. He found that the

Government had demonstrated a "compelling interest" in the information sought and that its investigation was "sharply focused." The judge ordered the women to testify.

In February 1977, Cueto and Nemikin, appearing before the grand jury, were asked: When did you last speak or otherwise communicate with Carlos Torres? Identify all N.C.H.A. funds that were directed openly or secretly to the FALN. Identify any person whom you know was involved or has claimed responsibility for the Fraunces Tavern bombing. Cueto and Nemikin declined to answer any questions, invoking their Fifth Amendment right against self-incrimination. Engel obtained court orders of immunity for the two, but they maintained their refusal.

Engel made motion before Federal Judge Marvin Frankel to hold Cueto and Nemikin in contempt. Frankel, who had been one of Engel's professors at Columbia Law School, had been a noted human rights advocate. Engel remembers, "I had enormous respect for Judge Frankel, but was concerned because of his liberal bent."

Frankel listened to defense arguments in a courtroom packed with avid supporters of Cueto and Nemikin. "They were ready to make trouble," Engel recalls, "and it was only the presence of U.S. Marshals that kept the peace in the courtroom." Frankel quickly decided in favor of the Government's motion, labelling the grand jury's questions "vital, proper and important" and opining that they were serving "a deep and urgent public interest." On the issue of violation of separation of church and state, Judge Frankel declared the situation analogous to the case of a murder in a cathedral where "the priest was asked 'Did you see anything?' That would be a proper law enforcement inquiry, not a violation of a constitutionally protected privilege." The judge found several other claims by the defendants to be frivolous, at one point telling their counsel, Elizabeth Fink, to stop "beating your gums."

The U.S. Court of Appeals for the Second Circuit upheld Judge Frankel's ruling, and the two women were jailed. Also found in civil contempt and imprisoned for refusing to answer grand jury questions was Pedro Archuleta, a community activist from New Mexico who had been a N.C.H.A. member. Archuleta defiantly told the grand jury, "I will not be used to help the FBI or the Federal Government smash the Chicano struggle in the Southwest or the Puerto Rican movement for Independence, or any other movement for liberation."

As the months passed, no concrete results followed. The FALN bombings and incendiary attacks continued, and the group's messages demanded that Cueto and Nemikin be released. "The FALN specifically targeted their communications to the grand jury investigation to intimidate us and to stop the proceedings," recalls Engel. Cueto and Nemikin were kept in jail for ten months, until another judge ruled that any knowledge they may have had become stale and was unlikely to advance the grand jury's investigation. Years later, in an interview with the *San Juan Star*, Cueto, of Mexican-American heritage, explained, "I found out that what the government was doing to my people was the same thing they were doing to the Puerto Ricans in the East. The government has a deliberate plan, and it is a matter of fighting against genocide. Therefore, the FALN has a legitimate right to exist."

Heading into the summer of 1978, the FALN had been active for four years. Several of its members had been identified but none arrested, a significant black eye for the FBI. Then another bomb detonated—this time unplanned.

# CHAPTER 18
## *William Morales*

*I once met Fidel Castro. It was at a reception and I said to him, 'Thank you.'*

—William Morales

ONE OF THE GREAT BENEFITS of growing up in New York City is the availability of free or highly subsidized, quality higher education in numerous four-year and community colleges sprinkled throughout the boroughs that together form the City University of New York (CUNY). In the 1930s and '40s, when these public colleges were comprised heavily of Jewish students from poor families—a popular joke was that CCNY stood for "College for Circumcised New Yorkers—they were major centers of socialist activism. Julius Rosenberg, executed for passing information on the atomic bomb to the Soviet Union, became a leader in the Young Communist League while at City College. Frank Connor knew his son, Michael, growing up. During the McCarthy era, CUNY colleges served as one of the few places where communists in the United States could organize openly. In the 1960s, CUNY students formed an early chapter of the Students for a Democratic Society. During 1964, many SDS members traveled south to participate in Mississippi Freedom Summer. One of them, Andrew Goodman of Queens College, was murdered by the Ku Klux Klan.

In the spring of 1969, lockouts and pitched battles forced CUNY to implement an open admissions policy and establish ethnic studies programs. One of the hundreds of City College students participating in the struggle was William Morales, who would later remark, "When I was involved in the student strike, I saw that talking wasn't accomplishing anything ... The more you talked, the stronger your enemy became."

Born in February 1950 to Puerto Rican parents, Morales was raised in the Taft public housing complex in East Harlem, where neighbors remembered him as a "cordial young man who said 'Hello' to them almost apologetically." He grew up to be a short, sinewy man with thick black hair and a mustache, known to friends as "Guillermo."

Morales' sensitivity to cultural background arose early in his life. He would recount to a reporter that when he was an elementary school student at P.S. 121 in Spanish Harlem, he asked for permission to write a report on Puerto Rican history instead of British or American history. "The teacher laughed and told me that Puerto Rican people had no history." As a young adult, Morales felt that, "Puerto Ricans, alongside black people and other minorities, were oppressed in the U.S. We feared speaking Spanish in the street. They taught us to almost hate ourselves for being Puerto Rican."

After two years at City College, where he studied political science, Morales attended Manhattan's School of Visual Arts, where he earned a B.A. in Arts and Cinematography. His graduation thesis was a documentary about the development of the Nationalist movement in Puerto Rico and the death of Pedro Albizu Campos. The increasingly radicalized Morales joined the FALN. He rose to a leadership position while working at odd jobs such as a freelance photographer, drug counselor, TWA Airline ticket agent (which assisted his travels to Chicago and Puerto Rico), and filmmaker. In early 1977, after he'd been identified as an N.C.H.A. member, Morales was interviewed by the FBI's Don Wofford and Lou Vizi about his knowledge and participation in the group. Morales admitted to joining the N.C.H.A. and knowing Carlos Torres, Julio Rosado, and Oscar López Rivera, although Morales portrayed the N.C.H.A. as a truly charitable organization. His calm, accommodating demeanor convinced Wofford and Vizi that Morales was not an FALN member. But NYPD detectives Elmer Toro and William Valentine, who also were on the FALN task force, were not deceived. They interviewed him several times, to the point where Morales alleged harassment.

That Morales was an FALN leader became known on July 12, 1978, a day during which there were incendiary attacks in Manhattan's Macy's and Korvette's department stores. It also was Frank Connor's birthday—he would have turned thirty-seven years old. Morales was sitting at a workbench in his two-room apartment in East Elmhurst, Queens, screwing the cap on his fourth pipe bomb of the afternoon. In what many in law enforcement considered *schadenfreude*, the bomb exploded in his hands, ripping through the apartment and blowing out doors and windows. Morales' jaw was fractured, his face was severely damaged, and he lost numerous teeth and his left eye. Also gone were his fingers except for the left thumb, torn off at the first knuckle and found stuck to the ceiling like burnt sausages. As Morales would later recount, "The pipe bomb was open on one side, so the whole blast escaped through that end ... If the pipe had been closed, I would have been dead."

A pipe bomb was and remains a common improvised explosive device, relatively simple to assemble because it requires only three primary components: the lead pipe itself, an explosive filler such as dynamite, and a fuse or timing device such as a cell phone or, back in 1978, a wrist watch. Sometimes attached to a tank of propane gas, it can be destructive, and its detonation is loud, readily causing panic. The settings on the wrist watches that served as timers for the bombs Morales was assembling had been prepared in advance by Carlos Torres. Morales later would accuse him of setting the wrong time on one of the devices, although FBI agents speculate that powder residue carelessly left in the grooves of the cap's pipe thread may have triggered the explosion.

Before being taken into custody, a bleeding, burned, and maimed Morales limped to the stove, blew out the pilot lights, and opened the gas knobs with his mouth, attempting unsuccessfully to convert the apartment into a suicide bomb. When firefighters arrived at the scene, they assumed a gas line had burst. Then they spotted galvanized pipe of the type used to make bombs and called in the NYPD Bomb Squad. The firefighters found Morales standing over the toilet. Undeterred by pain, Morales was busy tearing up his address book and other FALN documents with his teeth.

Morales was carried to an awaiting ambulance, to be rushed to Elmhurst General Hospital. A detective from the 110th Precinct clambered in beside him. On the way to the hospital, as recounted by Richard Esposito and Ted Gerstein in their book, *Bomb Squad: A Year inside the Nation's Most Exclusive Police Unit*, the following exchange occurred:

"What happened in there?"

"Fuck you. Fuck yourself."

"Fuck me?"

"Fuck yourself."

"It's you that are fucked, pal. You'll be wiping your ass with your elbows."

The cache of items seized in the apartment included massive amounts of explosives and ammunition rounds,

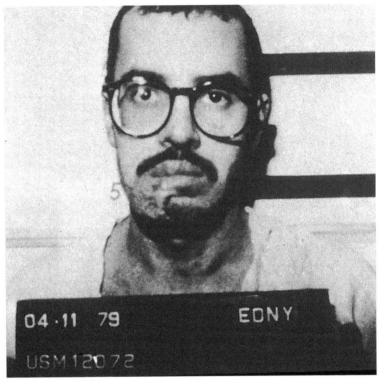

*William Morales mug shot*

watches, batteries, wires, machine screws and flashbulbs, potassium chlorate used for incendiary devices, propane-gas tanks, assorted weapons, and three pipe bombs ready for activation. These items were an exact match with the forensic evidence found in various FALN crime scenes. Also found in the wreckage was a mimeograph machine used to create the FALN's "communique stationery," which was later determined to have been purchased by Maria Cueto. Investigators further recovered a fifty-page

FALN manual detailing how to make and plant bombs and conduct terrorist activities. The manual described tactics that members "must learn, emulate, and practice" to elude detection, and provided instructions on when to use telephones and where to hold meetings. It included sophisticated directives for compartmentalized clandestine communications between different "cadres," or cells, as well as espionage counter-surveillance techniques. "One must observe religiously the rules and regulations of security in order to protect the organization, its cadres, its secrets, its documents, its arms, [safe] houses, and other instruments of work," the document instructed.

Morales had never been arrested, and days passed before he could be positively identified. Don Wofford visited Morales in the hospital. "I had sat across a desk interviewing Morales," recalls Wofford, "but when I saw him after the explosion, I couldn't identify him. His head looked like a basketball." Fire Marshall John Knox described Morales as looking "like a piece of rare roast beef."

The discovery that Morales' apartment had been rented by Carlos and Haydée Torres confirmed his ties to the FALN. Oscar López Rivera and Lucy Rodriguez were also identified by neighbors as having been seen at the apartment. Over the next few days, an intensive effort was made to find Torres and the other Chicago fugitives, but they again eluded capture. An apartment in Queens rented by López Rivera was located, but he and Lucy Rodriguez already had fled.

Lucky to be alive, Morales was arraigned while still being treated at Elmhurst General. Lying in a hospital bed, when asked if he was guilty of bomb-making, he spelled out "No" with his foot. Morales was tried early the following year in a federal court in Brooklyn crammed with both law enforcement officials and radicals supporting the FALN cause, on different sides of the aisle. The proceeding was held before a new judge, Eugene Nickerson, who would go on to preside over numerous famous cases, including a racketeering trial of the "Dapper Don," John Gotti.

Morales' interests were represented by Michael Deutsch of the National Guild, a group known to support radical causes. Deutsch told the press that Morales should not be viewed as a terrorist but, rather, as a "freedom fighter," which was the first of numerous times over the years that FALN members were to be characterized so favorably. Morales proclaimed himself a prisoner of war fighting against the crime of colonialism who should be treated according to the Geneva Convention, the first time that a Puerto Rican had asserted international law as a defense in the U.S. courts. "I was born a colonized subject," Morales stated, "and, as such, I have an inalienable right to fight for my nation's self-determination ... by any means necessary."

Morales unsuccessfully demanded to be transferred to an international forum and absented himself from the proceedings. He was convicted in late February 1979 of various explosives and weapons charges, among them reckless endangerment, possession of explosives, and transportation in interstate commerce of pipe bombs and a sawed-off shotgun. Morales was sentenced by Judge Nickerson to five concurrent ten-year terms.

Immediately after, Morales was placed on trial in a Kew Gardens state courthouse ringed with police armed with shotguns. Unlike in the federal court, where he did not have to appear and could stay in a back room, Queens Supreme Court Justice Kenneth Browne, who was the first African-American elected to the bench in the borough, insisted that Morales attend in person. Each day, Morales would be brought into the courtroom, only to disrupt the proceedings and be taken out. He quickly was convicted on State charges similar to the federal ones.

When Morales appeared for state sentencing before Judge Browne, the courtroom was packed with FALN supporters who earlier had demonstrated outside. Browne handed Morales a sentence of a minimum of twenty-nine years and up to eighty-nine years in jail, to run consecutively with his federal charges. An uproar ensued, during which Morales turned to the crowd, many of whom were agents and cops who had worked the FALN cases. Pointing to Detective William Valentine, the first to identify Morales at the hospital on the day of the explosion and later testified against him, he said, "There's the policeman who terrorized me when I was in a hospital bed." Then he openly boasted, "No jail is going to hold me forever." As Valentine was escorting Morales back to his cell, Morales told him, "You're a dead man."

Morales was held in the Federal Metropolitan Correctional Center in lower Manhattan, from where he called Maria Cueto dozens of times. Morales' attorney, Susan Tipograph, well-known for representing radicals and a part of the team of lawyers representing Cueto and Nemikin, was the domestic partner of former Weather Underground member Cathy Wilkerson. In the 1970s, Cathy Wilkerson was the lover of Ron Fliegelman, with whom she had a daughter. Fliegelman was the principal bombmaker for the Weather Underground. Bryan Burrough, in his book, *Days of Rage,* cites Fliegelman as confirming that the FALN's prototypical bomb design came directly from the Weathermen.

Tipograph also was closely connected to Lynne Stewart, the lawyer who later was convicted on federal charges of conspiracy and providing material support to Omar Abdel-Rahman, known as the "Blind Sheikh," whose prosecution for and conviction of seditious conspiracy grew out of investigations of the World Trade Center 1993 bombing. Stewart also represented Oscar López Rivera, who claimed she was the inspiration for his taking up painting during his years of incarceration.

Tipograph filed on Morales' behalf a federal lawsuit against various officials, including ones in the City's Correction and Police Departments, contending that he had been denied adequate medical care, such as "the right to artificial and reconstituted hands." Federal Judge Jack Weinstein subsequently ruled that it was "desirable" that there be a rehabilitation program for Morales, involving artificial limbs if appropriate. "We must bear in mind," Weinstein said, "that he is a human being. He must be afforded the fundamentals of civilized life, even in jail." Based on that ruling, Morales was moved to Bellevue Hospital's third-floor prison ward, waiting to be fitted with prosthetic hands. Tipograph, while continuously visiting Morales, wrote letters to the authorities complaining that the guards were needlessly frisking her, searching her belongings in violation of attorney-client privilege, and recording her conversations.

Just before the evening meal on May 18, 1979, Morales asked another inmate to tie a series of shoestrings around his waist to form a belt, so that a metal S-hook could be hung between his legs. Three days later, in the early morning, although he had only one functioning finger and his remaining eye afforded minimal vision, Morales cut through steel wire mesh on a cell window facing the back lot of the Bellevue complex using a surreptitiously obtained bolt cutter he had hung from the S-hook. He then shimmied down a forty-foot rope made from elastic bandages, falling the last few feet against a window air conditioning unit. Waiting to whisk him away were members of "The Family," a self-described Marxist revolutionary group formed by participants in the Weather Underground, Republic of New Afrika, and Black Liberation Army organizations. Six months later, the same group would use arms and a stolen van to free convicted murderer JoAnne Chesimard, also known as Assata Shakur.

The headline of *The New York Daily News* blared, "Handless Man Escapes From Jail." Morales' miraculous getaway was extensively investigated by the NYPD. Bill Valentine concluded that Morales had used Ace bandages to wrap one arm of the bolt cutter to his forearm while pressing its other arm against his body. "It works. We tried it."

After his escape, Morales called the NYPD's Arson and Explosion Unit and identified himself. Blaming Valentine for not saving his fingers and general harassment, Morales said, "Tell Valentine I haven't forgotten." Valentine responded through *The Daily News*, "He's hiding among 12 million people, and I'm going to find him." That prompted a call to the FBI from someone claiming to be a member of the FALN who warned that Valentine had been marked for "execution" unless he stopped his efforts to recapture Morales. Valentine became concerned not only for himself but, also, for his wife and five teenage children. "If they came after my family, I knew it would be with a bomb." Valentine's wife, upon learning of the threat, suffered a nervous breakdown.

Publicity of the escape and manhunt triggered excuses and finger-pointing. William Ciuros Jr., the city's Corrections Commissioner, acknowledged "sloppiness on our part," but added there was no evidence that any officer had intentionally aided Morales. Thomas Ryan, the officer guarding Morales, was accused of having been asleep and was suspended without pay for negligence, an action denounced by the Correction Officers' Union as scapegoating. The union alleged the Commissioner was at fault for failing to assign sufficient guards to the prison ward and for transferring Morales to a less secure facility. Queens District Attorney John Santucci chimed in to claim he had repeatedly warned officials that Morales would attempt to break out.

One member of The Family, Tyrone Rison, later became a cooperating witness who testified in multiple federal trials. Rison informed the FBI that Morales initially was taken to a safe house in East Orange, New Jersey. That house was run by Marilyn Buck, an American Marxist revolutionary and feminist poet who was later imprisoned for her participation in Shakur's prison escape as well as other violent felonies. Morales fled to Chicago, where he sought refuge in one of López Rivera's safe houses and returned to a leadership position with the FALN. By his own admission, Morales was a primary planner of several armed robberies and bombings subsequent to his escape.

Morales, listed as "America's Most Wanted Terrorist," had his scarred face displayed on post office walls from coast to coast. Concerned that his injuries made him recognizable, Morales decided to flee to Mexico, which had a long tradition of offering asylum to left-wing radicals. In September 1980, he was driven to El Paso, Texas, by Alejandrina Torres, stepmother of Carlos Torres, and illegally crossed the border at Ciudad Juarez. There, he contacted the Zapatistas, the revolutionary leftist political and military group, requesting assistance.

Via phone calls, Morales kept in regular contact with Alejandrina, who was a key figure in the Chicago FALN organization. Born in 1939 in the eastern Puerto Rican city of San Lorenzo, she was the ninth of ten children whose father died when she was a toddler. The impoverished family moved to New York in 1950, where Alejandrina attended public school and, in her view, became aware of the racial discrimination that Hispanic children were subject to. Years later, Torres described with lingering bitterness a junior high school experience. "One of my classmates lost his money and the teacher asked if anyone had seen it. Since I was the only Latina in the room, the teacher immediately began searching my pockets and book bag."

After high school, Alejandrina moved to Chicago to live with an older sister. There, she met and married Reverend José Torres, the father of Carlos Torres. She became active in the Puerto Rican community in Humboldt Park, an economically depressed neighborhood then rife with gang activity, crime, and drug abuse. By 1982, she was working as an executive secretary in the Department of Child Psychology at the University of Illinois Medical Center.

Alejandrina, whose fiery nature led FBI agents to dub her "Dragon Lady," spoke with Morales on a line being tapped by the Chicago Terrorist Task Force. "One Thursday evening in May 1983, we're listening to Dragon Lady yammering to some guy," recalls Jeremy Margolis, assistant U.S. attorney, "and we figure out that it's Morales. She's consulting with him about how to spring López Rivera from Leavenworth. They were even talking about bringing Morales, who was the one FALN member who had successfully broken out of jail, back to the States to help out." Before the two hung up, they agreed to speak again the following Thursday, May 26, at the same time.

The call was traced to a café that served as a phone center in the dusty town of Puebla, Mexico, 65 miles southeast of Mexico City, known for its clothing-factory sweatshops. Morales was living in a safehouse in Cholula on the outskirts of Puebla with other terrorist suspects. The FBI alerted the Mexican Federal Police, who planned to have Morales arrested away from the house when he called Torres, in order not to compromise the capture of the others. After Morales stepped into the café, the Federales moved in but were spotted by Morales' bodyguard, who opened fire along with accomplices in a nearby car. The bodyguard was killed, while two officers were seriously wounded, one of whom would later die from his injuries.

Upon being placed into a police car, Morales attempted to escape by jumping out and was locked in the trunk until arrival at the station. The Federales then drove to the two-story safehouse, where they were shot at from the inside of the building by Morales' girlfriend, Judith Virrio Anguiano. In the return fire that riddled the house with bullet holes, Anguiano was killed and her two-year-old son wounded.

The Puebla police beat Morales severely, breaking his ribs, and tortured him with electric prods. When NYPD officers and FBI agents who were members of the Joint Terrorist Task Force visited Morales' prison cell, he begged them to take him with them. Morales' mother, Lucy, also visited him in prison. "My son is still in pain from the torture he received," she told Mexican reporters. "He still has marks on his back of the blows he received."

Although the Justice Department demanded that Morales be extradited and presented their case before a Mexican court, the Mexican authorities retained custody. (Despite her son's brutal treatment in a Mexican prison, his mother urged Mexican authorities to grant him political asylum, alleging that he would be killed should he be returned to the U.S.) Because of his mangled hands, Morales had not fired any weapons himself. But he had shouted to his bodyguard in Spanish, "Kill the sons of bitches." As a result, Morales was charged with and convicted of aiding and abetting the murder of the police officer, as well as unlawful arms possession and entering the country illegally. He was sentenced to twelve years in prison, which was reduced after Morales' lawyers argued he was in ill health and disabled. Morales was granted further time off for good behavior and released early in June 1988 after serving only five years.

Despite a judgment delivered by a Mexican judge providing for the return of Morales to the U.S. once his sentence was completed, Mexico invoked the "political offense" exemption of the extradition treaty between the two countries. Pursuant to a deal brokered by Cuba, Morales was flown there and granted asylum.

Mexico's actions were spurred in part by its upcoming presidential and congressional elections. The ruling Institutional Revolutionary Party was concerned that extraditing him to the U.S. would make it appear weak. Morales' release also reflected the close relationship between that Party and Fidel Castro's Cuba. As described by former Mexican President Vicente Fox, "Throughout the Cold War, Mexico stayed close to Cuba to prove its independence in Latin America, like a teenage daughter who hangs out with a hoodlum boyfriend just to defy her parents."

Mexico was where Fidel and Raul Castro fled to in 1955 after being released from Cuban prison. One of the first friends Fidel made while in Mexico was Laura Meneses, the wife of the imprisoned Pedro Albizu Campos, whom Castro regarded as a hero. He also befriended Ernesto "Che" Guevara, a twenty-seven-year-old Argentine physician with Marxist ideas who had been expelled from Guatemala after a CIA-backed coup there the previous year. It was from Mexico where, in December 1956, the Castros, Guevara, and seventy-nine comrades sailed for seven days over twelve hundred miles in a battered wooden cabin cruiser to return to Cuba to complete the revolution. In 1961, the Mexican government led the protest of the Bay of Pigs invasion at the United Nations. Mexico repeatedly opposed the imposition of economic sanctions by the Organization of American States against

Cuba and in 1964 was the only OAS member to reject the U.S.-led effort to break diplomatic and commercial ties with Havana. In gratitude, Cuba abstained from supporting armed insurgencies in Mexico.

The Reagan Administration called Mexico's freeing of Morales "outrageous" and "inexplicable," and charged that it undercut the fight against international terrorism. The U.S. ambassador to Mexico was recalled to Washington to help the Administration convey this position in person to the Mexican ambassador to the U.S. The Mexican Foreign Minister responded that his government's refusal to extradite Morales to the U.S. "was in strict compliance with Mexican law" and should not be construed as a deliberate "anti-American act."

Puerto Rican *independistas* were ecstatic. Filiberto Ojeda Ríos declared, "No one can negate that this is an extraordinary victory ... the Mexican government's decision implicitly recognizes the Puerto Rican revolutionary movement as a legitimate force." Luis Nieves-Falcón, a sociologist and prominent activist for Puerto Rican self-determination, commented, "The decision by Mexico is the first official recognition by a sovereign nation of the international right of the Puerto Rican people to struggle against colonialism by any means necessary."

\*

In 1989, consistent with its radical tradition, City College was the site of student demonstrations and sit-ins over proposed tuition increases, which ultimately were vetoed by Governor Mario Cuomo. The protests spread throughout the City University of New York system, resulting in occupations at thirteen of its colleges. One of the concessions made to City College students was the designation of a third-floor room in the school's North Academic Center building as a community center. Unbeknownst to Joe Connor and most of the public, it was named the "Guillermo Morales/Assata Shakur Student and Community Center," in honor of the two infamous alumni. Throughout the years, students were granted autonomous control over the center, which had a separate funding and administrative structure from other clubs. The center was decorated with pictures of Che Guevara, Malcolm X, and other activists, and used as a meeting place by student and community organizations.

Morales and Shakur are connected in many ways beyond their link to City College. Shakur, born Joanne Deborah Byron (her married name was Chesimard) in Jamaica, Queens, spent most of her childhood in Wilmington, North Carolina, before relocating back to Queens. After graduating from City College, she changed her name to Assata Shakur—Assata means "she who struggles", and Shakur means "thankful one"—and became active in the Black Panther Party. Shakur later joined the Black Liberation Army, committing or being involved in numerous violent felonies, including armed bank robbery, kidnapping, and murder. Recounted by Detective Sergeant Jim O'Neil in his book *A Cop's Tale* is when Shakur walked into a real estate office in

*Shakur & Morales, Havana, 1989*

Brownsville, Brooklyn, announced "This is how the Black Liberation Army takes care of whities who exploit blacks," and put a bullet in an elderly realtor's head. Shakur also is suspected of helping to plan the 1972 BLA execution-style murders of New York City police officers Rocco Laurie and Gregory Foster.

Shakur's most notorious crime occurred on May 2, 1973, when she and two male BLA colleagues were stopped on the New Jersey Turnpike for driving with a broken tail light by State Trooper James Harper, backed up by another trooper, Werner Foerster, in a second patrol car. Harper asked the driver, Clark Squires, for identification, noticed a discrepancy, told him to get out of the car, and questioned him at the rear of the vehicle. Meanwhile, Foerster reached into the back seat, pulled out and held up a semiautomatic pistol and ammunition magazine, and yelled "Jim, look what I found." Shakur then emerged from the front passenger seat holding a handgun she'd hidden under her pant leg and fired at Harper, wounding him in the shoulder. Shakur continued to shoot at both troopers until she was wounded by Harper's return fire. The rear-seat passenger, James Coston, also fired at the troopers and was mortally wounded by Harper. Foerster, while engaged in hand-to-hand combat with Squires, was shot and severely wounded in his right arm and abdomen, and then shot twice in the head by Shakur at point-blank range with his own service weapon. Shakur's jammed handgun was found at Foerster's side. The German-born Foerster had spent his early years in a country ruled by Nazis and later by Communists, and finally escaped to start a new life in the West. Married and a father, he was only thirty-four.

Shakur, with gunshot wounds in both arms and a shoulder, and Squires were arrested at the scene. Squires was convicted of murder and in 1974 sentenced to life in prison plus twenty-four to thirty years. Three years later, after a widely publicized trial, Shakur was convicted of first-degree murder (of Foerster) and six assault charges, and sentenced to life imprisonment. After her escape in November 1979 from New Jersey's Clinton Correctional Facility for Women, Shakur lived as a fugitive before fleeing to Cuba in 1984. She was granted political asylum by "El Lider Máximo" and encouraged to make anti-U.S. speeches espousing revolution and terrorism.

In December 2006, a City College student, Sergey Kadinsky, took note of the center's name in a way that thousands of others hadn't. "I didn't know who Morales and Shakur were," he recalls. "And I'm pretty sure that most of the other students didn't know either." Kadinsky's online research led him to express his concern to the student government body about the inappropriateness of the center's name. Upon being rebuffed, Kadinsky sent a letter to the college newspaper, *The Campus*. Speaking of Shakur, he wrote, "Killing a police officer and escaping from prison does not make someone worthy of having a room named after them. Let them tell the family of Werner Foerster she's a good example for students."

Having received no response from the college's administration, Kadinsky sent his letter to *The Daily News*, which investigated. On December 12, the newspaper's front page displayed a picture of Shakur, next to which blared the headline: "Disgrace: Joanne Chesimard is a fugitive cop killer. Why is City College allowing her name to be honored on campus?" Inside the paper was an article reminding its readers of the criminal backgrounds of Morales and Shakur. The article quoted New York Patrolmen's Benevolent Association President Patrick Lynch on how "disgusting it was to honor a person whose life's goal was to kill people."

*Morales/Shakur Center*

The next day, CUNY Chancellor Matthew Goldstein released a statement making clear the Board of Trustees hadn't authorized naming the center after Shakur and Morales. Goldstein directed City College President Gregory Williams to remove the center's "unauthorized and inappropriate signage." Williams, who admitted the names on the door had meant nothing to him, first tried speaking directly to the students who headed the center. "Hopefully they will see the error of their ways, and will take it down." When this attempt proved futile, the college administration ordered security officers to remove the sign.

The story was picked up by major media outlets, and Foxnews.com made it the top national story under the headline, "Cop Killer Honored at New York College." Joe Connor was interviewed by Fox News, which he told, "My father grew up in Washington Heights and went to City College for several years ... They don't have a room named after him there."

City College was widely criticized. While Morales had once been America's most wanted terrorist, the focus was on Shakur. "We use tax dollars to support an institution that indemnifies a cold-blooded terrorist?" said David Jones, president of the New Jersey State Troopers Fraternal Association. "She's a cowardly, convicted murderer ... no different from those people who flew those planes into those towers and destroyed all those innocent lives." Three Republican New York City Council members released a letter to CUNY stating, "Unfortunately, this demonstrates that City College is woefully out of touch with the taxpayers who subsidize the university ... A terrorist is a terrorist period."

There was, however, strong pushback from several college student groups to the sign removal, spurring rallies and protests, with allegations made of "educational gentrification" and "ethnic cleansing." The Student Liberation Action Movement issued a press release stating, "We know that many black people who fought for better conditions in the 1970s were framed. We consider Assata Shakur to be one of them. And we consider her a hero and role model for standing up for our people and putting her life on the line." Posters advertising a rally on December 20 outside the City College Administration Building claimed the "attack" against the Morales/Shakur Center was a "blatant distraction from the vicious murder, in a hail of 50 bullets, of Sean Bell, an unarmed man on the night before his wedding." That incident, which occurred the previous month, had sparked fierce criticism of the police. In 2008, three of the five detectives involved in Bell's shooting were tried for first- and second-degree manslaughter and other charges. Each was acquitted by a judge on all counts.

Kadinsky, a Jewish immigrant from Latvia, was repeatedly maligned online by fellow students, who branded him, often with an anti-Semitic tone, as a snitch, a "right-wing fanatic," and a racist. "The only whistle that needs to be blown is on you, a supporter of Israel and apartheid," one post said. "You are in no position, as an apologist for the terror, to tell us who should be honored. You wish to denigrate our freedom fighters. For what reason, other than that they fought racism and imperialism that your beloved 'birthright' nation stands for?" Kadinsky remained unintimidated, responding, "I stand by my decision to blow the whistle by notifying *The Daily News*. Shakur and Morales are terrorists and do not deserve to be honored."

In January 2007, a group of City College students and associated community groups filed suit in federal court to force the college to restore the sign and prohibit the school from taking action against anyone who replaced it, or from evicting the groups that use the center. Because of the lawsuit and sympathetic City College faculty members, the center quietly remained in use by and under the control of the same leftist groups.

"City College said they would shut the place down, and the story died," recalls Joe Connor, "and I went on with my life. In the summer of 2013, something told me to check on it, so I Googled the center's name and called it. Sure enough, it was still there, so I went over and took pictures." Connor called the college's administration and sent them his photos, which showed the center's double red doors containing a large black painted fist, a poster with a picture of Shakur and the words, "Hands Off Assata," and a sign proclaiming it the "Morales-Shakur Student and Community Center."

With the issue revived, in October of that year, the administration determined the space being used by the center had been allocated to certain student groups without review and approval. The center was shut, to be reopened as an annex of the college's office for career and professional development. As described by the college's vice president of communications, the room would be "a quiet area where students can meet with outside employers and alumni to seek advice on careers."

Again, the college's actions became news. The *Daily News* observed, "City College has evicted its last vestiges of far-left delusion from a campus office that was a stain on the school's honor." A *New York Post* editorial said,

"The good news is that the Guillermo Morales-Assata Shakur Student and Community Center is no longer. Its presence had been a blot on CUNY's integrity for nearly a quarter of a century." The *Post* also ran a related story containing Joe Connor's reaction. "My father certainly deserved better than to have his killer honored at the college he attended ... I read about a student saying that he was 'torn in half' over this decision. Well, he should consider the people literally torn in half and the lives that were destroyed."

*

Soon after Morales' flight to Cuba, Connor began a campaign to have him extradited, writing letters to the Justice Department and making contacts with the NYPD, State Department, and Joint Terrorist Task Force. Meeting only frustration, he fought on, expanding his communications to Presidents George H.W. Bush and Bill Clinton, New Jersey Senator Bill Bradley, New York's Cardinal O'Connor, and Mayor Rudy Giuliani. "Over the years, anytime I ever spoke to anyone about getting Morales back to face justice, beyond sympathy, I was told it could never happen because we had no relations with Cuba, but that if we ever opened them, it would be a different story."

Joe's crusade marked the beginning of his activism to combat terrorism and bring terrorists to justice. Connor didn't tell his mother or brother about his effort initially.

"I was embarrassed. I guess I figured they would think I was naïve and stupid for believing that my letters could make a difference." When he later showed the letters to his mom, she told him how proud she was of him. As Mary would explain, "Joe worshipped his father, and wouldn't forget him. Or let the world forget him."

# CHAPTER 19
## *Death Knell*

*We knew the ten are in the same group. We knew the goals
of the group. We knew they're conspiring to bring about
those goals. We knew they're running around with weapons.
We knew they're frequenting safehouses that had explosives.
But we couldn't prove that a particular member put a
particular bomb in a particular spot, like Fraunces Tavern,
although all these people clearly shared responsibility.*

—Jeremy Margolis

IN SEPTEMBER 1979, President Jimmy Carter, as a "significant humanitarian gesture," commuted the sentences
of four imprisoned Nationalists—Lolita Lebrón, Rafael
Cancel Miranda, Ivan Flores, and Oscar Collazo—to time
served. (Another Nationalist, Andrés Figueroa Cordero,
had been released from prison in October 1977 because
of terminal cancer and died in March 1979.) They had
earlier refused to apply for parole, which they had become
eligible for, because of their political beliefs. It later was

alleged that the clemency was offered as part of a secret agreement with Fidel Castro that secured freedom for CIA agents imprisoned in Cuba.

The freed prisoners jointly embarked on a "victory tour." Appearing at rallies in Chicago, New York, and Puerto Rico, they proclaimed they had no remorse and could not rule out future violence in the name of Puerto Rican independence. Not long after their return to Puerto Rico, the four visited Havana as honored guests of Fidel Castro.

Carter's clemency grants, made without any attendant conditions and at a time when the FALN was active and had been publicly calling for the release of the Nationalists, were viewed by law enforcement officials and many Puerto Ricans as caving to terrorists. Puerto Rico's nonvoting representative in Congress, Baltasar Cortado del Río, pointed out that the assailants had been "kept in jail for their criminal conduct, not their political beliefs." The Governor of Puerto Rico, Carlos Romero Barceló, declared that Carter's action would encourage terrorism and undermine public safety.

By 1979, the FALN had united with other Puerto Rican terrorist groups to conduct a series of attacks in Puerto Rico. Those assaults, often timed to coincide with ones in Chicago and New York, included bombings of military installations, armored car robberies, the ambush murder of a U.S. serviceman, and rocket launches against a U.S. government office building and courthouse. Law enforcement realized that a large number of people were involved, as the actions required complex coordination of bomb makers, weapons procurers, financers, drivers, people to prepare and call in communiqués, and others.

One of the more brazen FALN attacks occurred in January 1980 when six members, led by Oscar López Rivera and Carlos Torres, attempted to steal machine guns and explosives from the Wisconsin National Guard Armory in Oak Creek. Employees were threatened at gunpoint and one round was discharged, but the effort failed when the FALN members were unable to open the door to the gun vault.

Two months later, the group tried a new, bizarre tactic when armed members forced their way into the Carter-Mondale presidential campaign office in Chicago. López Rivera, who earlier had joined that campaign as a volunteer to learn the lay of the land, announced the attack by declaring, "This is the FALN. We're taking this place over." Bruce Moran, one of the Carter-Mondale campaign staffers held hostage, first thought somebody was "playing a dumb campaign stunt" when he arrived for work and was confronted by a masked man waving a rifle at him. The FALN bound and gagged women and men while ransacking the facilities, spray painting the walls with Puerto Rican independence slogans, and stealing lists of delegates and supporters. In the days that followed, the group sent threatening letters to hundreds of people on those lists.

At the start of the new decade, the core of the highly disciplined FALN appeared unstoppable. But then came a call to police in the swank Chicago suburb of Evanston on Good Friday in early April 1980, shortly after the campaign break-in. Evanston had recently undergone a spate of murders and, in response, local police stepped up traffic patrols and encouraged citizens to call them whenever they saw something unusual. This effort paid off when an elderly woman living on a quiet, tree-lined street peered out her window and noticed a group of "suspicious-looking" men and women dressed as joggers. They were smoking what she guessed was marijuana and continuously entering and exiting a Budget rental truck (which had been stolen in a confrontational armed robbery). The police arrived in time to arrest nine FALN members, one with a dangling false mustache, plus two others who had stolen the truck.

The eleven FALN members had driven to Evanston that morning from a Milwaukee safe house where, the night before, they were briefed by the Chicago cell leaders, Oscar López Rivera and Carlos Torres. Also present in Milwaukee was William Morales, who was physically unable to participate in the operation. "The FALN members were heavily armed, and it was lucky they gave up instead of opening fire," said Don Wofford. "That could have been a disaster for them and the police." López Rivera was nearby when the arrests occurred but had not yet met up with the others and escaped arrest.

As part of the FALN's funding routine, the eleven appeared to be readying themselves to rob an armored truck carrying $200,000 in cash parked at Northwestern University's loading dock. An alternate theory is that they intended to kidnap wealthy industrialist Henry Crown or a member of his family, as the Crown residence was nearby and investigators later found an intelligence dossier on Henry Crown in a New Jersey FALN safe house.

Along with Carlos Torres, then number one on the FBI's most-wanted list, those taken into custody included his wife Haydée, Lucy Rodriguez, and Dylcia Pagan. Pagan had been suspected of being an FALN member in the aftermath of the Fraunces Tavern bombing. "We saw," recounts Wofford, "that she was articulate, animated, strikingly attractive, and very influential in the Puerto Rican community. But we found no concrete links at that time between her and the FALN."

Pagan was later identified as the woman with the Nuyorican Hispanic accent who had called in the report of a dead body that led to officer Angel Poggi's wounding. And it was learned that Pagan and her boyfriend, William Morales, lived up the block from the building where Poggi was injured, suggesting that she and Morales planted the bomb.

Pagan ostensibly was the most successful of the FALN members. Born in the El Barrio neighborhood of Manhattan in 1946, as a student at Brooklyn College she helped organize the Puerto Rican Student Union, which resulted in the formulation of a Puerto Rican Studies Department. By the early 1970s, Pagan began a career as a TV producer and writer, developing investigative documentaries and children's programs. She also worked as the English editor of the bilingual daily, *El Tiempo.*

Lucy Rodriguez was a Chicago native who in high school was elected the student-council president and captain of the cheerleaders. "I was involved in a lot of activities. I would participate in black students' meetings. That inspired me, how they related to their African roots. I saw how it made them stronger. Then I started to learn what was going on in Puerto Rico."

Several of those arrested were previously unknown to the FBI, including Freddie Méndez, a relatively new recruit to the FALN. Méndez's path to the FALN began with his joining the Puerto Rican Socialist Party and, later, the Movimiento de Liberacion Nacional (M.L.N.), which represented itself as a legitimate political organization advocating independence for Puerto Rico but, in fact, served as a training ground for FALN membership. It was during M.L.N. meetings when Méndez gradually was enlisted into the FALN by José López, one of Méndez's professors at Northeastern Illinois University and a master merchandizer of discontent.

Méndez was trained in terrorism techniques by José's brother, Oscar López Rivera, including how to conduct counter-surveillance, establish a false identity, and disguise appearance. Méndez would later testify that López Rivera once took him to the basement workshop of an FALN safe house, where he spent the day instructing

Méndez in the proper construction of various types of explosive and incendiary devices, the culmination of which was Méndez successfully building numerous timing devices and firing circuits. (López Rivera cautioned Méndez that Morales's bomb mishap had occurred because the watch on that pipe bomb had been incorrectly altered.) At López Rivera's direction, Méndez carried a bomb into the Democratic party headquarters in Chicago's Bismarck Hotel, with the intent of placing it in a washroom, but the offices had closed before he arrived.

Seized with the arrestees were a variety of stolen vehicles, weapons, disguises, and false IDs. Other evidence obtained led to the discovery of further safehouses in Newark, New Jersey, and Milwaukee, Wisconsin.

As later recounted by FBI agent Bill Dyson, the Evanston police initially didn't realize the eleven were Hispanic. "We had just broken relations with Iran and the police thought they were Iranians because none of them would say a word and they were dark-complexioned." Once the FBI was called in, law enforcement understood who they had in custody. Dyson and his colleagues were thrilled. "It's like us being kids in a candy store because these are the FALN people. I mean, we've got these wanted posters all around our desk and here we walk in and they're in various rooms."

Each of the eleven refused to cooperate with authorities. Immediate support for them came from Lolita Lebrón, the leader of the 1954 attack on the House of

Representatives who, while in San Francisco on a nation-wide tour, stood before a crowd of hundreds, in front of a banner reading, "Long Live the Heroic FALN. Free the 11!" and demanded their release.

Ten of the eleven would stand trial in Chicago. The exception was Haydée Torres, who together with her husband Carlos had operated a bomb-making safe house in Jersey City. Haydée was born in June 1955 in Arecibo, on a tip of the north coast of Puerto Rico, an ancient town established by the Conquistadores. She moved to Chicago with her parents when she was twelve. She became an activist, helping to found the Pedro Albizu Campos High School and participating in the Committee to Free the Five Puerto Rican Nationalists.

Haydée Torres was the woman who walked into the employment office on the ground floor of the Mobil Oil building back in August 1977 carrying a dynamite bomb hidden in an umbrella. After she hung the umbrella on a coat rack, Haydée filled out an employment application form—using the phony name of "Sandra Peters" and a made-up address—and, at the insistence of a Mobil employee, handed it in. She was identified through a fingerprint on that form which matched one of hers taken after she was arrested in 1973 during a demonstration in Chicago. Haydée's fingerprint was one of the few ever recovered from the methodical FALN members.

Haydée was returned to New York for prosecution for murder. At her arraignment, she described herself as a Puerto Rican freedom fighter. "I'm not going to participate in your so-called trial or, you know, circus, charade, whatever you want to call it." Haydée refused the appointment of counsel and informed the district court that she would neither present a defense nor participate in the proceedings. "I'm here representing myself and I don't need attorneys ... I have absolutely nothing, nothing to defend myself against because I have committed no crimes." Declaring herself to be a "prisoner of war," she demanded that her case be tried before an international tribunal. Michael Deutsch of the ACLU, an attorney who was one of Haydée's "advisers," informed the court that he had applied to the United Nations on her behalf for POW status. The district court denied Deutsch's request to stay proceedings until the U.N. responded.

During jury selection, Haydée spoke in Spanish to her supporters in the gallery, causing commotion and her removal from the courtroom. Convicted and sentenced to life imprisonment, Haydée did not participate in the court-initiated appeal on her behalf. Fifteen years later, though, her lawyers claimed she had been denied several of her constitutional rights and unsuccessfully appealed her conviction.

Back in Illinois, each of the remaining "Chicago Ten" was first tried and convicted in state court of various felonies and sentenced to terms of eight to thirty years. Then it was on to federal court. The prosecution team was headed by Jeremy Margolis. Short with a strong frame, bearded, and with "piercing eyes," Margolis' lawyerly demeanor was tinged with a wicked sense of humor.

Terrorism was not then a defined crime in the U.S. Margolis and his prosecution team weighed which formal charges to move ahead with, handicapped by an evidentiary inability to tie any single person, other than Haydée Torres, to any specific action. Certain counts, such as illegal possession of weapons and auto theft, were a given. But common conspiracy charges failed to reflect the severity of their actions.

Margolis decided to indict the group members for the commission of "seditious conspiracy," which carries much harsher penalties than common conspiracy. Seditious conspiracy was a felony that Pedro Albizu Campos and the four Nationalists who shot up the House of Representatives were convicted of. It also would be used during the same century against communists, radicals, neo-Nazis, and Islamic terrorists.

The indictment cited numerous bombings and incendiary attacks. One had occurred on June 7, 1976 in front of the First National Bank on Monroe and Dearborn streets. A couple—Richard and Fanny Schwartz—were standing before the building's famous Chagall mural when an FALN bomb exploded in a nearby trash can. A piece of shrapnel tore through Richard Schwartz' throat, cutting his vocal cord and leaving him choking in his own blood. Both he and his wife underwent surgery for eardrum replacement and remained plagued with hearing problems.

Of note is that these indictments addressed only the bombings that occurred in the Northern District of

Illinois, because the law required the acts charged to have taken place in the same district. Therefore, Margolis could not prosecute most of the FALN bombings, even those resulting in murder.

The U.S. Code of Federal Regulations defines terrorism as "the unlawful use of force and violence against persons or property to intimidate or coerce a government, the civilian population, or any segment thereof, in furtherance of political or social objectives." (The term "terrorism" comes from the Latin verb "terrere," which means "to frighten.") But, as Brian Jenkins, a noted author and expert on terrorism, has observed, terrorism also "is theater."

That maxim applied to the Chicago Ten trial. As with Haydée Torres, the accused refused to defend themselves or participate in the proceedings, although they accepted "assistance" from National Lawyers Guild attorneys who acted as "legal advisors" and made public relations gestures such as filing a petition with the U.N. Human Rights Commission. Nor did the defendants sit in the courtroom. They stayed in the "bullpen" area, leaving Margolis to present his arguments and evidence to a vacant defense table.

The courtroom itself, however, wasn't empty. FALN supporters packed it daily, chanting in Spanish and singing revolutionary songs. The presiding judge, Thomas McMillen, carried a revolver under his robe and was so concerned about retaliation against the jurors that he instructed them "not to reveal your fellow jurors' identity to anyone."

Margolis displayed his own dramatic flair. "At one point," Margolis recounts, "when FBI agents were carrying evidence out of a safe house, I noticed them holding a P-trap, the pipe that you find under a sink. The agents explained that they didn't need the entire sink, just the pipe, which contained some explosives residue. I said to them, 'Take the entire sink. This way, I can say in court that we took everything of evidentiary value, including the kitchen sink.'"

In his closing argument, Margolis said of the defendants, "What is dear and important to them are acts of terrorism. How proudly they claim credit for these bombings." After the jury had delivered its verdicts of guilt, Judge McMillen told them, "I admire you greatly for your perseverance in this case." As the judge handed down lengthy sentences, the defendants sang, shouted, and called him a "puppet" and a "clown." Lucy Rodriguez screamed at McMillen, "You say we have no remorse. You're right. Your jails and your long sentences will not frighten us." Carmen Valentin yelled, "You are lucky that we cannot take you right now. Our people will continue to use righteous violence. Revolutionary justice can be fierce, mark my words." Dylcia Pagan, the mother of William Morales' baby son, Guillermo (given up for adoption to friends in Mexico, who named him Ernesto Gomez-Gomez), warned the courtroom, "All of you, I would advise you to watch your backs." Judge McMillen, convinced the defendants forever would remain terrorists, said to them, "If there was a death penalty, I'd impose it on you without hesitation."

Following his conviction, but before sentencing, Freddie Méndez offered his cooperation to Margolis, in hopes of a reduced sentence and despite the imminent risk of retaliation by FALN members. Margolis told him, "If you have blood on your hands, I guarantee I'll make sure you die in prison where you belong. But if you don't, anything is possible." After extensive investigation, Margolis judged Méndez to be an idealistic young man who had sincerely believed, based in part on racism he had personally experienced, that police were oppressing Puerto Ricans and that the government in Puerto Rico was fascist. And that Méndez had not willingly crossed the thin line from militant activism to pointless violence. "Méndez's beliefs in social justice were betrayed by the movement," Margolis said. "He realized that the people he was involved with didn't care about human life and had no respect for it, which was something he wouldn't countenance." Margolis had a soft spot for Méndez based on Margolis' own family history. "My grandfather was a socialist in Russia before he immigrated to the U.S. He came to understand that the Bolsheviks had been disloyal to their own revolution."

Rick Hahn spent hundreds of hours over months debriefing Méndez, from whom he learned that Morales had been closely involved with the FALN's Chicago cell. Méndez had invaluable knowledge of how the FALN cells and underground operated. "I was bowled over by the fact that this guy's telling me how they were trained to dry-clean themselves, to use public transportation, and to change their appearance while they traveled. They'd go into a department store bathroom and reverse their jacket, put on a hat and some dark glasses, and walk out. Get on a bus and travel south when they really wanted to go north. Everything from how to avoid leaving fingerprints, to using code words, to using dead drops. All these spy versus spy type of things."

A period of inactivity followed the April 1980 arrests. In May of the next year, Freddie Méndez entered the witness protection program, which was understandable as the FALN had determined that Méndez was cooperating with authorities and released a "Wanted: Dead – Not Alive" poster with a large picture of him and the proclamation that he was a traitor to the Puerto Rican revolutionary movement.

Days later, a call was made to JFK Airport officials by a man who identified himself as a member of the "Puerto Rican Armed Resistance" (an alternate moniker for the FALN), warning that a bomb would detonate at the Pan Am terminal. After a frantic search, two bombs were discovered and safely removed. A third, left in a bag in a men's room, exploded before the terminal could be fully evacuated. The group's communique called for the release of the FALN members. Given this and other factors, law enforcement officials believe the bombing was the work of the FALN.

The third bomb claimed the life of Alex McMillan, a maintenance worker. He was twenty years old.

# CHAPTER 20
## *Oscar López Rivera*

*Before I got drafted, I was a happy-go-lucky Puerto Rican.*
*I enjoyed life. I wasn't paying attention to anything other*
*than me.*

—Oscar López Rivera

IN MAY 1981, IN Glenview, Illinois, police arrested
Oscar López Rivera, head of the Chicago branch of
the FALN, along with Wilfredo Santana, a member of
a sister terrorist group—the Movimiento de Liberacion
Nacional Puertorriqueño, formed by Puerto Rican and
Chicano activists. The pair was traveling in a green
Buick when they were stopped for driving erratically.
They presented drivers licenses that appeared altered.
A back-up officer standing next to the car noticed what
could be construed as burglary tools in the back seat,
including long-nosed pliers, alligator clips, wire connec-
tors, and field glasses. Upon searching the car, police

found a Browning handgun with its serial number filed off. They called the FBI, who identified López Rivera.

López Rivera, who had a look similar to Morales—wide face, unkempt long and thick black hair, and handlebar mustache—was born in 1943 in the mountainous town of San Sebastián in Puerto Rico. San Sebastián borders the town of Lares and became a key battleground in the failed 1868 Lares rebellion. When he was fourteen, López Rivera immigrated to Chicago, following in the path of other family members, and settled in Chicago's Humboldt Park neighborhood. López Rivera arrived on a brutally cold day. "I was dressed in the regular clothes I wore in Puerto Rico. I wanted to stay on the plane and go back."

After graduating high school, López Rivera commenced liberal arts studies at Wright Junior College in Chicago. He soon dropped out to help support his family, who had been abandoned by their father. In June 1966, López Rivera was drafted into the U.S. Army, He served seven months in Vietnam as an infantryman, earning a Bronze Star. López Rivera recounts, "It was two or three days at the base and then three or four weeks in operations. I fired thousands of bullets ... but I am very sure I did not kill anyone."

López Rivera arrived in Vietnam "thinking we were bringing freedom to Vietnamese people, but as soon as I hit the ground I realized that wasn't happening. We did sweeping operations getting villagers out of their homes, moving them off the rice paddies, body-searching them." He came to believe the Vietnamese to be "a humble and valiant people who resisted and rejected the only true invading force—the U.S. military and its allies. That spirit of resistance and struggle impressed me a lot. When I got back from Vietnam, I was ready to go to war for Puerto Rico."

Don Wofford believes that López Rivera's Vietnam service turned him "savagely violent" for the Puerto Rican independence cause. Another person who connected lessons learned from the war to the independence movement was Elizabeth Figueroa, a member in the 1970s of a Puerto Rican community group based on the West Side of Manhattan known as "El Comité," which was started by a softball team comprised of ex-gang members, factory workers, and Vietnam vets. Figueroa recalls, "It was the antiwar experience that drew me to want to know about my roots in Puerto Rico ... We were talking about Vietnam and suddenly someone would shout, 'USA out of Puerto Rico.'" The logic of the Vietnam War-Puerto Rican independence movement connection might be said to be: if the Vietnam War was waged by the U.S. to help the Vietnamese people maintain their own sovereignty, in the face of the Communist threat, then why shouldn't this ideal apply to Puerto Rico as well? (Of course, in the former case, the U.S. was fighting communism, while the FALN looked to spread it.)

López Rivera returned from Vietnam in early 1967 to a Chicago Puerto Rican community now unfamiliar. In June of the previous year, after the city's first Puerto Rican Day parade, the first "Division Street Riots" occurred in response to the treatment of Puerto Rican youth by a Chicago Police Department still racially and culturally oblivious. The trigger for the riots, which lasted three days, was the shooting by a cop of a Puerto Rican youth followed by the police beating with nightsticks and unleashing attack dogs on the crowd that came to his defense. López Rivera observed: "Something I could feel immediately was the radical change that had occurred in the community. It was no longer the silent and invisible one I had left behind. Even in the way that Boricuas walked, you could see the positive impact the riot had in our community ... They were becoming organized and radicalized. And it was these youths who gave the driving force and energy to the struggles that emerged after the riot."

Along with participating in anti-war protests, López Rivera became a community activist, helping to found a halfway house for convicted drug addicts and an educational program for Latino prisoners at Stateville Prison in Illinois. Felix Rosa, a member of the Latin Kings, a local gang, remembers López Rivera as a "kind of neighborhood hero."

One of López Rivera's fervent causes was the effort to culturally sensitize the school administration of Tuley High School, later renamed Roberto Clemente High School, on the city's West Side, which had a predominantly Puerto Rican student body. (Tuley's most famous former student is Knute Rockne—the author Saul Bellow also graduated from the school.) At Tuley, López Rivera met Carmen Valentín, a bilingual teacher and counselor who also would join the FALN. Valentín, like López Rivera, was born in Puerto Rico and immigrated with her family to the U.S. when she was young. While teaching at Tuley, she joined other community leaders in forcing the Chicago Board of Education to transfer out the principal, Herbert Fink, because of alleged racial insensitivity, and to introduce Puerto Rican history and culture into the school's curriculum.

López Rivera studied and came to idolize former Puerto Rican Nationalists such as Lolita Lebrón. "She was willing to give her life for Puerto Rico," he would tell *Latino USA* decades later. "I felt that I should be willing to do the same. To fight for the independence of Puerto Rico."

Soon after joining the FALN, López Rivera took on a leadership role. "How do we know this?" explains Rick Hahn. "We know from Méndez, who was trained by López. Méndez's veracity was tested not only by lie detector, but by the fact that his descriptions of the actions in which he participated with López Rivera match the facts determined by other investigations."

López Rivera was personally involved in numerous FALN bombing and incendiary attacks. He also was a prime recruiter of FALN members, a key trainer in bombing, sabotage, and other techniques of guerilla warfare, and the mastermind of the establishment of a series of FALN safe houses and bomb factories across the country. López Rivera had narrowly escaped capture in Evanston. He later plotted to free those captured, intending to kidnap President Reagan's son Ron, a ballet dancer living in New York City, and use him as a hostage. In López Rivera's residence, the FBI found a large quantity of dynamite and blasting caps.

López Rivera labeled his trial proceedings a "lie and a farce," and declined counsel to assist him with the "kangaroo court." Key to the government's case was the help of testimony by Freddie Méndez, who López Rivera himself cross-examined. Méndez testified to, among other things, the FALN's money-laundering operation:

> We were discussing bringing in money that we appropriate from armed robberies and using that money to buy buildings and ... put it into work for the struggle. Oscar said, "Yes, we done that before ... What we do is we take money—again, we rob in the underground—or they rob nationwide and in Puerto Rico and we bring it here and buy buildings."

López Rivera was convicted of several specific felonies, including conspiracy to transport explosives with the intent to kill and injure people and to destroy government buildings and property, armed robbery, aiding and abetting travel in interstate commerce to carry out arson, interstate transportation of firearms and a stolen vehicle, and possession of an unregistered firearm. He also was convicted of seditious conspiracy, a crime he rejected being capable of committing: "No Puerto Rican can seditiously conspire against the U.S. government because colonialism is a crime against humanity. International law makes that very clear." López Rivera and his FALN colleagues believed that their struggle for national sovereignty distinguished them from the pursuits of mere "terrorist" groups. "Every colonized person," López Rivera later argued, "has the right to exercise his or her free will and independence, using all available methods, including violence."

Judge Thomas McMillen sentenced López Rivera to fifty-five years in prison. "You are an un-rehabilitated revolutionary, and there's no point in giving you anything less than a heavy sentence."

\*

N.C.H.A. travel records obtained by the FBI demonstrated that López Rivera was staying in New York in late October 1974 when four FALN bombings occurred there. His whereabouts on the day of the Fraunces Tavern bombing, however, are uncertain. López Rivera has insisted he had nothing to do with that bombing, stating, "Up until January 26, 1975, when I heard the news in Puerto Rico, I had never heard of the Fraunces Tavern. I did not even know it existed." But is this true?

On January 24, 1975, Harry Hamburg, a *New York Daily News* photographer, was sitting in a car with his company driver having lunch on Water Street just around the corner from Fraunces Tavern when the bomb went off. "We heard this oomph sound," Hamburg recalls, "and the whole car lifted up. We looked at each other and thought, 'We got something.'"

Hamburg raced over to the Tavern. "I started shooting inside at first, but there was too much dust and smoke to take clear pictures. And then a cop I knew yelled out to me, 'Harry, you're standing on a body.'" Hamburg would end up snapping dozens of pictures, from different vantages. "Lots of people were hanging around the immediate area," he remembers. "The police didn't chase anyone away initially."

One of Hamburg's pictures, shown below, is of an injured man, wrapped in a blanket, being led away from the scene by emergency workers.

On the far right of the photo, two men stand by the side of the building. The shorter man bears a strong resemblance to Oscar López Rivera, as can be seen from the below picture of a young López Rivera followed by a blowup of the two men.

In another photo taken by Hamburg, shown on the following page, in the middle left, the same man bearing a strong resemblance to Oscar López Rivera can be seen in the front row of the crowd, his face turned directly toward the camera.

Antonio de la Cova is a professor of Anthropology and History at the University of South Carolina and a former San Juan reporter who has studied the FALN extensively. "It's not likely," Professor de la Cova explains, "that if López himself had planted the bomb, he would have stuck around. That would have violated the training the FALN members received from the Cubans and others. But it is quite possible that he would have been there to provide armed cover for the actual bomber, and to relish the devastation and mayhem." Tony Senft notes that it's not unusual for bombers or their accomplices to return to the scene.

As the date of publication of this book, the two pictures are being analyzed by the FBI and NYPD.

# CHAPTER 21
## *The Long Walk*

*I have two granddaughters who have Puerto Rican heritage, and I am proud of them, but I have never seen them. When they present me with crayon drawings and are pleased to show them to me, I have to pretend I can see them. When they ask me to go outside and play ball with them, I cannot. I don't have the fingers to hold the ball. I can't even see it coming."*

—Richard Pastorella, NYPD Bomb Squad

THE FALN RE-EMERGED IN the late evening of February 28, 1982 when the group planted four powerful bombs in the Wall Street financial district that damaged the Merrill Lynch and Chase Manhattan Bank buildings and New York and American stock exchanges. Witnesses spotted a car crammed with people speeding from the area moments after the blasts. In a multi-page communiqué left for police in a telephone booth, the FALN demanded the "immediate and unconditional release" of López Rivera and other prisoners, and decried 'imperialistic forces' opposing independence for Puerto Rico. (Mary Connor Tully would react to this repeated characterization by saying, "Frank was no 'imperialist.' He grew up in Washington Heights and went to college at night, pulling himself up by his own bootstraps.") Notably, the FALN expressed 'solidarity' with Weather Underground and Black Liberation Army radicals arrested the previous October after a bungled Brink's armored car robbery in Nyack, New York, in which two police officers and a guard were killed.

The FALN emitted its final tragic gasps on New Year's Eve of 1982, a brutally cold evening during which the core of the NYPD was patrolling in and around Times Square. In a span of ninety minutes, four powerful explosives detonated in lower Manhattan and Brooklyn at separate law enforcement targets. The first explosion occurred at 9:27 p.m. on the north side of 26 Federal Plaza, which houses the offices of the FBI and other federal agencies. Loud enough to be able to be heard in midtown, it knocked out windows on three floors and rained glass on the street but caused no injuries.

Thirty-three-year-old Rocco Pascarella, a uniformed police officer married with a daughter, was on security detail at the time at NYPD headquarters, four blocks away. In response to the first bomb, he was tasked with conducting a security sweep of the rectangular police headquarters building at One Police Plaza on Park Row, near City Hall and the Brooklyn Bridge, in the heart of the City's law enforcement hub. Wearing a nylon duty jacket, leather shoes, and light gloves that left him poorly protected against the bone-chilling wind, Pascarella, who wasn't trained in bomb detection, walked the dimly lit building perimeter, his plastic flashlight darting back and forth. At 9:55 pm, as he passed an unused rear entrance on the north side of the building, Pascarella spotted among the trash littering the ground a soiled paper bag filled with newspaper and a Kentucky Fried Chicken container. As he moved closer to investigate, his foot accidentally brushed against the container, which contained a bomb made of several sticks of dynamite, wires soldered to the back of the housing, alligator clips for securing the wires to a nine-volt battery, metal screw, a blasting cap, and a Bulls Eye pocket watch used as a timer.

The minute hand of the watch was touching the screw that had a wire soldered to it, but not quite enough to complete a simple circuit—a situation that bomb experts refer to as a "hang fire." The ever-so-slight jarring caused by Pascarella's uniform leather shoe was sufficient to complete the circuit.

Pascarella was found dragging himself on his elbows among shards of glass by two New York City Bomb-Squad detectives—Anthony Senft, thirty-six, a ten-year veteran, and Richard Pastorella, forty-two, a fifteen-year member of the police force—and their German Shepherd, Hi-Hat, trained in explosives detection. Pastorella and Senft had been called to the scene by the "Wheel," the nickname for

Bomb Squad headquarters. As Senft recalls, "Pascarella was ripped up like someone took a box cutter and shredded his face. We really didn't even know that he was a uniformed man until we found his weapon. That's how badly he was injured."

Pascarella was placed on a gurney by medics, who were frantically trying to prevent him from hemorrhaging and bleeding out. Despite his pain and shock, Pascarella insisted that he not be taken to the ambulance until he could speak with the Bomb Squad detectives. "Here was this incredibly courageous man," Senft remembers, "now blind in one eye, bleeding all over, his body torn apart, and he was trying to describe what he saw and warn us that sticks of dynamite had been planted in Kentucky Fried Chicken boxes."

Pascarella was rushed to Bellevue Hospital, where surgeons attempted without success to reattach his right leg, which had been severed below the knee. Meanwhile, a third bomb exploded outside the U.S. District Courthouse at 225 Cadman Plaza East in Brooklyn's Borough Hall section, directly across the East River, shattering windows in the building. The explosion reverberated throughout the neighborhood.

As this nightmarish scenario continued to unfold, Pastorella and Senft were asked by the NYPD Emergency Services Unit to investigate two additional suspicious packages partially wrapped in newspaper lying in the immediate vicinity. One was resting against a building column in St. Andrew's Plaza, which houses the

Manhattan federal courts and the offices of the U.S. Attorney for the Southern District of New York, adjacent to the Metropolitan Correctional Center and across Park Row from One Police Plaza. "The device lay next to building columns on a busy pedestrian thoroughfare for the Chinatown community," Pastorella recalls. "There were a bunch of Chinese people only twenty feet from them. I was now seeing the possibility of a lot of dead and injured. We had to take time to chase them away and set up a safe perimeter."

Pastorella and Senft were blessed by a monsignor who regularly attended to Bomb Squad members and had rushed to the area. Following protocol, Senft, a dog handler who was a week away from beginning his bomb technician training, brought Hi-Hat to the packages. They had been covered with steel-mesh Kevlar bomb blankets placed by Emergency Services Unit personnel. The dog, trained by Pavlovian conditioning methods to smell out the residual odor of nitrates in explosive devices without touching them, was brought to the package by Senft. The dog sniffed it and then turned away and sat, expecting to receive a food treat. This was a positive signal for the presence of explosive material. Senft led Hi-Hat back to the safe area and handed his leash to another officer.

The detectives, their hearts pounding, were helped into their bomb suits by ESU personnel. In those days, bomb suits were heavy and cumbersome, making movement difficult. Nor could one see clearly out of them on a frigid day because the faceplate fogged up. "They supplied a cream to keep the fog down," Senft recalls, "but it didn't work." As most bomb technicians chose to do at the time, Pastorella and Senft removed their face plate. They then started to take what Bomb Squad officers refer to as "the long walk" toward the device, with Senft carrying the tool box they would need.

At 10:45 pm, Pastorella knelt on his right knee and extended his right hand toward the explosive, intending to defuse it by preventing the blasting cap from going off without tripping a switch. Senft, on Pastorella's right side, bent over to observe. Pastorella gently lifted the blanket to get a close look at the device, which was the same type of bomb as Pascarella had encountered. As he did, Senft recalls, "I heard the explosion. And that is the last thing I remembered about it for a month."

The two officers were blown fifteen feet in the air, landing on their backs. Phil Messing, a young reporter for *The New York Post*, was on the scene. "I heard a kaboom that was the loudest noise I've ever heard. And I grew up on Coney Island, so I'm used to loud noises. This one sounded like an earthquake." Messing rushed toward the officers and recoiled when he caught sight of Pastorella. "It was the most awful thing I've ever seen. You wouldn't have known that he was a human being." Pastorella himself recalls, "I was literally on fire, and other cops physically rolled their bodies over on me to douse the fire."

ESU members helped medics cut off the bomb suits, not an easy task given their myriad straps, Velcro fasteners, zippers, buckles, and the like. Pastorella and Senft had been saved from death by the protective gear. But bomb suits at that time, consisting of Kevlar-like material and armor plates made of metal or fiber-reinforced plastic, were not sufficiently protective against the blast wave itself, which can cause lung and other potentially deadly internal injuries.

Pastorella later described how he "lost all of the fingers on my right hand, the sight in both eyes, and seventy percent of my hearing. I had to endure thirteen major reconstructive surgery operations on my face and my hand. I have twenty-two titanium screws holding my face together. I have shrapnel from that device embedded in my stomach, my shoulders, and my head."

Two NYPD buddies—Larry Riccio and Jeff Matlin—were at Bellevue when Pastorella and Senft were brought into an emergency treatment room. "Tony's bomb suit lay in the hallway," Riccio remembers. "It was smoldering and had this horrible acrid smell. Looking at it, I couldn't believe he had survived." Matlin recalls the moment when Mayor Koch arrived at the hospital. "He walked in, saw Richie and Tony, who were in adjoining rooms, and began crying and muttering over and over again, 'Those fucking FALN bastards.'"

Senft's injuries also were horrific. "On that day, I received a lifelong sentence without the opportunity for parole. My sentence includes five reconstructive operations on my face, the loss of all my sight in my right eye, sixty percent hearing loss in both ears, a broken nose, a fractured hip, and severe vertigo. My eardrums burst, and I had to keep putting cotton and Vaseline in my ears to allow water to go down. And I also had a brain injury that was like getting a hundred concussions at one time." Tony Senft's recovery was a long road. For years, he spent most of his day on the couch. "I had been an athlete, doing a lot of running and lifting. Now people had to help me tie my shoes. They'd tell me when to eat and when to shower." To this day, Senft says, "I sneeze or cough, it hurts. I can't touch the bad eye, that's how painful it is."

Senft admitted, "Before then, I had been skeptical about post-traumatic stress disorder. But it's very real. I was a mental and emotional wreck. I had horrible nightmares all the time. It took years of therapy, and the constant support of my loving wife, for me to get through it. I was so nervous and jumpy that I didn't venture out in public on my own for five years. It was a big deal for me to walk around the block. I lost my self-esteem."

During the months after the incident, Senft worried, "Would I be retired, or pushed into a job I didn't want? Would I still get a pension? But the NYPD was great to me." Reflecting back, Senft considers himself lucky. "They could have attached tacks, bb's, or nails to the dynamite. Each one would have become a bullet. In which case, I'd probably be dead."

Yet another bomb, wrapped in newspaper, was found by the entrance to One Police Plaza. Sergeant Charlie Wells and Detective Frank DeCicco were assigned to deactivate it. Wells was an ex-Marine who had cleared mine fields while serving in Vietnam. (Innumerable mines were planted during that war, and more than 100,000 people are estimated to have been injured or killed by unexploded mines since it ended.) He already was a Bomb Squad legend.

DeCicco had been on the squad for twelve years, and before that he defused bombs in the Army. Once, when asked whether he'd ever been injured, DeCicco laughed and replied, "You can't get hurt on this job or you're not on the job anymore."

Earlier, Wells, upon racing to the scene, was the person who found the fingers of Pastorella's right hand that had been blown off. On one of them was a ring containing a miniature detective shield with a small diamond center. Wells placed the ring on his own finger for good luck, and ordered Pastorella's fingers to be hurried to the hospital.

Wells and DeCicco felt that time was running out. The bomb was about to explode. Without bothering to don bomb suits, the two men approached the package wearing suits and ties, and kneeled toward it. They glanced at each other, blessed themselves, and with DeCicco holding the bomb, Wells precisely cut into the wires and defused it by removing the blasting caps. The two officers realized they'd been lucky the bomb hadn't gone off during their approach, as this pocket watch hand also had come in contact with the screw that served as the contact point, but the connection hadn't made the necessary linkage to fire the caps.

The device was placed in a bomb-disposal truck and taken to the Police Department's firing range at Rodman's Neck in the Bronx. As a Bomb Squad member would later relate, "The bomb was trademark FALN. But Willie Morales had learned from his mistakes in 1978. He taught others to make bombs as simply as possible, so there was less chance they would blow themselves up. And his simple design worked."

The New Year's Eve bombings had a silver lining—they spurred the development and use of robots as a means of examining suspicious packages, which the New York City Bomb Squad would avail itself of for the first time in 1983. Twenty-five years later, on New Year's Eve in 2007, the visitor's entrance at Police Headquarters was dedicated to Pascarella, Pastorella, and Senft. Those three also received the NYPD's highest honor, along with Wells and DeCicco. Charlie Wells would later serve as Detective Captain with Brooklyn North and commander of the Staten Island Detective Department's counter-terrorism efforts after 9/11. According to Richard Esposito and Ted Gerstein, in the month after 9/11, Wells was part of a team of Bomb Squad members who volunteered to defuse a nuclear device that al Qaeda reputedly was seeking to procure and detonate in either New York or Washington.

Pastorella and Senft would remain affiliated with the NYPD Bomb Squad, helping to screen new recruits. Two years later, Don Sadowy, a Marine Corps vet and NYPD patrolman, applied to join the Bomb Squad. He was required to meet with Pastorella and Senft. "They asked me why I wanted to join the squad," recalls Sadowy. "Richie takes my hand in his and says to me, 'I want you to feel and see the missing fingers.' And then he pulls off his sunglasses. 'I want you to look in my face. Notice that my eyes were blown out of their sockets, and that my face was rebuilt.' And Tony tells me to look at him, and he starts describing his injuries, internal, external, and psychological. And then they both asked again, 'Why do you want to come into this squad?'"

Sadowy was shaken but nonetheless joined the squad. He later would serve as one of the lead investigators in the 1993 World Trade Center bombing. It was Sadowy who, while digging through debris at ground zero, found a piece of burnt, mangled chassis frame containing a vehicle identification number that led to identifying the conspirators. And on 9/11, while working for Merrill Lynch's security department, Sadowy narrowly escaped death after being buried alive while exiting the collapsing North Tower after going up to the 20th floor to help evacuate people.

The New Year's Eve bombings were described at the time by the FBI's New York office as a "resurgence" of the FALN. Chicago law enforcement had another view.

# CHAPTER 22
## Dragon Lady and the Rabbit

*The armory was in the middle of Chicago's West Side barrio, so had they succeeded [in blowing it up], most victims of the blast would have been Hispanic. Although I often encounter such moral contradictions in my work, I never cease to marvel at them.*

—Candice DeLong, FBI

IN EARLY 1983, surveillance and analysis of wire taps uncovered two additional Chicago safe houses, one only blocks away from where Rick Hahn had grown up. The FBI began to track four persons who frequented them, a task made difficult by the intricate measures the FALN members used to avoid detection. Numerous agents, cars, and even helicopters were required. Jeremy Margolis obtained warrants to install cameras and microphones in the apartments. He brought in translators from Puerto Rico "to sit in the hole and monitor," because all the conversations were in Puerto Rican-style Spanish." Even then, the conversations were difficult to discern because loud music constantly played in the background.

"The surveillance technology we used wasn't ground-breaking," Margolis recounts. "Just basic Title Three microphones and video coverage. What was unique was that the wiretap authorization was purely circumstantial. We had no direct evidence or an eyewitness who could tell us about the safe houses. With the help of Méndez's testimony, we were able to successfully argue probable cause."

One day, after Alejandrina Torres and Edwin Cortes, the latter dubbed by the FBI as "the Rabbit," entered one of the apartments, located at 736 West Buena Avenue. Margolis and Hahn watched. "They're sitting with gloved hands at a kitchen table cluttered with magnifying glasses, pocket watches, strands of wire, pliers, screwdrivers, and batteries, building firing circuits and timing devices for bombs," Margolis remembers. "But they had walked in emptyhanded. And they later walked out emptyhanded. So, we had this huge, 'Oh, shit' moment, realizing that we'd missed something."

Margolis obtained another search warrant, allowing FBI agents to return to the apartment while the subjects were away and searched it meticulously. They found, under a sink, a false cabinet bottom concealing a treasure trove of weaponry, bomb-making materials and manuals, disguises, false identification papers, and body armor. "We kept Rick Hahn in the apartment all night long so the warrant wouldn't expire, through use of the rule of constant possession." Concerned that the weaponry might unexpectedly be used or a bomb might accidentally go off, harming others in the building, but not wanting to comprise the surveillance effort, the FBI brought in explosives experts. "They rendered the dynamite safe," Margolis explained. "The bullets were made harmless with inert material. We replaced the firing pins in the guns with ones that were a little short. Rendered the fuses and caps unusable. Everything looked exactly like it should, except it wouldn't go bang. This methodology, which was suggested by Rick Hahn, was unique." In 1984, United States Attorney General William French Smith awarded Hahn the Attorney General's Award for Distinguished Service for his efforts in disrupting and dismantling the FALN.

For weeks, each evening, the law enforcement team gathered to review the day's events. "They were planning potential terrorist acts in real-time," recalls Margolis, "and we needed constantly to be able to frustrate them in real-time without them knowing. Every day that we stayed operational, we might miss something that would allow someone to be harmed or even killed. There might have been other safe houses we didn't know about. Or a terrorist plan that we might fail to prevent. We constantly had to do this cost-benefit analysis of whether the risks of continuing our secret surveillance outweighed the likely benefits. And there was never a clear answer. We went on gut feel and intuition."

The four suspects were overheard planning to rob a Chicago Transit Authority mobile safe operator of the daily collections. One of them, Alberto Rodriguez, born in the Bronx but raised in Chicago, discussed ways of confronting the CTA guard. "We may have to shoot him, which makes a noise." Later, Rodriguez was observed surveilling a CTA station. The FALN members also plotted to storm the Correctional Center in downstate Pontiac with machine guns to free FALN member Luis Rosa.

In early June 1983, the FALN members detailed the layout of a National Guard Armory and were observed surveying it as well as a Marine base training center and two military motor pools. It became evident they intended to blow up the armory on July 4.

A week before Independence Day in 1983, Margolis and Hahn determined the flow of information was drying up, and there weren't any new plots to compromise. By then, more than seven hundred hours of surveillance video had been recorded. The FBI arrested Torres, Cortes, Alberto Rodriguez, and another Rodriguez—José Luis. At their arraignment the following month, the four raised clenched fists, prompting sympathizers who had filled the courtroom to applaud and sing an independence song before the room was cleared.

The defendants' trial began in July 1985 in the Dirksen Federal Building before Judge George Leighton, a black man of Portuguese descent who had been a civil rights attorney with notable clients such as Martin Luther King. The charges against them included seditious conspiracy, unlawful possession of firearms, storing explosive materials, conspiring to make firearms, stockpiling weapons and blasting materials, operating bomb factories, planning prison escapes, and planning to rob the CTA money collector.

During the proceedings, the *Chicago Tribune* interviewed members of the Puerto Rican community. Angelina Rodriguez, a fifty-year-old woman born in Puerto Rico, angrily told a reporter, "I think [the defendants are] communists. They should be put in jail." But her twenty-six-year-old daughter, standing next to her, "rolled her eyes and sighed in exasperation at her mother's comments. 'Don't believe her,' she asserted. 'They're fighting for Puerto Ricans, for our rights and for the rights of our children.'"

Judge Leighton ordered extensive security measures, including package searches and restricted access to the courtroom. Each of the four defendants was guarded by two marshals, with another marshal assigned to the courtroom and two more standing watch in the corridor. The courtroom was checked twice a day by canine units trained to sniff out explosives, and a special route was used to take jurors in and out of the building. Fearing for his own safety, Leighton, a World War II veteran, wore a gun under his robe as Judge McMillen had.

One day outside the courthouse, a pro-FALN demonstration was led by José López, the brother of Oscar López Rivera, who shouted at a passing FBI agent that he'd better watch out for revenge by Los Macheteros ("the Machete Wielders"), a sister independence group. The trial was interrupted when five spectators were removed from the courtroom after making throat-cutting gestures toward Freddie Méndez as he was testifying. They wore T-shirts, each bearing a single letter that together spelled the Spanish word "chota," which means "stool pigeon." During the third week of the trial, dozens of FALN sympathizers demonstrated outside the Dirksen Federal Building to commemorate the anniversary of the U.S. occupation of Puerto Rico.

The prosecution team sought to show the jurors the black-and-white, silent videotape of Torres and Cortes huddled over a cluttered kitchen table manufacturing bomb timing devices. Judge Leighton ruled the videotape inadmissible because its viewing would constitute an invasion of privacy. But his ruling was overturned by the Court of Appeals on the ground that privacy rights did not extend to making bombs at home.

When the trial opened, Cortes and Torres characterized their homeland as a "bleak world where the American government systematically effaced a rich, proud Puerto Rican cultural heritage and where the powerful, shadowy hand of the Wall Street capitalist dictated the country's politics and exploited its citizens and natural resources." They referenced the large-scale human trials of the first birth control pill, Enovid, carried out in Puerto Rico in the mid-1950s by the pharmaceutical company G. D. Searle & Company. (The experimental dosages were many times higher than the legal dose today, and the women who volunteered typically were not fluent in English, illiterate, and unaware of the risks, which included blood clotting. Three women died, igniting controversy over the ethical standards used in the trial.) During the last day of testimony, Torres, Alberto Rodriguez and Cortes accused government authorities of enslaving Puerto Rican nationals in a "cocoon of ignorance." They invoked the names of freedom fighters from Northern Ireland, Nicaragua, and elsewhere, ignoring that over the years the people of Puerto Rico have consistently and resoundingly voted to reject proposals for gaining independence.

In his summation, assistant U.S. attorney James Ferguson countered, "There may be something heroic about someone who dies for his beliefs, but there is nothing heroic about someone who sneaks out into the dead of the night, plants bombs, and then slinks back into the sanctuary of a safe house before the bomb detonates."

All four defendants were convicted of seditious conspiracy, and three—Torres, Cortes, and Alberto Rodriguez—on a variety of additional charges. After the verdicts were announced, dozens of supporters in the courtroom stood with raised clenched fists and sang the separatist version of "La Borinqueña," the Puerto Rican national anthem, before being escorted out by U.S. marshals.

On sentencing day, demonstrators marched outside the courthouse, urging support of the FALN and chanting slogans in Spanish and English such as, "Grand jury, FBI—U.S. justice is a lie." Torres, Cortes, and Alberto Rodriguez each was handed a thirty-five-year prison term. José Luis Rodriguez, who denied he was a member of the FALN and was the only defendant represented by an attorney, received a suspended sentence and five years' probation. At sentencing, Judge Leighton observed that the case "represents one of the finest examples of preventive law enforcement that has ever come to this court's attention in the twenty-odd years I have been a judge and in the twenty years before that as a practicing lawyer in criminal cases."

The capture and conviction of a large number of FALN members effectively ended the group's reign of terror, which had been made possible because of the FALN's organizational and operational sophistication. By then, the FALN had been linked to over 140 bombings, incendiary actions, and other attacks, six deaths, more than a hundred injuries, and tens of millions of dollars in property damage. None of which advanced its stated cause of independence, which the clear majority of Puerto Ricans rejected and which was cover for the FALN's real objective—to subject Puerto Ricans to traditional Marxism modeled after Castro's Cuba.

# CHAPTER 23
## *Leavenworth*

*They didn't care, really, how many people were killed in this whole operation."*

—Bill Dyson, FBI

OSCAR LÓPEZ RIVERA'S NEW HOME was Leavenworth, the first federal prison ever built. Known as the "Hot House," the penitentiary is isolated and imposing, built in a radial design with four cell blocks emanating from a domed structure known as the "Big Top" that is modeled after the U.S. Capitol. Leavenworth reflects an idea, new and bold at the turn of the twentieth century, to make prison a "city within a city." It is completely self-contained within sixteen acres, and surrounded by thirty-five-foot-high walls. The prison has an illustrious list of alumni, among them "Whitey" Bulger, Al Capone, "Machine Gun" Kelly, James Earl Ray, and Michael Vick. At the time of López Rivera's incarceration, Leavenworth was a maximum-security prison whose twelve hundred inmates were considered to be America's most dangerous.

In early 1983, the FBI-Chicago police task force uncovered a plot to have López Rivera feign serious illness requiring him to be transported to a nearby Veteran's Administration hospital. Awaiting his arrival would be armed FALN members who were prepared to kill López Rivera's guards. The FBI allowed López Rivera's cohorts—including Dragon Lady and the Rabbit, both of whom were wearing disguises and bulletproof vests—to believe that López Rivera was being transported to the hospital. They were photographed and surveilled as they moved about the hospital's parking lot and ambulance entrance, and later charged with aiding and abetting an escape from prison.

That same year, López Rivera befriended fellow inmates Kojo Bomani-Sababu (born Grailing Brown, a New Afrikan Black Panther Party member convicted for murder and bank robbery), David Bryant, and Richard Cobb. They bonded over a shared interest in leading campaigns of "armed struggle" and discussions of weaponry needed for subversive actions. López Rivera boasted that he was the Chicago leader of the FALN and remained in communication with his free colleagues through visits, mail, and coded telephone calls.

By the summer of 1984, their focus shifted to escape. Cobb told Bomani-Sababu he'd heard from another inmate that a helicopter could fly into Leavenworth yard and pick up prisoners, if certain other measures were concurrently taken. Bomani-Sababu relayed this idea to López Rivera, who agreed to present it to "his people." Dora Garcia, López Rivera's former sister-in-law and a community activist, repeatedly visited him to discuss how funds would be obtained to purchase the weapons. Several weeks later, López Rivera told Cobb that the FALN had given him permission to participate in the escape and would provide a helicopter, pilot, and various needed materials. From late 1984 to mid-1985, López Rivera, Bomani-Sababu, and Cobb met daily to work out the details. Occasionally, Bryant joined in. They consulted an aerial photograph of Leavenworth, a surveyor's map, and a coroner's inquest containing information describing a similar helicopter escape attempt at Marion Penitentiary.

Their plan, in its final form, was summarized by FBI agent Bill Dyson:

> They were going to blow up one of the towers at Leavenworth Penitentiary to create chaos. While this was going on, they were going to attack all the military helicopters at Fort Leavenworth, the military base, because they had the feeling that they would support the prison. So, they were going to try to take them out. They were also going to have a helicopter swoop down and take them away.

According to the subsequent Victim Impact Report, López Rivera intended to "riddle guard towers with rounds from automatic weapons, and throw grenades in the path of those who pursued them." Smoke grenades would be used to obstruct the guards' vision, and fragmentation grenades would be thrown against the guard tower. Once out of prison, the escapees would steal cars and drive to a safehouse located in Des Moines, Iowa. There, they would then accumulate funds through robbery or counterfeiting to buy explosives and firearms. López Rivera promised to bring in FALN members to help train the men.

In September 1984, López Rivera revealed the plan to George Lebosky, another Leavenworth inmate. Lebosky bragged to López Rivera that he knew of a Houston lawyer who had a weapons contact in Louisiana. Bomani-Sababu then approached Lebosky with a list of weapons that included grenades, rifles, plastic C-4 explosives, and LAW (light-anti-armor) rockets. Lebosky was instructed to contact the attorney to find out the cost and availability of the weapons. The problem was—the Houston lawyer didn't exist.

Faced with exposure as a liar, Lebosky informed prison authorities of the plot. The FBI was brought in. In March 1985, Roger Rubrecht, the FBI undercover agent assigned to play the role of the weapons dealer, met with Jaime Delgado, a counselor at Northeastern Illinois University and FALN sympathizer, at the Dallas Airport, to discuss the purchase of the weapons on Bomani-Sababu's list. Rubrecht placed himself at great risk, as López Rivera had instructed his conspirators to murder the seller if he didn't give them a "fair price."

In May 1985, Rubrecht met with a weapons procurer arranged by Delgado, who turned out to be former

Weather Underground member Claude Marks. Rubrecht sold Marks thirty sticks of fake C-4 explosives. During their meeting, FBI agents bugged Marks' rental car. When Marks picked up fellow Weather Underground member Donna Jean Willmott, he was overheard telling her about the weapons purchase. Marks and Willmott were tracked by the FBI to Pomona, California, where they had stored explosives.

In June 1985, Cobb was released from Leavenworth prison to a halfway house in Denver. He quit his involvement in the conspiracy and began cooperating with the FBI, including recording telephone calls from Bomani-Sababu and López Rivera. In October 1987, once the FBI considered that it had obtained enough evidence, López Rivera, Bomani-Sababu, Delgado, and Garcia were put on trial amid heavy security in the Chicago courtroom of U.S. District Judge William Hart. (Marks and Willmott escaped arrest and were placed on the FBI's Ten Most Wanted List. They assumed new identities, married separately, had children, and remained in hiding for nine years until, tired of living on the lam, they negotiated a plea agreement and turned themselves in.)

Defense attorneys scoffed at the claims by Assistant United States Attorney Deborah Devaney that their clients engaged in violent schemes, and alleged that the trial was a "dance of deception" by the government. López Rivera once again asserted a prisoner-of-war status and contested the court's jurisdiction over him. He delivered a lengthy speech to the jury, during which López Rivera charged that the United States illegally gained control over Puerto Rico in 1898 and, ever since then, has waged a campaign of "cultural and racial genocide." As he spoke, his sympathizers, who had packed the courtroom, clapped repeatedly.

After a ten-week trial, the jury found López Rivera, Bomani-Sababu, Garcia, and Delgado guilty of various charges, including participating in a multi-goal conspiracy to effect the escape of inmates from Leavenworth, to transport weapons and explosives with intent to kill and injure people, and to use explosives to destroy government buildings and property.

López Rivera's sentencing report stated, "His level of remorse, rehabilitation, and positive regard for this court's process is minimal, if non-existent. He demonstrates a sustained, consistent commitment to the use of violence and weapons ... He is beyond rehabilitation. He has shown nothing but contempt for the judicial system and the lives of his fellow citizens." Judge Hart handed López Rivera a fifteen-year sentence, to run consecutively to the prison sentence he was already serving. "Those who take up the sword die by the sword," Hart told López Rivera.

Dora Garcia drew a three-year sentence. When she pleaded for leniency, contending that she was "generous and loving," Devaney responded, "What compassion did she show for the guards at Leavenworth who were going to be riddled with bullets?"

# CHAPTER 24
## *Who Placed the Bomb in Fraunces Tavern?*

*The Yanki government is trying to terrorize and kill
our people to intimidate us from seeking our rightful
independence from colonialism. They do this in the same
way as they did in Vietnam, Guatemala, Chile, Argentina,
Mexico, the Congo, Algeria, and in many other places
including the United States itself.*

—FALN communiqué

RICK HAHN BELIEVES IT WAS leaders of the Weather
Underground who chose Fraunces Tavern as the FALN's
target. It wasn't probable the FALN would have known
about the Anglers Club or its import, as most members
of the public didn't. And the communiqué issued in
connection with the bombing is focused on fighting
colonialism globally.

The dynamite for the bomb carried into Fraunces
Tavern likely was stolen from the Heron Dam construction

site in New Mexico and the cases driven to New York. This may well have been done by Pedro Archuleta, a former National Commission on Hispanic Affairs member who was fanatically dedicated to Chicano rights and the Puerto Rican independence cause. Archuleta, who in the 1970s was held in contempt and jailed for refusing to testify, defiantly announced to the grand jury, "I will never talk to you because I am proud of being a Chicano and fighting for justice." New Mexico was Archuleta's home state, and he had found work in the community of Tierra Amarilla, near the dam site.

Another suspected dynamite supplier is Ricardo Romero, a long-time Denver, Colorado, community activist in the "Chicano/Mexicano" movement, who also served on the board of N.C.H.A. Romero had clear ties to the FALN, having been identified by the FBI as the purchaser of a carbine rifle found in an apartment rented by William Morales. Like Archuleta, Romero was jailed for refusing to testify before a grand jury. The whereabouts of both Archuleta and Romero are long unknown.

As for who crafted the bomb, there are numerous suspects. The manner in which a bomb is fashioned— its parts, wiring, and overall design—is its "signature," reflecting how the maker was trained and his predispositions. Signatures, like fingerprints, are valuable investigatory clues. For example, the Unabomber's bombs were known for containing parts carved out of wood. Signatures can help law enforcement connect seemingly unrelated bombings. Therefore, agencies worldwide maintain extensive databases on bomb signatures.

In the hours after the Fraunces Tavern bombing, FBI explosive experts sifted through debris, finding items such as a watch back plate, a mutilated latch from the case that held the bomb, and a piece of a valve stem from a propane tank. (Today, DNA evidence would be searched for as well.) This evidence suggested the bomb had Morales' signature, which included the use of certain components like a Bulls Eye pocket watch and nine-volt battery, and the way in which the wires were connected. Plus, recovered in Morales' East Elmhurst apartment was a link to the Fraunces Tavern attack—a Gestetner wet-ink copy machine whose imperfections matched exactly the related FALN communiqué. Morales wasn't charged with participating in the Fraunces Tavern bombing in part because there wasn't a need to, as his conviction on a variety of federal and state weapons charges had already earned him a lengthy sentence.

The Fraunces Tavern bombing occurred more than three years before Morales was identified as the FALN's chief bombmaker. Don Wofford believes that in early 1975, Morales hadn't yet been sufficiently trained in bombmaking and that it's more likely the bomb was fashioned by Carlos Torres. There is also the possibility that the Weather Underground crafted the bomb.

While every FALN member shares guilt for the murder of four men at Fraunces Tavern, the question remains—who was the man who carried the gray duffle bag into the restaurant? Again, there are numerous candidates.

Charlie Murray spotted the bomber near the end of the lunch. "The guy was on the short side with light brown skin and a wide face. He was wearing a hat and glasses, and holding a bag. He seemed clearly out of place." Murray recalls that the man walked into the room and soon turned around, fumbled with an exit door handle, and was gone.

Based on descriptions by Murray and other restaurant witnesses, images were sketched by police artists of two Hispanic men seen roaming Fraunces Tavern before the bomb went off. Professor de la Cova has reviewed the sketches and matched them against the pictures of every known FALN member. De la Cova concluded that the suspect depicted in one sketch closely resembles Filiberto Ojeda Ríos.

Ojeda Ríos, after helping to found both the FALN and Los Macheteros, while in hiding in the 1970s and early 1980s had several encounters with Puerto Rican law enforcement. In August 1985, a group of FBI agents, wearing bulletproof vests and supported by snipers located on adjacent rooftops, knocked on the door of Ojeda Ríos' apartment building in Luquillo, on the northeast coast of Puerto Rico, seeking his arrest. Ojeda Ríos refused to let them in. In the meantime, his wife burned incriminating documents in the apartment's bathroom. When Ojeda Ríos noticed agents climbing a ladder to reach the second floor, he let loose from the stairwell with an Uzi sub-machine gun. One agent was struck in the eye. Ojeda Ríos kept firing until he was disabled by a bullet that hit his Uzi and pushed it into his chest, knocking him to the floor.

Ojeda Ríos was charged for his part in planning the 1983 robbery of a Wells Fargo depot in West Hartford. The theft, which took place on September 12, 1983, the anniversary of Pedro Albizu Campos' birthday, resulted in seven million dollars being taken, at the time the largest bank heist in American history. While awaiting trial, Ojeda Ríos' attorneys argued he had been denied the right to a speedy trial, although the delay in bringing him to trial was largely the result of defense motions. Ojeda Ríos was released from prison on a one-million-dollar bond and ordered to wear an electronic monitoring bracelet. He promptly cut off the device, left it at the door of the offices of *Claridad*, a Puerto Rican pro-independence newspaper, and disappeared. Two years later, he was convicted and sentenced in absentia to fifty-five years in prison.

As with most *independentistas*, Albizu Campos was a role model for Ojeda Ríos. One of the actions taken by Albizu Campos upon assuming leadership of the Nationalist Party was to annually commemorate El Grito de Lares on its anniversary, September 23, as the first major revolt against Spanish rule in Puerto Rico and the birth of the concept of Puerto Rico as a distinct nation. Every year on September 23, Ojeda Ríos would issue taped statements on various aspects of the independence movement. He also granted several radio interviews to island media outlets. In one given in 1998, he admitted to many violent acts committed by Los Macheteros, including planting bombs at several banks throughout the course of a general strike. (Reporters conducting the interview were transported blindfolded to Ojeda Ríos' hideout.) That same year, the FBI increased its reward for information leading to his capture to $500,000. Ojeda Ríos issued a statement advising that anyone who provided information to the police regarding his whereabouts would be considered a "traitor" and would "pay with his life."

In September 2005, the FBI received a tip that Ojeda Ríos, who had assumed the identity of Don Luis, a rose gardener, was hiding in a farmhouse in the hilly town of Hormigueros, eighty-five miles west of San Juan. On Tuesday, September 20, a team of agents began surveillance of the farmhouse, planning to wait until the weekend to make the arrest. On Friday, in Ojeda Ríos' annually recorded El Grito de Lares speech, which was broadcast on radios throughout the island, he called for unity among pro-independence groups. Ojeda Ríos asked his followers to focus on three issues: the United States stop military testing in and controlling access to the El Yunque rainforest, Puerto Rico's water supply not be privatized by American or multinational companies, and for support for the anti-military and counter-recruitment movements among Puerto Rican youth.

By Friday afternoon, the agents suspected they had been spotted, and decided to move in. As they approached, Ojeda Ríos opened the front door and fired nineteen rounds, eight of which struck FBI agents, wounding one seriously in the abdomen. The agents returned fire and established a defensive perimeter. Fearful the house was rigged with explosives, they waited eighteen hours for an explosives expert to arrive on a flight from the Quantico Marine Corps base in Virginia before attempting a tactical entrance into the house. Encountering no resistance, they found Ojeda Ríos, dressed in combat boots and a bulletproof vest, dead on the floor from a bullet that had pierced his neck and exited through his back. An autopsy found he had bled to death.

Ojeda Ríos was buried in his hometown, in a wooden casket adorned with a machete. Hundreds attended his wake, waiting in a line that stretched several blocks. In the room where his open coffin lay, patriotic music was played and speeches given. At the same time, San Juan's main avenue was blocked to demonstrate against his "assassination."

The circumstances of Ojeda Ríos' death drew widespread criticism, including from Puerto Rican government officials. Among the allegations were that Ojeda Ríos had sought to surrender, did not fire first, did not receive prompt medical attention, and that the FBI did not properly coordinate with Puerto Rican police and deliberately timed their action to coincide with El Grito de Lares. FBI Director Robert Mueller asked the Justice Department's Office of the Inspector General to investigate. After an extensive review, the Inspector General concluded that Ojeda Ríos initiated the gunfight, that the agents were justified in returning fire, that the agents' use of force in the Ojeda Ríos operation did not violate the Justice Department's Deadly Force Policy, and that the delay in entering the house after Ojeda Ríos was shot was based upon a legitimate concern for agent safety.

\*

The sketch of the second man closely matched another FALN member, Luis Rosado, whose distinctive face included pockmarks on his cheek, a prominent nose, and a scar on the right side of his scalp. (Rosado resembles the man standing next to Oscar López Rivera in the picture discussed earlier.) Luis Rosado, along with his brothers Julio (a former newspaper reporter for *The San Juan Star* who was an enthusiastic advocate of Puerto Rican independence) and Andrés (a bomb technician), had been leaders in the Puerto Rican independence movement since the formation of M.I.R.A. in the late 1960s. When Don Wofford and the FBI began investigating the Fraunces Tavern bombing, Wofford developed a chart of suspects that he kept above his desk. "From the first day, Julio Rosado was always in my top five, sometimes number one, because he was the main guy in New York."

*In 1978, Luis Rosado, Pedro Archuleta, Andrés Rosado, and Julio Rosado refusing to testify before a New York grand jury investigating the FALN* (courtesy of latinamericanstudies.org)

After the Fraunces Tavern bombing, Wofford had dispatched agents to interview the Rosados. The agents who interviewed Julio Rosado described his pale, stunned face and shaking hands when they identified themselves, his breaking into a sweat, and his halting, stammering responses to their initial questions, like a man caught in the act.

The brothers' first serious brush with the American criminal justice system came in November 1976 after Chicago police discovered the Haddon Street safe house and the letter linking FALN suspects to the National Commission on Hispanic Affairs of the U.S. Episcopal Church. The three Rosados, because of their known ties to the Commission, were subpoenaed to testify before the investigating grand jury. They refused to answer the grand jury's questions and were indicted on criminal contempt charges, but those were dropped on a technicality. After the deadly Mobil Oil building bombing in August 1977, the three brothers were detained as suspects. This time, they were represented by William Kunstler, who gained fame in the 1960s defending Vietnam War protestors, and whose clients included the Black Panther Party and the Weather Underground. Kunstler's defense of the "Chicago Seven," radicals accused of conspiring to riot during the 1968 Democratic Convention, led *The New York Times* to label him "the country's most controversial and, perhaps, its best-known lawyer." After refusing to provide fingerprints, handwriting, or voice samples requested for comparison to other evidence gathered in the FALN investigations, the brothers again were held in contempt of court. This time, they were imprisoned for ten months. Upon being released, they posed together on the steps of the federal courthouse along with Pedro Archuleta, each raising a clenched fist. Two weeks after their release, more FALN bombings occurred.

Julio Rosado visited William Morales shortly before his escape from Bellevue, and Rosado's fingerprints were found in Morales' Queens bomb factory. And in June 1981, Rosado was arrested in Brooklyn after being observed spray painting the letters FALN on the wall of a Teamsters Union local. A briefcase carried by Rosado was found to contain photographs of Morales as well as counter-surveillance photos of members of the Joint Terrorist Task Force.

Julio Rosado, along with Oscar López Rivera, constituted the FALN's "central command," and must be considered a candidate to have been the man who placed the bomb in Fraunces Tavern. But Don Wofford believes that his brother Luis is a more likely suspect. "You have to think of who among the FALN and their sympathizers had the violent temperament, the fanaticism, and, frankly, the balls to have walked into the restaurant with a live powerful bomb. I think Luis had those characteristics in spades. More than Julio did, and on par with Morales."

The links between Luis Rosado and William Morales are numerous. Both were born in Chicago to Puerto Rican parents. They attended school together and became close friends. Luis Rosado was instrumental in Morales' escape from the Bellevue medical ward in 1979. His brother Andrés had been an employee of Bellevue in the mid-1960s, and after Morales' transfer there, Luis Rosado rented a corner apartment on First Avenue, opposite the Bellevue ward. From the kitchen, he sketched diagrams of the grounds and logged the movements of guards. After Morales escaped and, while in hiding, recovering from being wounded by his fall onto the air conditioner, Luis visited him.

Luis Rosado supported himself driving a cab, selling cars, and as a porter. And through theft. In December 1980, Rosado, along with an accomplice, Felix Rosa, robbed a salesman at a car dealership in the Chicago suburb of Highland Park at gunpoint and stole a van. Following a high-speed police chase, both were arrested and charged with armed robbery, kidnapping, and aggravated battery. Inexplicably, they were released on bond. Luis Rosado failed to appear for his March 1981 trial.

On New Year's Eve in 1982, a man called a local New York City radio station, WCBS, and declared, "This is the FALN. We are responsible for the bombings in New York today." A tape of the call was played to Freddie Méndez, who recognized the voice as Luis Rosado's. Méndez told the FBI that he had spoken with Luis on many occasions "and had heard him speak publicly on matters relating to the independence of Puerto Rico." Based on an affidavit sworn to by Méndez, a complaint was filed in Federal District Court in Brooklyn accusing Rosado of conspiring with others "to participate directly or indirectly" in the New Year's Eve bombings. New York City Police Commissioner Robert McGuire announced a reward for information leading to the arrest of Luis and his conspirators, which soon swelled to $250,000, of which $200,000 was put up by the New York City business community. But Rosado was never located, and in April 1995, the Clinton Administration dropped the charges against him on the belief that he had fled to Cuba and could not be tried. The investigation into Rosado's whereabouts ended.

The Rosados, Pedro Archuleta, Ricardo Romero, and William Morales had escaped justice. But the victims and their families could take comfort in the fact that the law had caught up with Oscar López Rivera and many of his FALN comrades. Their punishment, in the form of decades of incarceration, appeared certain.

# CHAPTER 25
## *The Push for Clemency*

*I know the chilling evidence that convicted the petitioners,
the violence and the vehemence with which they conspired
to wage war on all of us. They made every effort to murder
and maim. A few dedicated federal agents are the only
people who stood in their way.*

—Deborah Devaney, former Assistant U.S. attorney

CLEMENCY, WHICH IS THE exercise of leniency toward
persons who have committed crimes, dates to the oldest
known legal code—the Code of Hammurabi. Several
forms of clemency have evolved, including full pardon,
commutation of sentence, elimination of fines and forfei-
tures, delay of full punishment, and the grant of amnesty
to a group. Pardon amounts to forgiveness of a crime,
which lessens the stigma arising from the conviction and
removes restrictions on the right to vote, hold state or
local office, or sit on a jury.

In the U.S., the clemency process was carefully designed by the framers of the Constitution when they drafted the Pardon Clause in 1787, which bestows on the president the power to "grant Reprieves and Pardons for Offences against the United States …". Among other considerations, they debated the potential for Presidential abuse and whether one or both branches of Congress should play a role in the process. In the end, they rejected proposals to check the power through Congressional oversight because, in the words of Alexander Hamilton, "one man appears to be a more eligible dispenser of the mercy of the government than a body of men." Hamilton believed that the President's "sole fiat" to grant clemency would be tempered by "scrupulousness and caution; the dread of being accused of weakness or connivance, would beget equal circumspection." The result is that the president's award of clemency is absolute and unreviewable, nor can future presidents rescind a grant. It is, arguably, the only power in the Constitution not subject to check and balance. Therefore, the clemency process ordinarily is held to strict guidelines to protect against corruption and undue influence.

The founding fathers crafted the Pardon Clause with multiple purposes in mind, including the potential to diffuse unpredictable situations and serve societal goals beyond the individuals affected. "In seasons of insurrection or rebellion," Hamilton wrote in the Federalist Papers, "there are often critical moments when a well-timed offer of pardon to the insurgents or rebels may restore the tranquility of the commonwealth." Among the numerous examples of the use of the pardon power to "restore tranquility" are Washington's pardoning the leaders of the Whiskey Rebellion, Jefferson's pardoning of deserters from the Continental Army, Andrew Johnson's 1868 forgiveness of Confederate soldiers for treason, and Carter's 1977 blanket absolution to Vietnam draft dodgers.

Arguably the most famous pardon issued for public policy purposes was granted by President Ford to Richard Nixon. Notably, Ford went to great lengths to justify his action, including making an historic and voluntary appearance before the House Judiciary Committee. "Surely we are not a revengeful people," Ford said. Nixon "already is condemned to suffer long and deeply in the shame and disgrace brought upon the office he held." The crux of Ford's reasoning was that the trial of a fallen president would be divisive and divert the nation from the many challenges it faced.

Over the years, some have argued that the clemency power constitutes a challenge to the rule of law, by allowing the ends to justify the means. Hamilton thought the reverse was true, that clemency is a way of correcting the law's inherent imperfections by tempering justice with mercy. As Chief Justice Rehnquist wrote in a 1993 Supreme Court decision, "Clemency is deeply rooted in our Anglo-American tradition of law, and is the historic remedy for preventing miscarriages of justice where judicial process has been exhausted." A classic example of clemency being used to achieve a fair result is if a person is later found through DNA evidence to have been wrongly convicted, yet a court will not overturn the sentence. But the tension between justice and mercy can be difficult to reconcile. What's the proper balance? If you reduce a prison sentence, by how much? And what else should be required?

*

Soon after Bill Clinton assumed office, Luis Gutiérrez, a new Congressman from Illinois, discussed with the president freeing the imprisoned Puerto Rican *independistas*. "Clinton would sit down and talk to you as a member of Congress when you went to petition him for a pardon, and he would talk about the political situation." During the same period, the activist Luis Nieves-Falcón began corresponding with Bernard Nussbaum, Clinton's White House Counsel and a long-time friend of the First Lady, about the status of the FALN prisoners. Nussbaum's support led Nieves-Falcón, in March 1993, to write to the president, Attorney General Janet Reno, and Margaret Love, the Pardon Attorney at the Justice Department, requesting "immediate and unconditional release from prison of Puerto Rican independence fighters in U.S. jails and prisons." In her reply letter, Love informed Nieves-Falcón that clemency is considered only "upon formal application by the individual who has been convicted."

In November of that year, Nieves-Falcón, working within a campaign called Ofensiva '92, filed a petition for executive clemency with Love on behalf of eighteen prisoners. The campaign would consistently emphasize that "they were fighting for the independence of Puerto Rico, their imprisonment was unjust, and their sentences were disproportionate."

An argument in the petition was that the Justice Department should compare the Puerto Rican prisoners to the forefathers of the United States who fought for independence from Great Britain—many of whom presumably frequented Fraunces Tavern. This logic would have us believe that all violence, including harming civilians, committed in the name of understandable political impetus is justifiable. As stated by former Secretary of State Colin Powell after the Islamist extremist May 2003 bombings in western compounds in Riyadh, "We should not try to cloak their ... criminal activity, their murderous activity, in any trappings of political purpose." Loran Lomasky, the noted American philosopher, has observed, "Possession of grievances in no regard distinguishes terrorists from the remainder of humanity. Bad luck and injustice are, to one degree or another, the common human lot."

Over the next few years, Ofensiva '92 organized a sweeping letter-writing campaign for clemency, sending more than 75,000 signatures of support to the White House. As the petitioning continued, the movement's leaders obtained numerous face-to-face meetings with sympathetic top government officials. Among them were members of the Interagency Working Group on Puerto

Rico, co-chaired by Marcia Hale and Jeffrey Farrow. In October 1994, Mayra Martinez-Fernandez, a special assistant to Farrow, wrote Farrow a memo on the "Puerto Rico Political Prisoners," the title of which alone demonstrated administration favoritism. In it, Martinez-Fernandez stated that the prisoners, "have been persecuted because of their commitment and activism in support of Puerto Rican independence ... They are truly good people who are where they are for wanting their country to be free. That is not a crime." Her memo continued on to discuss the political benefits to the Clinton Administration of granting clemency. "The release of these Puerto Rican men and women ... will have a positive impact among strategic Puerto Rican communities in the U.S."

Politicians and activists joined the clemency crusade, framing the issue in terms of human rights. They included former New York City Mayor David Dinkins and Coretta Scott King, as well as two former island governors, several Democratic lawmakers from New York and the three Congressmen of Puerto Rican descent—Nydia Velázquez and José Serrano of New York, and Luis Gutiérrez. In a meeting with Clinton's chief counsel, Jack Quinn, Velázquez claimed, "If there is one issue that unites all Puerto Ricans, it is getting these people out of jail." She added, "The sentences these men and women are serving are too long. They're clearly political prisoners."

Many prominent persons lobbied on behalf of the prisoners, with the White House mischaracterizing some of their comments. One example was President

Clinton's statement about Archbishop Desmond Tutu, a Nobel Peace Prize winner: "He wrote to seek clemency for the petitioners, since they have received 'virtual life sentences' and 'have spent over a decade in prison, while their children have grown up without them.'" But Bishop Tutu did not make those comments. He only asked the president, on behalf of his "brother Bishop in Puerto Rico" to <u>consider</u> clemency (emphasis added).

John Cardinal O'Connor, the Archbishop of New York, also weighed in, writing to Attorney General Janet Reno in March 1996 to ask her to review the cases of imprisoned FALN members for possible pardon on humanitarian grounds. The Cardinal's support for clemency was touted by its advocates but doubted by Joe Connor. Connor wrote to the Archbishop asking him to publicly state his true position. "These people were knowing participants in murder and terrorism. And none have ever expressed regret or offered an apology." The Cardinal responded, "I believe that this kind of terrorist action must be condemned. My request was for a review of these cases. I believe that there are many factors which must be considered, including renunciation of violence as a means of achieving political ends. I also believe that an expression of remorse for these crimes should also be considered in determining humanitarian release."

The most influential backer of clemency was Jimmy Carter who, while president, had presided over a foreign policy that enabled Iranian radicals to overthrow the Shah and establish an Islamic terrorist regime. In the decades since leaving office, Carter has compiled a sizable record of appeasement of terrorism. Among numerous examples, in January 2015, after the Charlie Hebdo attack in Paris, in which a roomful of cartoonists and satirists were slaughtered, Carter suggested that a root cause was the "Palestinian problem." Carter has long backed Hamas, designated by the State Department as a terrorist organization, meeting in person with its leaders and stating that, "Only by recognizing its legitimacy as a political actor can the West begin to provide the right incentives for Hamas to lay down its weapons." Carter made no distinction between freedom fighting and terrorism. As pointed out by Benzion Netanyahu, the father of a future prime minister of Israel, "In contrast to the terrorist, no freedom fighter has ever intentionally attacked innocents. He has never deliberately killed small children, or passersby in the street, or foreign visitors, or other civilians who happen to reside in the zone of conflict or are merely associated ethnically or religiously with the people of that area."

In February 1997, Carter urged Janet Reno to recommend to President Clinton commutation of sentences for all imprisoned FALN members. In his letter, Carter pointed to the precedent he set in 1979 by reducing to time served the sentences of four Puerto Rican Nationalists. "[Granting clemency] would be a significant humanitarian gesture." Carter argued, "And would be viewed as such by much of the international community." Joe Connor, in response, wrote and placed many calls to

Carter's office, seeking to set the record straight. None was returned. Nor did Carter ever contact any of the FALN victims or their families.

As the hundredth anniversary of Puerto Rico becoming a U.S. territory passed in 1998, clemency was a popular topic of discussion on the island and mainland. In July of that year, Carter wrote a second public letter to Reno in which he stated that he had "read some of the prisoners' recent statements and ... there seemed to be a process of reflection going on in their thinking." Carter might have listened to Bill Newhall, the Fraunces Tavern bombing survivor, when he testified before the Senate Judiciary Committee in 1999. Newhall stated, "We've heard how much these self-styled 'freedom fighters' sacrificed and lost because of their political beliefs. To the contrary, those who truly paid for the FALN's beliefs were their dead victims. Men of character, humor, and promise, they will never return to their loved ones, or receive a hero's welcome." To his friends, Newhall would admit, "Hardly a day that goes by that I don't think of the men I was with that day. I keep seeing a moving picture of them, like a mini news reel."

Carter asserted to Reno that, "If a clear, democratic path to independence had existed at the time, it's quite likely that they would not have chosen to act as they did." Carter's statement was disingenuous, and ignorant of the facts. There existed at all times a clear, democratic path to independence, namely, public referendums, of which four have been held since 1967. In both the July 1967 and

November 1993 referendums, voter turnout was high, a majority chose to keep the existing commonwealth status, and an overwhelming majority (more than 95 percent) rejected independence. Tellingly, William Morales deemed the 1993 plebiscite to be "irrelevant." He added, "To me, there is no choice in the matter. Puerto Rico must be free, to quote Malcolm X, by any means possible."

In the December 1998 referendum, when voters were given a multiple, confusing choice among statehood, independence, free association, being a territorial commonwealth, or "none of the given" options, a majority selected the last option. (The limited vote for maintaining commonwealth status reflected concern that the definition of that status was misleading.) A November 2012 non-binding, two-part plebiscite asked Puerto Rican voters if they wished to keep their current U.S. commonwealth status. Seventy-nine percent of eligible voters turned out, an extremely high turnout percentage. A slim majority voted no. Voters then were asked if they wanted Puerto Rico to become a state, an independent country, or a freely associated state. Over sixty percent chose statehood (although nearly half a million voters left the second question blank), and once again only a small percentage voted for independence.

Contradicting Carter, *The Daily News* stated, "The terrorists are simply people who turned to violence when the votes didn't go their way." Or as former Puerto Rico Governor Carlos Romero Barceló said, "The basic crime [the FALN] committed was to try to impose their aspirations on the people of Puerto Rico against their will."

While he was president, Carter was responsible, under Article II of the Constitution, to "take care that the laws be faithfully executed." The president must enforce all federal laws regardless of his administration's view of their wisdom. As another president, Abraham Lincoln, once said, "Let every man remember that to violate the law is to trample on the blood of his father, and to tear the character of his own and his children's liberty." Yet Carter suggested in his letter to Reno that unlawful and violent acts may be justified. Democrat Representative Henry Waxman reacted to Carter's statement. "I must say that I'm offended by [it]. It may be his view, but whatever reasons these people had, [they] ended up in the loss of human lives. I was also troubled by the idea that [clemency] would be considered a humanitarian gesture. I don't think we have to make gestures of humanitarianism. I think what we need in this country is justice."

Carter's argument, in his mind, was morality based. So was the approach taken in May 1994 by Federal Judge Kevin Duffy when he faced four men convicted of the 1993 World Trade Center bombing. Duffy imposed the extraordinary sentence of 240 years on each of them, with no possibility of parole. In doing so, he consulted actuarial tables to ascertain the life expectancies of each of the six persons who died in the blast, and added the years that each of them presumably lost, arriving at a figure of 180, which involved the first six counts of the indictment. Two other counts, including assault on a federal officer, carried mandatory sentences of 30 years each, adding another sixty years to the 180, totaling 240 years.

Over time, numerous entities and individuals spoke out against clemency. One was the FBI, whose Director, Louis Freeh, a Clinton appointee, advised the Justice Department of the Bureau's "unequivocal opposition to the release of these terrorists under any circumstances." Freeh wrote to Henry Hyde, the Chairman of the House Judiciary Committee, that clemency "would likely return committed, experienced, sophisticated, and hardened terrorists to the clandestine movement for Puerto Rican independence, and would psychologically and operationally enhance" the FALN.

Clemency also was opposed by officials of the Federal Bureau of Prisons, which monitored the FALN members' visits, telephone calls, and letters, and concluded that if they were released from prison, they might resume their criminal behavior even after renouncing it. Michael Cooksey, the Bureau's Assistant Director of Corrections, believed that some of the prisoners had an "extreme propensity to violence or escape." He noted that the Bureau hadn't been asked for its advice by the White House.

Every major police organization in the country opposed granting clemency, including the Fraternal Order of Police, whose president, Gilbert Gallegos, sent a letter to President Clinton expressing "incredulity that he would even consider releasing terrorists who are committed to achieving their separatist goals through violence." Howard Safir, New York's Police Commissioner, commented, "This type of action will encourage terrorism worldwide. We should never make deals with terrorists." Safir later added, with the New Year's Eve bombings in mind, that, "The message this sends to police officers is that they're disposable." The United States Attorneys in Chicago and Hartford—each of whom had prosecuted FALN members—were consulted; both recommended against leniency.

Frank Keating also spoke up. Keating was a former FBI agent who assumed the governorship of Oklahoma in 1995. Three months later, the Alfred P. Murrah Federal Building in downtown Oklahoma City was bombed, killing 168 people and injuring more than 680 others. The attack was, at the time, the deadliest terrorist attack in American history. President Clinton visited the site days later and quoted from Proverbs 11:29: "Those who trouble their own house shall inherit the wind," presumably referring to the futility of purpose of the bombing.

The Oklahoma City bomb was planted by Timothy McVeigh, who would later be executed. Terry Nichols, McVeigh's active co-conspirator, was at home in Kansas with his family when the bomb went off. Keating later drew an analogy to the proposed FALN clemencies. "The terrorists were convicted of crimes that directly supported bombers and killers ... and very similar to those committed by Mr. Nichols in support of Mr. McVeigh.

They deserve to serve the sentences imposed on them by American juries."

In December 1996, Margaret Love, still the Pardon Attorney, recommended to President Clinton that he deny the clemency requests. But in July 1997, Eric Holder, U.S. Attorney for the District of Columbia since 1993, succeeded Jamie Gorelick as Deputy Attorney General under Janet Reno, winning confirmation by a unanimous vote. As stated by John Fund and Hans von Spakovsky in their book, *Obama's Enforcer,* "Even early in his career, Holder showed a permissive, casual, and dangerous attitude toward terrorists, particularly when doing so could be advantageous for political patrons."

One of Holder's first acts was to fire Love and replace her with Roger Adams, a member of his staff. Holder instructed Adams to revise the clemency report with "the desired objective of recommending that the president grant clemency to the extent it would result in the prisoners' serving [a maximum of] twenty years in prison."

The U.S. Attorney's Manual cites five factors in considering whether to recommend a pardon, one of which is "acceptance of responsibility, remorse, and atonement." Holder subsequently met with various persons and groups who supported clemency but, like Carter, never with the victims or their families. One such meeting occurred in April 1998 with members of the religious community, during which the clemency supporters handed Holder a "Statement from the Puerto Rican Political Prisoners." It read, "Our actions, for the most part symbolic, have had the objective of focusing the attention of U.S. government on the colonial condition of Puerto Rico, and not of causing terror to the citizens of the U.S. or Puerto Rico. <u>However, that is not to deny that in all liberation processes, there are always innocent victims on all sides.</u>" (emphasis added).

In August 1998, Adams raised directly with Holder several concerns about the proposed clemency. Among them were that it would run against the strong recommendations of two U.S. Attorneys, have a negative impact on pending prosecutions and investigations, including the Fraunces Tavern bombing, fly in the face of FBI Director Freeh's testimony to Congress indicating that the FALN was a source of domestic terror, disregard victim impact, and ignore the range of offenses committed by members of the group.

Holder stood firm. Typically, each clemency recommendation is written in one of three ways: "summary denial," "full denial," or "favorables." Holder ignored precedent by asking Adams instead to prepare a memo for the president that contained no specific recommendations, only an analysis for each prisoner and multiple options ranging from unconditional release to no leniency. This approach would allow the president to grant the commutations without appearing to go against the Justice Department's wishes. But it violated the Justice Department's own regulation requiring that in every clemency case, the Department "shall report in writing [its] recommendation to the President, stating whether in [its] judgment the President should grant or deny the petition."

On June 4, 1998, Jeffrey Farrow, whose White House service dated back to the Carter Administration, told the *San Juan Star*, "We expect that the Department of Justice will complete its review and submit its recommendations in a few months." But not until July 1999 did the Justice Department transmit its second clemency report. By then, Puerto Rico's colonial status was a prominent news story due to massive protests against the continued use by the U.S. Navy of Vieques for military purposes, which were spurred by the death of a Puerto Rican security guard from an errant bomb.

In August 1999, Joe Connor calculated that he had reached the exact age to the day his father was when he was killed. "Kind of morbid no doubt, but I think most men reflect on reaching their father's age and compare themselves to him. I wondered how I could possibly be as old as my old man."

# CHAPTER 26
## *A Month's Wait*

*As a Puerto Rican, I feel I owe them for their sacrifice.*
—Mayra Martinez-Fernandez, Clinton White House staffer

ON AUGUST 7, 1999, the one-year anniversary of the U.S. embassy bombings in Africa that killed 224 people and wounded more than 5,000, President Clinton vowed he "will not rest until justice is done." And Secretary of State Madeleine Albright promised to wage "an all-out war against terrorism." Four days later, while Congress was on summer recess, the Justice Department announced in a brief press release that the president "has agreed conditionally to commute or remit the sentences of 16 individuals for crimes committed in the 1970s and early 1980s." The clemency requirements included agreeing to renounce the use of violence and abiding by all conditions of release set by the Parole Commission.

None of the prisoners was required to agree to cooperate in ongoing investigations. Twelve were former

FALN members, while the other four were comrades who belonged to "Los Macheteros." Like the FALN, Los Macheteros, more formally known as the "Boricua Popular Army," was started by Filiberto Ojeda Ríos and other *independistas* who desired a sister Puerto Rico-based organization. As explained by author and sociologist Ronald Fernandez, an expert on Los Macheteros, they were not only Puerto Rican nationalists but, also, "socialists with a distinct Leninist tinge ... Acting on the advice of Lenin, they are an exceedingly methodical and thoroughly trained group, with written guidelines for everything."

Los Macheteros was established on July 26, 1976, a date chosen because it coincided with the most significant day on the Cuban revolutionary calendar—Castro's failed attack on an army facility in the city of Santiago de Cuba on July 26, 1953. Los Macheteros' publicly stated goal was obtaining independence for Puerto Rico through armed struggle against the United States government.

The Macheteros' history of violence within Puerto Rico was vast. Among many examples, in August 1978, they ambushed a police patrol car in an attempt to steal weapons, uniforms, and the car itself. One of the officers was killed as he resisted while the other, stripped of his uniform, was left handcuffed to a tree at the side of the road. In December 1979, the Macheteros attacked a U.S. Navy transport bus at Sabana Seca, on the island's north coast, near San Juan. The bus, carrying nineteen unarmed sailors, was blocked on a public highway by a pickup truck, whose driver shot and killed the Navy bus driver. A van then pulled into the opposing lane of traffic and its passengers sprayed the side of the bus with automatic weapon fire, killing another sailor and wounding ten more. And in January 1981, the Macheteros used explosives to destroy jet aircraft at the Muñoz Air National Guard Base, resulting in more than $50 million in damage. At the time, that domestic terrorist attack was the costliest in U.S. history. In later years, their actions included firing a stolen anti-tank weapon at the FBI office in Hato Rey and rockets at the U.S. courthouse in old San Juan.

By 1999, the FALN and Macheteros together had inflicted more harm on American persons and interests than any other terrorist organization in history. Yet none of the sixteen prisoners was asked to express contrition. Adolfo Matos, one of the Chicago Ten, was taped in phone conversation only months before the clemency offers as saying, "I have nothing to be ashamed of or feel that I have to ask for forgiveness ... My desire [for the cause] has gotten stronger, to the point where I want to continue to fight and get involved with my people, because I love them." Matos admitted this despite being fully aware that all phone calls by federal prisoners are monitored, except when speaking with their lawyers.

In issuing the clemency grants, President Clinton broke with his own precedent. Approaching August 1999, Clinton had taken a less generous approach to clemency than any president since John Adams. More than three thousand clemency petitions had been filed with the Justice Department during his tenure, yet the president had approved only three of them, and each of those involved the commutation of a length of original sentence far less than for the FALN or Los Macheteros prisoners. Two were for drug offenses, while the third was given to a Nebraska hog farmer who'd been convicted of perjury in a bankruptcy proceeding. Clinton's pardon power had gotten him into trouble in 1980 when, having lost his re-election bid for the Arkansas governorship, he granted dozens of pardons before the end of his term. One of them was for a murderer who promptly killed again.

The president's rationale for commutation followed the Ofensiva '92 petition language; namely, the "unduly severe" sentences being served by the sixteen and the lack of "meaningful purpose" to their continued incarceration. Administration officials also insisted that none of the "activists" offered clemency were involved in any deaths. In response, Dick Morris, a long-time friend of the Clintons who worked as their pollster and political consultant, quipped regarding one of the sixteen—Los Machetero leader Juan Segarra-Palmer, who was the admitted organizer of the U.S. Navy sailor killings—that he was "about as non-violent as Jeffrey Dahmer [an American serial killer who raped, murdered, and dismembered seventeen men and boys]."

A White House representative, in the period leading up to the clemency offer, officiously told Deenie, now Deenie Berger Ettenson, "In this country, we do not have guilt by association." This also was stated by Bill Clinton himself during a press conference the day before the prisoners were released.

The Administration indicated that the president had acted based on reports prepared by the Justice Department and former White House Counsel Charles Ruff, who had overseen clemency issues. (A *Washington Post* reporter, Michael Kelly, called Ruff's defense of Clinton during the impeachment process "a masterwork of arguing black into white.") But Cheryl Mills, Deputy White House counsel and later a Hillary Clinton aide, asserted executive privilege to shield those reports from public disclosure, arguing that Congress "had no authority over the matter." A swift reaction came from Orrin Hatch, chair of the Senate Judiciary Committee, which oversees the Justice Department. "The White House and the Justice Department are hiding behind their tired old ploy of executive privilege ... If the President has confidence that his decision was the right one and a just one, then he ought to be willing to hold it up to public scrutiny."

Clinton used executive privilege for only the fourth time in his presidency. He had done so to avoid disclosing embarrassing information about scandals involving Travelgate, Monica Lewinsky, and Agriculture Secretary Mike Espy. A wide swath of lawmakers was angered, including New Jersey Democratic Senator Robert Torricelli, one of Clinton's most notable boosters, who "greatly regretted" the decision to assert executive privilege. Torricelli also lashed out at the clemency offers, saying directly to FALN victims and their family members, "This is a better government, and those of us who serve in Congress are better people than this outrageous action would indicate. There are no words sufficient to apologize to those who will live their lives with these wounds to explain this release from prison."

Joe Connor had been following developments closely. "We had begun to hear rumors in 1998 that clemency was being petitioned on behalf of FALN convicts. An article appeared in March 1998 in *Newsday* describing the efforts of Dylcia Pagan's son Guillermo and others pushing for clemency for Pagan. Her son complained that he did not have the benefit of his mother while growing up. *Newsday* published our reply to the article in which we empathized with the young Pagan as we, too, had to live without a parent during our formative years. Unfortunately, the reason we didn't have our father was because his mother conspired to murder him."

Prior to the clemency offer, Mary Connor Tully wrote a letter to the editor of her local newspaper, *The Bergen Record*, in opposition to the push for the prisoners' release. Instead of merely publishing the letter, the paper did a story on the Connor family. Little did the interviewer know this was the first time that Mary, Tom, and Joe had spoken openly about the most tragic event of their lives.

Over the years, Joe's wife Danielle had been struck by the Connors' stoicism. "In my family, we talked about everything. Joe's family was the opposite. They quietly focused on Tom and Joe staying in school, not getting in trouble, and succeeding in life. They would go to church on the anniversary of Frank's death, but, although Mary pushed the boys to go for counseling, they refused. In some ways emotionally, they put blinders on." "Joe characterizes it as "a very Irish way of coping. We each had cried in private so many times, but not with each other. We had never shared how upset we were, or how much we missed him. When we did, all that we had bottled up finally came out. We left our hearts on our sleeves."

On the day of the clemency offer, Joe and Danielle had taken their two children and Tom's two young sons to the local zoo. "The phone rang shortly after we returned home. I could hear Danielle talking to Tom's wife, Regina, with a concerned look on her face. From the few words she spoke, I instinctively knew what had happened. Clinton had done the unthinkable."

Word of the prisoners' release sent shock waves through the law enforcement community as well. Rocco Pascarella was told the news that day by his brother-in-law, who had heard it on the radio. "At first I didn't believe him. I didn't think it was possible that no one in the government would tell me in advance."

During the next few days, as the issue grew in national attention, Tom and Joe Connor were guests on several radio talk shows, as well as on Laura Ingraham's MSNBC TV program, *Watch It!* While the brothers waited backstage to appear with Ingraham, Henry Kissinger, who was scheduled to appear on the show immediately after them, ambled down the hallway. "Although I knew he would be on," Joe admits, "I was a little awestruck when he sat in the little cubicle right next to us, and could offer little more than a shy 'Good Morning, Dr. Kissinger.' As if he had known us for years, he asked, 'So what are you guys here for?'" Tom answered, "Clinton released the terrorists that killed our father at Fraunces Tavern." Kissinger shook his head. "Oh, the clemency. It's a goddamn disgrace." When asked by Tom "Why do you think he did it?" Kissinger responded, "I have so little respect for the man that nothing he could do would shock me."

There was much pushback to the clemency offers from both ends of the political scale. On the one hand, it included the largest demonstration in Puerto Rican history demanding the unconditional release of the prisoners. But many questioned the president's stated rationale. Peggy Noonan—author, columnist, and presidential speechwriter—observed, "Was it compassion for the prisoners that motivated the president? Clinton is not known for this ... as governor, he had even allowed a retarded man, Ricky Ray Rector, to be put to death in Arkansas in 1992 rather than face what he imagined would be political heat in the presidential race for being soft on crime."

Among the Democratic Party critics were Chicago Mayor Richard Daley, three-time New Jersey Senator Bill Bradley, and former New York City Mayor Ed Koch, who predicted that Clinton's obituary will include, "along with the section on Monica Lewinsky, a major reference to his inexplicable granting of clemency to terrorists." Koch had urged Clinton to drop the idea "like a hot potato." Various prominent Puerto Ricans also spoke up. Miriam Ramirez, a candidate for the island's Senate, told the *Washington Times* that the clemencies would only embolden Los Macheteros. The Resident Commissioner and former Governor of Puerto Rico, Carlos Romero Barceló, pleaded with Clinton not to release the terrorists. Romero Barceló, an avid supporter of statehood, asked, "How can we responsibly set them free? What if they kill somebody else? What do we say? 'Too bad'? And how can we ask for equality for Puerto Rico if in Puerto Rico people defend those who have declared war on the United States?"

The Clinton Administration fed wood to the fire when, on August 24, the Justice Department announced the release of Silvia Baraldini, an Italian-born freelance radical who had been sentenced in 1983 to forty-three years in prison for conspiring to commit two armed robberies, including the Brink's one, and driving a secondary getaway car during the prison break of Assata Shakur. Baraldini had been linked by physical evidence (a carbon copy of a communiqué) to the FALN. Technically, Baraldini was remanded to the custody of the Italian government, which pledged to keep her incarcerated until 2008, but the sham was exposed by the hero's welcome she received upon returning to Italy.

To quell the spiraling controversy, President Clinton wrote a five-page letter to Representative Henry Waxman, the ranking Democrat on the House Oversight and Government Reform Committee, the principal investigative committee of the House. Clinton insisted that, "My decisions were based on our view of the merits of the requests—political considerations played no role in the process."

But prevalent in the assertions by detractors was that Clinton had made the clemency offer in light of his wife's anticipated campaign for Senator of New York in 2000. Hillary was not a native New Yorker and had few ties to that state. New York's 1.3 million voters of Puerto Rican heritage were a key constituency. (Hillary Clinton did run successfully for the vacant New York Senate seat, initially against New York City Mayor Rudy Giuliani, who eventually withdrew upon learning of his prostate cancer diagnosis.) Staten Island Borough President Guy Molinari observed that the grant of clemency was made over the objections of many federal agencies. "This is part of a trend of abusing the Department of Justice for political purposes in order to achieve points for Hillary. There is no other reason that makes any sense." Senator Phil Gramm, chairman of the Senate Banking Committee, stated on ABC's *This Week* program, "This was an effort by the President, and the First Lady, to manipulate politics in New York." Raoul Lowery Contreras, a journalist and talk show host, wrote, "The President insults all Hispanics with his pandering for support. He insults the intelligence of Puerto Ricans with this cheap grab for Puerto Rican votes." Brit Hume of Fox News might have phrased it best. "We have papa panda bear in the White House and now mama panda bear running for Senate. It is just a case of pandering."

Tom and Joe Connor penned an op-ed piece in the *Wall Street Journal* pointing out that Frank Connor "grew up in the same neighborhood, was faithful to the same religion, and went to the same college as several of the convicted terrorists. Yet he, as the supposed representative of 'colonial oppression,' was the target of their bomb." Their article ended with, "It is our hope and belief that all New Yorkers will see through this craven political act and send a message to the first family that their votes cannot be bought through the release of those with our father's blood on their hands." Bill Newhall agreed, labeling the clemencies as "grandstanding parading as compassion."

Hillary Clinton repeatedly denied any "involvement in or prior knowledge of" the decision to offer clemency. Her husband backed her up. "She didn't know anything about it until—as far as I know—until someone called and asked her for a comment, because I did not discuss it with her." Clinton's statement was mocked by many, including William Safire, the noted author and presidential speechwriter, who in a reference to Clinton's infamous denial of a relationship with Monica Lewinsky wrote, "It is as if Bill Clinton looked us directly in the eye, and waggling his finger said … I never discussed clemency for terrorists with that woman, Ms. Clinton. Not a single time. Never." Dick Morris added, "Here she was, running for Senate in the state that had the largest Puerto Rican population in the nation. The clemencies directly affected how she would be perceived in that community ... It is just not credible that he didn't tell her."

In October 1999, José Rivera, then a New York City Councilman, undermined Hillary's account in an issue of *The New Republic* in which he said that Hillary met with him and other supporters two days before the clemency announcement. During that meeting, he handed her a packet of information about the prisoners along with a letter asking her to "speak to the President and ask him to consider granting clemency" to them.

Clemencies granted for political purposes were not new. In 1946, New York Governor Thomas E. Dewey pardoned Charles "Lucky" Luciano for "wartime services to the country," after which Luciano was deported to Italy. Ten years earlier, as a district attorney, Dewey had prosecuted Luciano and sent him to prison. Dewey, who was gearing up for his 1948 presidential run, was never able to adequately explain how Luciano, while in jail in the U.S., helped the war effort. Although word spread that Dewey and Luciano had worked together to protect American docks and prevent ships from being sunk, World War II military leaders denied that happened. Instead, it was widely alleged that Luciano's large contributions to the Republican Party had greased the wheels for his release.

This clemency controversy was unique for a number of reasons. One was that Hillary Clinton herself flip-flopped on her position on the clemency offer, coming under attack both by Puerto Rican leaders and by groups that opposed the release of the prisoners. She initially backed it. On August 14, three days after the clemency offer, Hillary's spokesman Howard Wolfson insisted she was "absolutely not" involved, but that "she's supportive, provided that the terms are strictly adhered to."

But after more than three weeks of the terrorists refusing to renounce violence and public outcry, Hillary changed her position. On Saturday, September 4, while on vacation with her husband at Camp David, Hillary asked for the offers to be rescinded. "When the administration first offered these prisoners clemency, I made it very clear that I had no involvement in or prior knowledge of the decision, as is entirely appropriate, and that the prisoners should not be released until they renounced violence. Their tardy response speaks volumes about their continuing advocacy of violence as a political weapon." Within an hour of her statement, the White House set a deadline of 5 p.m. on the following Friday for the prisoners to accept in writing the conditions for their release.

Hillary was blasted by several Puerto Rican leaders, including Representative José Serrano, a Bronx Democrat, who said he felt "grave disappointment and anger" at her "intervention," and was withdrawing his support for her candidacy for the Senate. As *The Daily News* put it, "Instead of getting credit for going against her husband and taking an unpopular stance among her backers, Clinton comes off as a novice who waited too long to take a stand." Days later, while speaking to the World of Women Leaders Conference in Manhattan, comprised largely of black, Hispanic and Asian women, Hillary told the audience that her decision to oppose clemency may have been too hasty, and that "the consultation process was not what it should have been, and that will never happen again."

Another suspected motive for the clemency offer was to bolster Hispanic support for Vice President Al Gore, who was gearing up for his 2000 presidential run. The House Government Reform Committee, chaired by Dan Burton of Indiana, after subpoenaing White House and Justice Department communications and other records relating to the President's decision, produced an internal White House memorandum written by Jeff Farrow in which he stated, "The V.P.'s Puerto Rican position would be helped" by clemency. In the memo, Farrow urged President Clinton and Vice President Gore to meet with the three Puerto Rican members of Congress on the issue. Gore denied knowledge of the document, and announced that he would not "stand in judgment" of the clemency decision. The Committee also produced an e-mail sent by Maria Echaveste, White House deputy chief of staff, to Charles Ruff. Attaching Farrow's memo, she wrote, "Chuck—Jeff's right about this—very hot issue," Ruff and senior Justice Department officials subsequently met with the three Puerto Rican Congressmen.

New York's senior Senator at the time, Daniel Patrick Moynihan, once famously said, "To be Irish is to know that in the end the world will break your heart." On August 30, Joe Connor reached out to Moynihan's niece, a Sullivan and Cromwell lawyer who represented the business in which Connor worked. She, in turn, contacted the senator, whose seat Hillary Clinton would succeed to. The next day, he became the first Democratic senator to publicly oppose the grant of clemency.

On the same day, Joe Connor and the three policemen severely injured in the 1982 New Year's Eve bombings joined Vito Fossella, a Republican member of the House of Representatives from Staten Island for a press conference on the steps of the Capitol building. Fossella had contacted Connor after the clemency offers were announced, when it seemed to Joe that "the world was literally against my family and me and other victims' families. Vito was a person willing to speak and take action on behalf of what is right. He gave us voice when we had been largely ignored by our government, and lent immediate credibility to us."

Connor admits, "I was unsure what exactly 'the steps of the Capitol' actually meant." "We had no script, few notes and basically no idea what to say. The congressman just told the police officers and me to speak from the heart. As I stepped in front of the cameras, reporters, and microphones, I was at once exhilarated and scared. Looking at the reporters' faces, I wondered if they thought

I was a good guy or not." Connor told them, "It is painful to think that my father's life is worth less [to Clinton] than his wife's election." Anthony Senft added, "These terrorists Clinton has released were not caught detonating a bomb—that almost never happens—but they were caught red-handed, with bombs and with bomb-making components and paraphernalia, and some of them actually were caught on videotape making bombs. They were not convicted of many of the bombings that we think they perpetrated, but it is wrong for the media to state as fact that they are innocent of these crimes."

Connor took notice of one "intense female reporter above all the others. She had dark hair, a dark complexion, and deep, thoughtful, emotional eyes. I first thought that she was Puerto Rican and that she wasn't friendly." That reporter was Deborah Orin of *The New York Post*," who published a lengthy review of the clemencies in which she argued forcefully that President Clinton had made a major misjudgment. "The Clinton White House forgot one key thing," wrote Orin, "the FALN bombers had real victims who still suffer horribly."

Orin's articles, and others, helped provoke a storm of legislative protest. In September, twenty-one members of Congress wrote to Clinton telling him that clemency "is a mistake of overwhelming magnitude." That was followed by Fossella filing a House resolution denouncing the clemency offer as a "deplorable" act and "an affront to the rule of law, the victims and their families, and every American who believes that violent acts must be punished to the fullest extent of the law." The House approved the resolution by a 311–41 margin that included ninety-three Democrats (seventy-one Democrats abstained). Days later, the Senate passed, by an even more overwhelming proportion of 95–2, a resolution of condemnation stating that President Clinton had made "deplorable concessions to terrorists, undermined national security, and emboldened domestic and international terrorists." Even the Puerto Rico House of Representatives weighed in with its own resolution expressing "the clearest and most vehement message of repudiation on behalf of the four million United States citizens residing in Puerto Rico of any act of violence of terrorism committed to further political or social causes."

Senate Foreign Relations Subcommittee Chair Paul Coverdell, who within months would die from a cerebral hemorrhage, wrote to FBI Director Louis Freeh asking for the underlying documents to see "why this decision has been made against the advice of the Justice Department, the FBI, and the U.S. Attorneys who originally prosecuted these individuals." Coverdell, along with Burton, also sent document demands to Attorney General Janet Reno and the Federal Bureau of Prisons. Other legislators called for the Clinton administration to hand over the reports that had been considered in making the clemency offer. They included Chuck Schumer, the junior Democratic Senator from New York, who said it was impossible for him to know if Clinton's offer was justified without seeing them, and explained that the White House's stonewalling was a key reason for his voting in favor of the Senate resolution denouncing the clemencies.

The days dragged on with no clarity as to which, if any, of the sixteen would accept the clemency terms before the September 11 deadline. As observed by Debra Burlingame, the noted activist and sister of Charles "Chic" Burlingame, the pilot of hijacked American Airlines Flight 77, which crashed in the Pentagon on 9/11, "Committed and unrepentant militants who did not accept the authority of the United States, they refused to apologize for activities they were proud of in order to obtain a clemency they never requested."

Initially, rather than accept the clemency offers, the prisoners publicly raised various objections, which included: (1) neither Oscar López Rivera nor Juan Segarra-Palmer would be immediately released from prison; (2) the condition to renounce violence might impede their ability to "join Puerto Rico's civic and political life," and (3) they would be prohibited from meeting with each other (although the two sisters in the group—Alicia and Ida Luz Rodriguez—were allowed to live together). Their spokesman, Nieves Falcón, labeled the clemency terms "punitive," and cited Jimmy Carter's pardons of five Puerto Rican Nationalists in 1979 without condition.

The left side of the political spectrum piped up as well. Congressman Luis Gutiérrez, a former member of the Puerto Rican Socialist Party, stated, "When one seeks peace and reconciliation, one doesn't place conditions." His position was echoed by Nydia Velázquez, a New York Democratic Congresswoman. "The political nature of the charges gave way to disproportionate and unjust sentences—placing conditions on them now is a continuation of the injustices that began almost two decades ago." Jesse Jackson went even further, bizarrely asserting, "To free them under those conditions is to give them a life sentence." Lolita Lebrón, pardoned by Carter, alleged that Clinton had "insulted the dignity of the Puerto Rican nation and those who fight for its liberty." The White House, forced to defend itself against attack from the left as well, stated through a spokesman, "The president tried to take a balanced approach. These were serious crimes for which they were convicted."

Although clemency is an individual, not group, grant, the administration, anxious to have the terms accepted and out of the news, arranged unprecedented joint conference calls for the sixteen, who were locked up in eleven different facilities. On September 7, close to thirty days after the clemency offer had been made, the White House announced that fourteen of the sixteen terrorists had agreed to the clemency conditions, including renouncing violence. As Lucy Rodriguez put it, "We decided that we wanted now to continue our lives out of prison. It was as simple as that."

One of the two who rejected the terms was Oscar López Rivera, who still had ten more years to serve before being released because the clemency offer did not extend to his conviction for attempting to break out of prison. López Rivera later claimed that he had refused the offer because it was not extended to Carlos Alberto Torres. The Justice Department's explanation for this was that Torres "was identified as the leader of the group, and had made statements that he was involved in a revolution against the United States and that his actions had been legitimate." The same, however, could have been said of others who were offered clemency. López Rivera's choice to remain in prison was the act of a leader—the captain going down with the ship.

The other to decline was Los Machetero member Antonio Camacho-Negron, who had been involved in the 1983 Wells Fargo robbery. The key to the theft was Victor Gerena, a Hartford-born Wells Fargo security guard, born to a mother who was an ardent supporter of Puerto Rican nationalism. After the day's pickups were done, Gerena turned a gun on his two co-workers. He tied them up, injected both with a sleep-inducing substance, and packed bales of currency into his rented Buick. Gerena was smuggled into Mexico City and eventually flown to Cuba.

The Wells Fargo robbery was yet another demonstration of the ongoing links between the Puerto Rican independence movement and Cuba. Jorge Masetti, a former Cuban diplomat who would defect to the United States, testified that, weeks before the robbery, he delivered $50,000 to the Macheteros on orders from his superiors in Castro's Department of the Americas, the Cuban agency created to support revolutionary movements. Some of the money went to the purchase of a motor home used for sneaking Gerena into Mexico. Masetti himself waited at the border and helped disguise Gerena, handed him a Cuban passport, and arranged his flight from Mexico City to Havana. Cuba kept about half the stolen money, according to conversations the FBI later intercepted among Los Macheteros members.

Camacho-Negron had been released from prison the year prior to the clemency offer, after which he flew to Puerto Rico and told a large adoring crowd that he had no intention of abiding by parole conditions and was willing to die for Puerto Rican independence. When he did violate parole by associating with people active in the independence movement and becoming involved again himself, he was re-arrested and returned to prison.

Joe Connor received phone calls at work from newspapers, law enforcement officials such as Howard Safir, and television stations telling him of the mass acceptance of the clemency offers. "It was devastating, and it came at a time when the stress at home was mounting and my job was suffering. Danielle knew I had to do what I was doing but she understandably was getting frustrated because fighting the clemency was all encompassing. It seemed whenever we sat down to eat, the phone would ring. We could not watch TV without the topic arising and ultimately dominating. Even the kids were affected. Though our son Frank had only turned two years old that May, he spoke very well and told me not to talk to the TV people because 'they are going to hurt you.'"

# CHAPTER 27
## *Release*

*We say we are not going to negotiate with terrorists. Are we going to let the Unabomber go now?*

—Terry Hillard, Chicago Police Superintendent

ON SEPTEMBER 10, 1999, almost twenty years to the day of Jimmy Carter's unconditional release of four Puerto Rican Nationalists, eleven of the fourteen who accepted Clinton's clemency walked out of federal prisons around the country, with most eventually making their way to Puerto Rico. Los Machetero leader Juan Segarra-Palmer, who was convicted of a variety of charges related to his involvement in the Wells Fargo theft, accepted the commutation offer and had his fifty-five-year sentence reduced. But he would have to wait until 2004 to be released. (Segarra-Palmer, a Harvard graduate who attended the university during the heyday of the radical student movement, would go on to write a screenplay about how he planned the robbery.) The two remaining

Los Macheteros members, who had also been involved in the armored car robbery, were already out of prison and had the unpaid balance of their fines expunged. This news led to a new round of condemnations. But there also was celebration, in a manner validating what Richard English, the noted Irish historian, has observed as the "inherent rewards" of belonging to a terrorist group—prestige, status, a sense of identity, pride, intense friendship, and redemption. That night, The National Committee to Free Puerto Rican Political Prisoners rallied in Humboldt Park. Puerto Rican flags were pasted to utility poles and the sounds of a mariachi band filled the air. "Que viva Puerto Rico libre," shouted Luis Rosa, released from Leavenworth, as he played conga drums.

Rosa was born in Chicago in August 1960. On the day of his birth, his father died, and Rosa grew up poor. Only nineteen at the time of his arrest in April 1980, he was a student at the University of Illinois and a star baseball player, recruited by professional teams. But his sports passion had been exceeded by his activism and involvement in the Puerto Rican student movement, where he rose to become president of the Union for Puerto Rican Students and a ready target for recruitment by the FALN.

Another of the ex-prisoners, Alberto Rodriguez, told the cheering crowd, "I am happy, but my happiness is shattered. When I walked out of the Terre Haute Penitentiary this morning, I left behind a very beautiful person," he said, referring to López Rivera as his "comrade, friend, and family." William Morales told a

*New York Post* reporter in Havana that he was elated at the releases, especially for Dylcia Pagan, the mother of his son.

On the Sunday after the prisoners' release, Joe and Danielle were dressing for a wedding when a friend called to tell Joe to turn on *Meet the Press.* He watched as Tim Russert interviewed Ricardo "Dickie" Jimenez, one of the released FALN members. Jimenez, a Tuley High School alumnus, in 1974 had been chosen by Mayor Daley as Chicago's "Senior High School Student of the Year." He had ridden away from jail in a gold Mercedes.

Referring directly to Joe and Tom Connor, Russert asked, "Would you apologize to them this morning for what your organization did?" Jimenez responded, "We had no intentions of doing that purposely. We had never intended … to terrorize people. We have had much compassion." Russert tried again. "If you, in fact, are part of an organization that sets off 140 bombs, isn't there a pretty strong possibility that innocent people are going to be hurt and killed? Jimenez replied, "No. I think all precautions were taken, you know, to make sure that all human life was preserved. And, in the end, the measures were not taken that were necessary by the people who owned those establishments."

"There was not an ounce of contrition for what he had done," Connor recalls. "He was given a chance to apologize, but instead he blamed Fraunces Tavern and showed that he remained a cold-blooded killer. These are the sociopaths the Clintons released on America. I was so sickened by what I had seen and heard that I physically broke down. Danielle went to the wedding by herself."

Democrat Senator Dianne Feinstein reacted publicly to Jimenez's comments. "If you participate in a terrorist network, you actually participate in the commission of the planting of the bomb, although your hand may not have actually planted that bomb ... Mr. Jimenez's statements defy any reasonable analysis."

The following night, Joe Connor appeared on *Hardball*, the MSNBC show hosted by Chris Matthews, along with Congressman Fossella and Juan Garcia Passalacqua, a well-known Puerto Rican political analyst. "Immediately before the show began, I decided to shave off the five o'clock shadow and predictably cut just under my nose with the razor. Blood began to pour as the studio manager informed me that it was two minutes to airing. I was no longer nervous about what to say during the interview. Thankfully, the make-up guy was awesome. I don't know what kind of potion he caked under my nose, but literally ten seconds before the cameras rolled, the blood stopped, and my heart resumed."

Matthews directed most of the questions toward Passalacqua, who repeatedly claimed that the terrorists were not responsible for the Fraunces Tavern attack. "For the first time during the TV and radio interviews," Connor recalls, "I was visibly and audibly irate as I went back at the Puerto Rican antagonist who was defending the indefensible by justifying murder as 'retaliation.'"

For Joe Connor and his family, the clemency saga opened and aggravated "an indescribable wound." "My children looked at pictures of my dad and asked who he is. My wife and I told them he is in Heaven watching over us. But, when they asked why he was killed, what answer could we give? And when our kids got older, how could we explain the clemencies?"

# CHAPTER 28
## *Aftermath*

*Americans should be able to go about their daily lives feeling safe and secure, but we can't, because on the eve of the next century, the threat of global terrorism is greater than it has ever been ... The World Trade Center and Oklahoma City bombings are just the latest examples, but more are sure to follow.*

—Tom Connor

JOHN RAWLS, THE GREAT American philosopher, opined that justice "is the first virtue of social institutions." The Clinton clemencies, with their echoes of cynicism and corruption, turned on its head the famous Latin legal dictum "Fiat justitia ruat caelum," meaning "Let justice be done though the heavens fall."

On September 14, 1999, Senator Paul Coverdell's Subcommittee on Western Hemisphere Terrorism of the Senate Foreign Relations Committee held a hearing on the clemency decision. Coverdell invited witnesses from the Justice Department as well as the FBI and Bureau of Prisons. But Cheryl Mills delivered a letter the night before indicating that no one would be made available due to another assertion by the president of executive privilege. An FBI official told CNN on the day of the hearing, "They pulled the plug on us."

Joe Connor was among those testifying, telling the senators, "These people never allowed my dad to see my brother and me play sports in high school or to take pride in seeing us graduate from college or get married. They took from my mom the promise of growing old with her first love." Reflecting on that day, Connor says, "It should not be underestimated how difficult and emotionally draining it is for a regular guy, a private citizen, to publicly oppose the president. To sit before a Senate Committee and openly, nakedly, express the pain, torment, and anger that my family and I have felt. How frustrating it is not to be able to stop this miscarriage of justice."

After giving his testimony, Connor asked an FBI agent he'd become friendly with if he should be scared for his young family because he tried to keep terrorists in prison only to have them now free. "The agent looked at me quizzically and said, 'The terrorists won't come after you. You should be more afraid of the Clintons.' Those words shook me."

Similar testimony was given by family members and law enforcement officials a week later before Dan Burton's House Committee on Government Reform. Vito Fossella introduced Deenie Ettenson. "[She] suffered what is probably the most fearful thing any family can suffer. Her husband left work one morning, attended a lunch, and never returned." In her testimony, Deenie said, "I refuse to be insulted by those who say that these people weren't proven to have caused bodily harm. They were captured before more innocent lives were lost. Acts of random terrorism ceased after these people were imprisoned." She asked, "Why was clemency granted to sixteen violent criminals who show no remorse for their conduct?"

Tom Connor spoke next. He told the Committee members, "Right now, when the United States should be leading the world in fighting terrorism, the president decides to offer clemency to sixteen members of two of the most violent groups ever to wage war against the U.S. from within our borders." Tom added, "By granting this clemency, President Clinton has endangered America ... The next indiscriminate bombing in this country probably will not harm me or anyone else in my family, but it may harm someone you know or love. And whenever that happens, I, unlike the president, will feel the pain of the victims, and he will be partially responsible for it." Tom's prediction that his family would not be involved in the next terrorist attack proved to be wrong.

Assistant FBI Director Neal Gallagher was allowed to appear at Burton's hearing and opined about the released FALN and Los Macheteros members, "I think they're criminals and terrorists and represent a threat to the United States ... To the degree that [clemency] would ever send a message that persons who are not the actual placers of a bomb or those who pull a trigger on a weapon are not as serious a threat as those that would support the terrorist organization, I would agree that this is a significant national security issue."

Also testifying was Carlos Romero-Barceló, by then Puerto Rico's Congressional Representative, who repudiated any notion that "this group of terrorists" speaks for Puerto Ricans. He pointed out that Amnesty International did not consider them prisoners of conscience because the acts they were accused of were violent in nature.

During the hearing, an exchange arose regarding the administration's assertion of executive privilege worthy of inclusion in a Marx Brothers movie. Representative Bob Barr from Georgia was questioning Jon Jennings of the Justice Department as to why even the final recommendation of the Justice Department to the president was not disclosable. (This was prior to the Committee learning that the second Justice Department report did not make any recommendations to the president.) Jennings cited the "chilling effect" such disclosure might have on the future ability of administration officials to offer candid assessments. Barr reminded Jennings that the Committee was not asking for "all of the different conflicting advice and all of the minutes, just the recommendation itself." Jennings asserted, "It's not, I think, for me to answer that in the sense that it is covered by the president's privilege assertion." Barr responded, "It becomes rather circular—the chilling effect is the chilling effect is the chilling effect sort of thing."

Another person appearing at the hearing was Reverend Dr. Thomas Dipko, executive vice president of the Board for Homeland Ministries of the United Church of Christ. (A young Barack Obama was then a member of Chicago's Trinity United Church of Christ, whose activist pastor was the Reverend Jeremiah Wright, Jr.) Throughout the 1990s, the United Church of Christ's national office had been an active lobbyist for release of the FALN prisoners. Dipko was asked by Chairman Burton, "You took great pains to go to prison to talk to these people ... Did you by any chance take any time to go talk to any of the victims?" Dipko answered in the negative.

Barr noted that the Church's literature described the FALN members as "prisoners of war" and that one of them, Alejandrina Torres, was to be honored and bestowed with "great accolades." Barr asked Dipko, "What was it that makes her honored?" Dipko replied, "Because she had convictions about the self-determination of the peoples of Puerto Rico." Barr played the surveillance tape showing Torres and Cortes crafting bombs. After viewing it, Dipko admitted, "If that is an accurate record of what happened and what she was doing, the church would wish to, of course, disassociate from it." Nonetheless, after her release, Alejandrina Torres received an award from the Church.

The Committee would condemn President Clinton and his administration for its handling of the clemencies. "Granting clemency to violent terrorists is a matter of national significance. This is particularly true when the President of the United States not only withholds information from the people, but also uses the immense power of his office to mislead. This, in essence, is what occurred in the aftermath of the offer of clemency to the sixteen terrorists."

Lou Vizi, Don Wofford's right-hand man in the FALN investigations, had recently retired from the FBI. He called Deenie Ettenson soon after the eleven walked out of prison. "He wanted me to know," Deenie recalls, "how important the FALN case was to the FBI agents, how hard they all worked on it, and how much it meant to them to bring the terrorists to justice. Lou told me about agents who had breakdowns, who hurt their marriages, who put their families at risk because the case was so consuming and frustrating and the FALN members so dangerous. And I realized, more than I ever had, what a toll it had taken on them."

Many FBI agents called Rick Hahn, saying, "Can you believe this?" and "Why did we bother to spend years of our lives tracking them down?" Hahn himself observed, "There was so much resource and effort put into the FALN investigations over a decade, only to have it all unraveled because of some cheap political motive."

Reflecting back seventeen years later, Jeremy Margolis said, "It bothers me to this day. Not only was it done for evil reasons, but stupid ones as well. Puerto Ricans don't want independence, so why would the White House think that the clemencies would endear Hillary to the main-stream Puerto Rican population, even after they were misled into thinking that the terrorists were non-violent?"

On October 20, 1999, Eric Holder and Roger Adams each appeared before the Senate Judiciary Committee to explain further the rationale for the clemency grants. Holder began his testimony by extending his "heartfelt sympathy" to the victims and their families. Four different senators asked Holder why he had not reached out to any of them. To the Committee Chair, Orrin Hatch, Holder admitted, "I think we could have done a better job here." Hatch snapped, "You didn't do anything here." Holder declined to answer various questions, on the grounds that he was bound by the White House claim of executive privilege. A frustrated Hatch finally blurted out, "Why can't this White House just be open and tell the truth?"

At the start of the hearing, the Judiciary Committee revealed Attorney General Janet Reno's written conclusion the prior month that the impending release of FALN members is one of several factors "which increase the present threat from these groups." When asked about Reno's evaluation, Holder denied that she was referring to the same terrorists who'd been granted clemency. Yet when Holder was asked to identify who Reno was talking about, he responded, "I don't know that. We might be able to get you some more information on that …" But neither Holder nor the Justice Department ever provided any additional names.

Issues raised regarding the clemency grants were comprehensively addressed in a report issued in December 1999 by the House Committee on Government Reform. This Committee found that the sentences imposed on the FALN and Los Macheteros prisoners were fair. It cited analysis from the U.S. Sentencing Commission that "the federal sentencing guidelines generally would call for sentences as long as or longer than those actually imposed if the defendants had been sentenced under current law." Of note in this regard is that, in the mid-1990s, passage of a special federal sentencing enhancement allowed district courts to significantly increase the penalty for activity that fell into a defined category of terrorism.

The Committee highlighted that those offered clemency were violent offenders who were "very unlikely" candidates for clemency, President Clinton had been "extremely fastidious in granting clemency up until that point," none of the sixteen had personally requested clemency, they had not renounced violence until such repudiation became necessary to get out of prison, and they remained unrepentant, with some being "openly belligerent."

The White House was criticized for appearing "to want clemency more than the terrorists did." The Report noted the frequency with which White House staff referred to the sixteen as "political prisoners," the numerous meetings held by those staffers with clemency advocates, and the "eagerness" with which staff provided assistance. "It is highly inappropriate that members of the President's Working Group on Puerto Rico and the Justice Department would either organize outside support for the clemency or reach out to prod proponents of clemency to do things that made it easier for the President to find in their favor."

Other findings of the Committee included that law enforcement organizations had not been adequately consulted and the decision undermined the U.S. position in the international fight against terrorism. The Committee pointed out that no one in the Justice Department ever inquired whether the FALN and Los Macheteros prisoners might have information relevant to open investigations, such as the Fraunces Tavern bombing, or the apprehension of fugitives.

Deenie Ettenson reached out to the NYPD over the years to learn of any changes in the Fraunces Tavern case. "I was always told that it was an inactive file, so you can understand my shock upon receiving a phone call telling me of the clemencies." Anthony Senft began writing letters to the White House and his Attorney General in 1997 in opposition to clemency. None was responded to. As Joe Connor, who had been writing to the Justice Department for years, testified, "Had we been properly notified, we would have requested the delivery of our opinion on the issue through a personal meeting with Janet Reno, as the pro clemency supporters were granted. God willing, if Ms. Reno had been fully informed, there is a chance, however small, that she would have vehemently objected to the clemency offer ever being made by the President."

Overall, the Committee found that, "victims were unable to get meetings with the White House or Justice Department. Some had tried ... they were simply rebuffed. Activists seeking clemency did get such meetings. Furthermore, while clemency supporters were updated regularly on the progress of the petition, victims were not even informed of the clemency decisions." This disregard of the victims and their families violated the Victims' Rights and Restitution Act of 1990, which provides, "After trial a responsible official shall provide a victim the earliest possible notice of ... release from custody of the offender." It also contradicted Bill Clinton's statement in March 1997 that "When someone is a victim, he or she should be at the center of the criminal justice process, not on the outside looking in."

President Clinton's politicization of the clemency process would be reaffirmed in the last hours of his presidency in January 2001. After keeping the Pardon Office up through the night, Clinton issued 140 pardons as well as dozens of commutations, an explosion of cronyism that came to be known as "Pardongate." It became apparent that many of the pardons had been secured outside official channels through the intervention of individuals with direct access to the President, and that at least some of these persons had been paid handsomely for their efforts. One example was the pardon received by Almon Glenn Braswell, convicted of mail fraud and perjury, who paid $200,000 to Hillary Clinton's brother, Hugh Rodham, to press his case. Rodham returned the payments after they were disclosed.

More evidence of the president's weakness in addressing terrorism were the pardons granted to Linda Evans and Susan Rosenberg, former members of the Weather Underground. Linda Evans had been convicted in a plot to bomb the U.S. Capitol in 1983. Rosenberg, who worked in a drug counseling program run by the Black Panthers and the Young Lords and later was a member of a youth work brigade in Cuba, drove the getaway car during the infamous 1981 Brink's truck robbery and assisted in Assata Shakur's escape from prison.

The clemency process was particularly damaged by the pardon given to Marc Rich, a fugitive billionaire indicted on federal charges of massive tax evasion, wire fraud, racketeering, and trading with the enemy. Rich's actions included reaching a deal with the Ayatollah Khomeini regime during the Iranian hostage crisis to purchase oil for arms and handheld rockets, and trading Soviet and Iranian oil to the apartheid government in South Africa in exchange for Namibian uranium. The uranium was sold back to the Soviet Union in 1991 in connection with Castro's efforts to escalate Cuba's nuclear weapons program. That pardon appeared to have been granted in return for the substantial donations to the Clinton Library Foundation and to Hillary Clinton's senate campaign made by Rich's former wife, Denise Eisenberg Rich, a major Democratic Party fundraiser, with the coup de grace being her presenting Bill Clinton with a new saxophone at a black tie dinner in Manhattan only weeks before. A February 15, 2001 memo from the FBI's Criminal Division "White Collar Branch" noted that then-Deputy Attorney General Eric Holder was the "only person" at the Justice Department notified of the Rich pardon.

In the years after Pardongate, senior Bush and Obama administration officials acknowledged that the furor over the Rich pardon had made them much more cautious about using the clemency power. Kenneth Lee, who served as associate White House counsel during Bush's second term, said Marc Rich was always on the minds of those vetting pardon applicants. "We probably would have recommended a lot more pardons to the president, but we were reluctant to do so if DOJ didn't recommend them." Mark Corallo, formerly the Republican communications director of the House Committee on Oversight and Government Reform, said that in a moment of "bad judgment" Clinton had "damaged the ability of future presidents to pardon."

\*

Fallout from the clemency grant continued through the end of the millennium and into the presidential election year. On February 8, 2000, Joe Connor participated in the introduction by Orrin Hatch of a bill, entitled "The Pardon Attorney Reform and Integrity Act," designed to require the Justice Department's Office of the Pardon Attorney to gather law enforcement and victim information once the President asks it to conduct a clemency investigation, including facts and opinions about the risks posed by any release from prison. Hatch stated, "We found that the decision to release these criminals re-victimized the families of those injured or killed," and wanted to "make sure that crime victims are not ignored by the clemency process or by hearing of a grant of clemency to their perpetrator on television." Connor was struck by the acronym for the bill—PARIA. "A coincidence, although I liked to think it was a subtle shot at our outgoing president."

Arriving at the Dirksen Senate Building before the presentation began, Connor met Deenie in person for the first time. "Through our phone conversations, I had grown to greatly respect her. We embraced and cried a bit." After an introduction by Senator Hatch, Connor spoke. "This bill requires the voices and opinions of victims of crimes for which executive clemency is being considered to be heard ... And it's intended to be a guarantee that the President is making an informed decision fully disclosed to the American people." Connor again warned about the encouragement that would-be terrorists must have received from the FALN clemency grants.

Deenie followed Connor with an emotional plea for an end to partisanship and for support of the bill from both sides of the aisle. "A beautifully moving moment, and then it was over," recalls Connor. "Deenie and I shook a bunch of hands, posed for pictures with Senator Hatch and Representative Fossella, and walked to Union Station to catch the Amtrak. We were used by the Washington legislators, and we used them. Except for Fossella, I never heard from any of them again."

The White House condemned the bill, calling it "partisan" interference with the President's long-standing pardon authority. Within a week, the Justice Department, known for taking strong positions in favor of executive rights, wrote to Orrin Hatch stating its opinion that the bill was an unconstitutional infringement on the President's exclusive pardon power. "Because the President's pardon authority is plenary, even statutes that create what may seem to be only minor incursions on the President's discretion are unconstitutional." Yale University constitutional law professor Akhil Amar, who had advised the drafters of the bill, countered that much of the Department's opinion was "irrelevant and overwrought," and that if its position was correct, the entire Office of Pardon Attorney "as it currently exists" would be unconstitutional. Professor Amar pointed out that the bill affected only how that Office, a congressionally created and funded one, performed its investigation, and the bill's requirements would apply only when the President asked the Pardon Attorney to investigate a particular clemency request.

The bill was passed on to the full Senate. And Vito Fossella introduced the bill to the House Judiciary Committee as well. But although it had support from a number of victim and law enforcement organizations, the bill was destined to die in Congress, a casualty of concerns regarding its constitutionality.

\*

In September 2000, Joe Connor received a phone call from the Republican National Committee asking that he and his brother join Mayor Giuliani at a press conference at City Hall Park marking the one-year anniversary of the release of the FALN prisoners. Tom and Joe were invited to meet with the mayor beforehand. "The mayor's office," Joe recalls, "was impressive for its sports stuff. There were Yankee and Jet memorabilia everywhere, including a baseball bat, a Jets helmet, and many pictures of the mayor with various players. There was also an imposing painting of Fiorello LaGuardia hanging behind his big dark wood desk." In their pre-conference chat, Giuliani appeared pleasantly surprised when Joe told him that a former colleague of the mayor was his dad's first cousin, Andrew J. Maloney, the U.S. Attorney for the Eastern District of New York, best known for prosecuting and convicting John Gotti.

During the conference, Joe and Tom were given the opportunity to "describe what happened in 1975 and why the clemency was so wrong. After we spoke, the floor was opened for questions, and we were immediately verbally attacked by a seemingly insane Latino man." But the most striking moment came at the kickoff of the conference, when Giuliani said, "we're here to point out the one-year anniversary of one of the most disgraceful things that's been done in the last hundred years by a president of the United States."

# CHAPTER 29
## *Prelude to 9/11*

*When you're not being held sufficiently accountable, what's the fear? To my mind, actions like the FALN clemencies paved the way for 9/11.*

—Jean Schlag Nebbia

MUCH HAS BEEN WRITTEN ABOUT President Clinton's tough talk but eventual weakness, reactive strategy, and lack of focus in fighting terrorism, even though numerous serious attacks against the U.S. occurred during his two terms. One example is the 1993 World Trade Center bombing, about which the 911 Commission Report concluded that Clinton and his principal advisers didn't adequately "press the question of whether the [law enforcement] procedures that put the Blind Sheikh and Ramzi Yousef behind bars would really protect Americans against the new virus of [terrorism]." After that attack, Clinton declined to visit New York City to view the damage, stating, "I would discourage the American people from overreacting to this."

Clinton named James Woolsey as his first CIA director but never met privately with him after their initial interview. When a stolen Cessna 150 plane crashed on the South Lawn of the White House in September 1994, the joke among administration officials was, "That must be Woolsey, still trying to get an appointment."

In October 2000, al Qaeda bombed the Navy guided-missile destroyer *USS Cole* while refueling in Yemen's Aden harbor, killing seventeen U.S. sailors. Osama bin Laden took credit for the attack, even writing a poem about it that he read aloud during the January 2001 wedding of his son, Hamza. At the memorial service for the *Cole* victims, Clinton promised, "To those who attacked them we say: You will not find a safe harbor. We will find you and justice will prevail." Osama bin Laden prepared for U.S. retaliation, evacuating Kandahar and escaping into the desert, but Clinton rejected military action, claiming the evidence against bin Laden was not strong enough. And his State Department warned that attacking bin Laden would "inflame the Islamic world." Years later, Bill Clinton told the 9/11 Commission he felt that before he could launch strikes on al-Qaeda, he needed the CIA and the FBI to "be willing to stand up in public and say, we believe that bin Laden did this."

Ali Soufan, former FBI agent who was integrally involved in the *USS Cole* investigation, states in his book, *The Black Banners*, of being told by an al-Qaeda member who had served as bin Laden's driver and confidant, "You [the United States] brought 9/11 on yourselves; you didn't respond to the *Cole,* so bin Laden had to hit harder." Many expert commentators have concluded that the success of the brazen action against the USS *Cole* encouraged al-Qaeda to prepare for an attack on the U.S. itself.

Florida Senator Marco Rubio echoed a common sentiment. "I believe that if Osama bin Laden had been killed, al Qaeda as an organization would not have grown to the point where it could have conducted 9/11." In *Dereliction of Duty,* Robert "Buzz" Patterson, a presidential aide and carrier of the "nuclear football," describes President Clinton's unavailability and indecisiveness in the fall of 1998 after being advised that the military had located bin Laden in Afghanistan and had "a two-hour window to strike." It was a year in which Clinton was enmeshed in the Monica Lewinsky scandal and an impeachment battle. By then, bin Laden had been tied to many murderous attacks on Americans, including the bombings in November 1995 of a U.S. Army training facility in Riyadh, in June 1996 of the Khobar Towers military barracks in Dhahran, Saudi Arabia, and in August 1998 of two U.S. African embassies.

Most telling are the comments that Bill Clinton made only ten hours before the first plane hit the World Trade Center on 9/11. During a speech to a group of businessmen in Melbourne, Australia, he was asked about international terrorism. With full knowledge that the entire session was being recorded, Clinton spoke about bin

Laden, bragging that he "nearly got him once." "I could have killed him, but I would have had to destroy a little town in Afghanistan called Kandahar, and that would have meant killing 300 innocent women and children, and then I would have been no better than him. And so, I didn't do it."

A defining aspect of terrorism is the inevitable randomness of its violence. Secular and religious notions of morality uniformly condemn harming blameless persons. One example is the Koran, which states that anyone who kills an innocent person shall be treated "as if he had murdered all of mankind." This concept logically applies to our government's responses to terrorists as well.

Nonetheless, Clinton's words ring hollow. Kandahar is a large city. The president presumably was referring to "Tarnak Farms," the walled compound where bin Laden and his wives, bodyguards, and command team lived along with their families. The adult residents were committed to the al-Qaeda cause, which targets the innocent. (Al-Qaeda believes that any innocent Muslims will be rewarded in heaven for their sacrifice. "Innocent non-Muslim" is an oxymoron, and such a person is not even worth consideration.) As told by Navy Seal Mark Owen in his book, *No Easy Day*, recounting the raid in May 2011 that killed Osama bin Laden:

> The door cracked open slowly, and I could hear a woman's voice calling out. That didn't mean we were safe. If she was coming out with a suicide vest

on, we were dead. This was bin Laden's compound. These were his facilitators.

Every person in Tarnak Farms, excluding children, may be said to have constituted a threat to all Americans. To use a term coined by the noted philosopher Jan Narveson, the "moral arithmetic" argued strongly in favor of Clinton taking the recommended action against bin Laden, which would not have tainted America's ethical standing.

Clinton's 1999 clemency grants were made in the context of a snowballing level of domestic and transnational terrorism through his years in office, highlighting his inability to perceive the growing threat. And they disregarded a fundamental rule in addressing terrorism to never negotiate deals with terrorists. Many others had issued a similar warning during the 1999 Congressional investigation—that the release of unrepentant terrorists would only embolden terrorists to strike us again.

\*

On the morning of 9/11, Joe Connor commuted through the PATH station at the World Trade Center. Like thousands of others, he witnessed the towers explode and burn, in his case from his office on the 36th floor of 60 Wall Street. He quickly called his mother to tell her he was okay. "My mom, as anyone would imagine, has been extraordinarily sensitive to the ramifications of terrorist acts. After the first World Trade Center attack in 1993, she was inconsolable, afraid for her sons and nephew who worked near there."

Joe also reached his wife and brother. "Tom had seen people jumping from the floors above the impact. He was shaken." Joe found in his rolodex the number of his cousin Steve Schlag, who was Frank Connor's godson. "Steve's office phone just kept ringing. I left a message on his cell phone for him to call me." Steve would have been at work early, as his firm, Cantor Fitzgerald, was a key player in the Government securities marketplace, in which trading begins by 7 a.m. In New York, by the time the attacks began, more than $500 billion worth of trading had occurred.

Joe and Tom found each other amid a frenzied crowd at a pre-arranged spot, a Wendy's on Water Street. After withdrawing as much cash as they could from an ATM and observing that the wind was blowing south, which would take any biological or chemical releases with it, they walked uptown. They camped out for a while in the Angelica Theatre on Houston Street, which had opened its lobby for people to take refuge in, and then headed west. "When we reached the West Side Highway, we found thousands of refugees like ourselves walking north as an endless stream of fire trucks, police cars and trucks, ambulances, and emergency vehicles poured south toward a massive black cloud obscuring lower Manhattan. The brave first responders headed toward the carnage while we moved away from it."

Joe and Tom were able to board a boat at Chelsea Piers, where aid workers were passing out cold water and offering shelter from the sun to the frightened masses. It carried them to Weehawken, across the Hudson River. There, buses awaited to transport them to the Giants Stadium parking lot. "Some passengers cried, some to our horror were laughing and joking, but most were very quiet, perhaps in shock, or deep in thought or prayer about their own lives or the tens of thousands of lives that we believed were lost."

Later that night, as President Bush addressed the nation, Joe drove Steve's car from the Radburn train station in Fair Lawn, where Frank Connor's car was parked the day he was murdered, to the Schlag house in Franklin Lakes. He and Tom had earlier joined family and friends in waiting for word on Steve, a vigil disconcertingly similar to the one for their father decades earlier. "While his wife, Tomoko, his parents, friends, and sisters held out hope, Tom and I kept a positive face although we knew optimism was futile."

Two weeks later, hundreds of Steve's family and friends gathered for a memorial service. All except Grandma Connor. "My cherished grandmother had broken her hip and was confined to a nursing home nearby," recalls Joe. "We told her about the Trade Center attacks but not about Steve's death. We knew she'd be with her son and Steve all too soon."

Joe, the second-to-last speaker, listened to the many eulogizers before him and was struck by how well they captured Steve's qualities. As Connor began, he was moved by the faces of Steve's children staring up at him. "The two boys, Dakota and Garrett, were the same age as Tom and me on our September 11. But the face etched in my mind was little Sierra's, a beautiful six-year-old girl."

A month after 9/11, Margaret Connor, the family matriarch, died. Margaret, who had told Mary after Frank's murder that she didn't want to live anymore, survived to the age of ninety-seven. All the while, she kept her faith in God and remained a churchgoer, chuckling, "You've got to pay the Man." Eulogizers told of how Grandma Connor, right after losing her only child, would pointedly advise Mary about her two sons, "We don't want them to grow up with hate in their hearts." Tom Connor said of his grandma, "She was the best person I have ever known."

\*

Destroying capitalism and the free markets vital to our society and way of life has been a common terrorist objective for many years. Prior to the Fraunces Tavern bombing, the worst assault in U.S. financial history occurred on September 16, 1920, when a horse-drawn buggy loaded with 100 pounds of dynamite and 500 pounds of cast-iron slugs exploded on Wall Street, across from the headquarters of the J.P. Morgan Bank, killing 38 people and injuring hundreds more. One time when Frank brought his sons into the City for the employee Christmas Party, he pointed out the remnants of the damage from the 1920 bombing still visible on the 23 Wall Street building. Those pocks in the stone façade left an indelible mark on both the building and the boys, with Joe remembering "feeling especially bad for the horses."

While there is no comparison in terms of scope or impact between the Fraunces Tavern bombing and 9/11, similarities exist, including the merchandizing in discontent that is at the core of terrorist recruitment. Another parallel is the foreign element, as the FALN was backed by Cuba and co-founded by a Cuban intelligence officer, Filiberto Ojeda Ríos. Moreover, in both attacks, "Wall Street" was a target. Almost a third of the firms located in buildings affected by the World Trade Center collapse were in the financial services business, and close to three-quarters of those killed worked in that industry. A part of the complete 9/11 narrative is that it presented the financial industry with the greatest operational crisis in its history.

*

In September 2014, the scope of Bergen County's annual 9/11 Memorial ceremony in Leonia, New Jersey, during which the name of each of the country's 154 residents who died on that day is read, was expanded to honor Frank Connor. In an interview before the service, Mary Connor Tully said of Frank's godson, Steve Schlag,

"It breaks my heart to hear his name read." When Mary spoke, she addressed her late husband. "Frank, it's thirty-nine years since we lost you, but you're forever a thirty-three-year-old dad to Tom and Joe." After the ceremony, Mary was asked if she'd achieved some closure. "That is the biggest joke I ever heard," Mary responded. "There is no closure when somebody is killed at that age. You go on with life, because you don't have much choice."

*Memorial plaque for Frank Connor and Steven Schlag*

# CHAPTER 30
## *Return to Fraunces Tavern*

*It is not true that one man's terrorist is another man's revolutionary. The right to throw off the bondage of colonialism is a right to engage the presiding government that subjugates. It does not provide any moral justification for attacking innocent civilians. That's a glossy sheen to hide the truth of terrorism.*

—Rick Hahn

DICK MORRIS SERVED AS Bill Clinton's political advisor for twenty years and was campaign manager for Clinton's 1996 re-election before being forced to resign amid personal scandal. In 2005, Morris published *Rewriting History*, a stinging rebuttal to Hillary Clinton's biography, *Living History*. In his book, Morris refers to and quotes Joe Connor's reaction to the Clinton clemencies. After Connor read Morris' book, he called Morris to introduce himself. "I figured if he put me in his book, he should at least know who I am."

That initiated a regular correspondence between Connor and both Dick Morris and his wife, Eileen McGann. In early 2007, Morris asked Connor if he would be willing to appear in an upcoming documentary about Hillary Clinton, entitled *Hillary: The Movie*, to discuss his views on the FALN clemencies. The film was being produced by Citizens United, a conservative non-profit advocacy group led by David Bossie. Bossie, a Republican activist, had worked for Dan Burton when Burton was chairman of the House Committee on Government Reform and Oversight, as chief investigator of the Clinton campaign finance abuses.

The documentary, comprised largely of interviews with a who's-who cast of conservative figures such as Newt Gingrich, Larry Kudlow, Mark Levin, Robert Novak, and Ann Coulter, reviewed various Hillary Clinton scandals. On its Web site, Citizens United promoted the film as featuring a "cast to end all casts," and promised, "*Hillary: The Movie*' is the first and last word in what the Clintons want America to forget!"

Connor agreed to participate. "I went into this for a simple reason. To have the truth told about the Clintons." In June 2007, Connor met with the Citizens United team led by Alan Peterson, the film's director, and Rick Hahn, retired from the FBI, to film the clemency segment of the movie at Fraunces Tavern. The lead-in to that segment of the film is a silent home video of Frank Connor and his young family together with a voiceover by Joe telling of his idyllic childhood and the qualities of his dad. Later in the piece, Rick accompanies Joe to Fraunces Tavern. "It was profoundly emotional," Connor remembers, "having Rick give me a tour of Fraunces Tavern and describe where my poor dad was sitting, how the terrorist walked in the bomb while looking in the faces of those he would murder, and the impact and devastation. It took me back to the nine-year-old eagerly anticipating a birthday celebration. I felt my dad's presence again, as I do whenever I need him."

After filming at Fraunces Tavern, the crew moved to the Fair Lawn park where Connor played and rode bikes with his father. "Danielle, Frank, and Kathleen came to the park to watch. It was painful but important to share this moment with my family." During the shooting, Connor gazed at the spot where he and his brother had been playing on the day of his father's murder. "My last innocent memory was there."

None of those who participated in the making of *Hillary: The Movie* could have anticipated the significance it would take on. Citizens United sought to promote the film before and during the presidential primary season and to distribute it through video-on-demand on cable TV beginning the night before the Democratic primaries in January 2008, in which Hillary Clinton and Barack Obama were the leading candidates.

But the organization was concerned about the possible constraining effect of the McCain-Feingold law (formally known as the "Bipartisan Campaign Reform Act," or BCRA). Passed in 2002, the statute was designed to reform the way money is raised and spent on campaigns by banning unrestricted, or "soft money" donations, to political parties made directly by wealthy donors. It did so through imposing a prohibition on corporations and unions from using their general treasury funds to make independent expenditures for speech expressly advocating the election or defeat of a candidate. The BCRA also limited the advertising that unions, corporations, and non-profit organizations could engage in up to sixty days prior to an election. The BCRA provided an exemption for such "electioneering communications" if done by nonprofit corporations, but their requirement to publicly disclose donors remained.

In December 2007, in connection with its planned release of *Hillary: The Movie,* Citizens United filed a complaint in the District Court for the District of Columbia challenging the constitutionality of BCRA provisions restricting corporate sponsored electioneering communications, and asking the court to enjoin the FEC from enforcing its funding, disclosure, and disclaimer regulations against the film. (It was not possible first to go directly to the FEC for a ruling, as at the time the Commission only had two members, insufficient for the plurality needed for an advisory opinion.) A favorable declaratory judgment would have allowed Citizens United to freely show its movie as well as the promotional ads for it. But a special three-judge panel rejected the group's argument that the documentary was akin to news or information programs such as PBS' "Nova" or CBS'

"60 Minutes." Rather, the court found the film effectively to constitute a 90-minute campaign ad and there was "no reasonable interpretation [of the movie] other than as an appeal to vote against Senator Clinton," making it an "electioneering communication."

The BCRA did not cover all forms of media distribution, and despite the FEC and court rulings, Citizens United was able to advertise on the Web, sell the movie on DVD, and show it in theaters. The film's theater premier was in Washington on January 14, 2008. "I squirmed in my seat," Joe Connor recalls, "anticipating the last segment of the film, and felt sick when the special effect of the bomb exploding shook the theater."

*Hillary: The Movie* opened in New York on January 24, 2008, the 33rd anniversary of Frank Connor's murder. The extended Connor family attended along with many friends. "The anticipation of our segment and the depiction of the Fraunces Tavern bombing was so difficult for our family to watch," Connor recalls. "I felt especially sad for Don and Pat Schlag," Connor remembers, "as they watched the part of the movie telling how Clinton could have taken out bin Laden and saved their son's life." Jean Schlag-Nebbia, seated near Connor, was focused on him rather than the events on the screen. As she tearfully recalled years later, "I so felt for Joe at that moment. What I saw was a little nine-year-old boy—vulnerable, scared, and not fully understanding what had happened to his dad."

Citizens United appealed the District Court's ruling to the Supreme Court. The following January, in an opinion written by Justice Anthony Kennedy, the Supreme Court ruled five-four in *Citizens United v. FEC* that the First Amendment allows both corporations and unions unlimited expenditure through nonprofit organizations to pay for the broadcast of issue advocacy ads and electioneering communications, and there should not be restriction of when they can be shown. "The First Amendment does not," the Court majority said, "permit laws that force speakers to retain a campaign finance attorney, conduct demographic marketing research, or seek declaratory rulings before discussing the most salient political issues of our day."

The Supreme Court's ruling was a landmark decision that transformed the campaign finance landscape by overturning certain spending limits in the BCRA and paving the way for essentially unlimited contributions by corporations and unions to political action committees. One sentence in the lengthy decision best summed up the Court's logic. "Because speech is an essential mechanism of democracy—it is the means to hold officials accountable to the people—political speech must prevail against laws that would suppress it by design or inadvertence."

# CHAPTER 31
## *Clemencies Redux*

*I realized that, in many ways, I am angrier at the
Clintons, Eric Holder, and all those craven politicians
for exploiting our father and our family than I am at the
terrorists themselves, who on some level had a conviction,
a goal larger than themselves, and never claimed to have
our best interests at heart.*

—Joe Connor

THE CLINTON CLEMENCIES WOULD be the subject of
Congressional scrutiny one more time—during the
January 2009 confirmation hearings for Eric Holder to
become the country's Attorney General. Press reports, bol-
stered by new interviews and an examination of previously
undisclosed Justice Department documents, reminded
the public of Holder's prominent role in the 1999 grants
of clemency. Pardon Attorney Roger Adams recounted
telling Holder of his "strong opposition to any clemency"
in several internal memos and meetings, noting, "But

each time Holder wasn't satisfied." A spokesman for the Obama administration, in defense of Holder, countered that "President Clinton made the ultimate decision to commute these sentences."

Before the Senate Judiciary Committee confirmation hearing, Joe sat for an interview with Brian Darling of *Red State*, a conservative blog. "United States Attorneys General can neither be stooges to their president, releasing terrorists against their better judgment, nor have such poor judgment and values as to unleash dedicated terrorists with no concern for the American people. His record shows that Holder clearly does not have the judgment, character, or values to be Attorney General." Connor described Holder's actions as akin to playing "Russian roulette with the American people," a charge he would revisit in September 2014 when Connor joined the opposition to Fred DuVal's unsuccessful campaign for Governor of Arizona. DuVal had been co-chair of the White House Interagency Group on Puerto Rico during the clemency period.

The ensuing confirmation hearing covered a wide range of issues, including waterboarding as torture, the treatment of prisoners in Guantánamo, second amendment rights, and racial profiling. But the Clinton pardons received much attention. Patrick Leahy, Chair of the Committee, began the hearing by noting his strong disagreement with the Rich pardon. He asked Holder, "How do you respond to those that say it shows you do not have the character to be an independent attorney general?"

Holder admitted that "my actions in the Rich matter was a place where I made mistakes ... I should have not spoken to the White House and expressed an opinion without knowing all of the facts with regard to that matter."

Pennsylvania senator Arlen Specter pressed further. "When you take a look at the facts, it's a little hard for me to see how you came to the conclusion you did, even conceding that none of us is perfect." Specter noted the evidence that Holder had told Jack Quinn, former White House counsel, that Quinn could go directly to the White House with the pardon application, which cut the Justice Department out of the normal process. Holder denied giving this advice to Quinn.

Specter continued. "The indicators are that you were very heavily involved, and yet you testified you were only casually involved." He asked, "Now, if this were some underling or somebody who wasn't too bright, or wasn't too experienced, you'd slough it off as a mistake. But given your experience and your background and your competency ... how do you explain it beyond simply, 'It's a mistake'?" Holder responded, "I knew it was a substantial tax fraud case. I knew that he was a fugitive. I did not know a lot of the underlying facts that you have described." Holder admitted that, given the opportunity to handle the Marc Rich pardon again, he would act differently. "I should have made sure that everybody, all the prosecutors in that case, were informed of what was going on. I made assumptions that turned out not to be true."

Back in 1995, when Holder was U.S. Attorney for the District of Columbia, his office investigated Rich and his questionable business interests. And, in the same year, Holder's office successfully sued Clarendon Ltd, a Swiss company, for fraudulently obtaining government contracts by concealing its ties to Rich, whose status as a fugitive made him legally ineligible to receive such deals. By January 2001, Holder knew Rich and his background well and should have applied that awareness to his consideration of Rich's pardon.

Alabama Senator Jeff Sessions (later U.S. Attorney General under President Trump) brought up the FALN clemencies, describing them as "inexplicable." Sessions added, "I believe that it reversed the recommendation of Margaret Love, a very fine pardon attorney who I believe you removed, and imposed and allowed this to go forward in a way that I think is unjustifiable." Texas Senator Cornyn followed up by asking Holder if he recommended clemency for the FALN terrorists to President Clinton. After Holder answered affirmatively, Cornyn said, "Was that a mistake?" Holder replied, "No, I don't think it was a mistake." Under further questioning, Holder admitted that, post-9/11, he would have viewed the FALN clemency grants differently.

At the request of Iowa Senator Chuck Grassley, the now well-known FBI surveillance video showing Edwin Cortes and Alejandrina Torres in a Chicago safe house apartment building a bomb was played. Grassley asked Holder, "At the time you directed the pardon attorney to draft a neutral options memo, had you ever seen this video before?" Holder answered negatively. Grassley followed with, "Do you believe that it is fair to characterize Cortes and Torres as 'non-violent,' and, therefore, deserving a clemency?" Holder responded that none of those granted clemency "had themselves been directly linked to a murder or directly linked to a crime that involved an injury to somebody." Grassley countered that the only reason Cortes and Torres didn't hurt anyone is because the FBI caught them first.

Holder's echo of the old canard that none of the FALN members had been convicted of a specific violent crime was a semantic and meaningless defense. Holder well knew there were no passive FALN members. Freddie Méndez had testified that, "everybody in the organization has to know how to make bombs." Presumably, Holder, a former judge and a U.S. Attorney, understood that, under the law, direct involvement in violent acts is not the sole prerequisite for being liable for their consequences. The FALN members operated within a clandestine structure that made it virtually impossible to identify individual people committing specific crimes. But it's clear each member understood and participated in achieving the group's goals, which were to use fear and violence to change American government policy. As Jeremy Margolis said, "Our prisons are filled with thousands of people convicted of drug smuggling conspiracy without a shred of evidence they actually sold or delivered anything."

Joe Connor, testifying on the second day of the hearing, commented with regard to Holder's role in the FALN clemencies, "He claimed he didn't know about a lot of the issues that were raised, from the surveillance tape to their threat of Judge McMillen at their sentencing, and that alone was disturbing ... How then could he know enough about the case to feel comfortable in releasing them? What does that say about his judgment?" Connor urged the Senate to "review Mr. Holder's record, put aside any politics, put themselves in the shoes of ordinary Americans who have given them their trust and their vote, and decide if this man ... who released unrepentant terrorists should be charged with protecting our fellow citizens."

Rick Hahn also testified, concluding by saying, "The granting of clemency in these [FALN and Los Macheteros] cases stands out as one of the greatest compromises of the American justice system in history. It is my view that anyone in the government who proactively worked to bring about the clemencies betrayed their office, the victims and the American people."

In spite of the various concerns, Eric Holder was quickly confirmed as Attorney General, a position crucial in the fight against ever-growing terrorism.

# CHAPTER 32
## *Parole Hearing*

*He talked, and he talked, and he talked, and every word
out of his mouth was a blatant lie. It was so difficult to sit
there and not scream.*

—Deenie Berger Ettenson

IN APRIL 2009, HAYDÉE TORRES, the murderer of
Charles Steinberg, was paroled. That was followed in
July of the next year by the freeing of her husband, former FALN leader Carlos Alberto Torres. Both had been
incarcerated for three decades. Mere hours after being
released, Carlos, wearing a black guayabera shirt and a
scarf adorned with the word "patriota," waded through a
joyous homecoming in Humboldt Park. During the rally
in his honor awash with Puerto Rican flags, he danced
to the thumping of plastic buckets and the chants of
hundreds of supporters.

By the time of his release, Carlos was divorced from
Haydée. He first moved to San Sebastián, Puerto Rico,

where he started a pottery workshop. In 2016, he returned to Chicago to open a bakery on Division Street. With their releases, the sole remaining FALN member imprisoned was Oscar López Rivera. In 2013, he published an autobiography, *Oscar López Rivera: Between Torture and Resistance*. In it, López Rivera whitewashes his terrorist activities, compares himself to Christ, and paints himself as a victim. In the book's limited references to the FALN, he grouses about the grand jury "fishing expeditions" against the group and the jailing of his brother José for refusing to cooperate with a grand jury investigation. López Rivera describes his decision to join the FALN as being in the "long tradition of clandestine political action dating back two thousand years from the early days of Christianity ..." Much of López Rivera's discourse complains about his "torture of imprisonment" in the "gulag" of the U.S. prison system.

In assessing just treatment for López Rivera, one may look to the concept of "restorative justice," which emphasizes healing the victims, in contrast with a more traditional focus on punishing the criminal. It fosters dialogue between victim and offender, which can lead to greater victim satisfaction and offender accountability. Victims take an active role, and offenders are encouraged to take responsibility for their actions.

As observed by Howard Zehr, the father of restorative justice, "Crime is defined as against the state, so the state takes the place of the victims. Yet victims often have a number of specific needs from the justice process." Forgiveness is not a primary goal, but often an outcome.

The specter of forgiveness lurked in January 2011 when a two-hour parole hearing for Oscar López Rivera was held in the Federal Correctional Institution in Terre Haute, Indiana, a high-security prison whose notable alumni included Timothy McVeigh, executed there in June 2001. (Under the Sentencing Reform Act of 1984, Congress eliminated parole for federal defendants convicted of crimes, but only for ones committed after November 1, 1987.) Ahead of the hearing, more than 16,000 letters supporting his release were sent to the Parole Commission, thanks to intensive lobbying by organizations such as the National Boricua Human Rights Network and the Comité Pro Derechos Humanos. The four members of Congress of Puerto Rican descent, including Pedro Pierluisi, Puerto Rico's non-voting delegate, sent a letter to the Parole Commission, stating, "Notably, of all the Puerto Ricans convicted for politically motivated activities in the early 1980s, Mr. López Rivera is the only one who remains in prison."

The victims and their families, who were not notified of the hearing by the government but, rather, by Rick Hahn, took action. Joe and Tom Connor, Deenie Ettenson and her husband, Alan, Bill Newhall (who still moved with a limp when he tired), and Don Wofford (Rick Hahn was unavailable) flew to Indianapolis the day before the hearing and met in a Terre Haute motel.

At night, they gathered in the lobby bar to compare the victims' impact statements that Joe, Tom, Deenie, and Bill would present. Newhall remembers, "We were happy to finally have the opportunity to present our case the way we should have been allowed to give it in 1999 before the clemencies were granted."

The next morning, the group enjoyed breakfast in an IHOP. "That was such a normal, ho-hum setting," Joe recalls, "so different from the foreboding place we entered a half hour later." Deenie found being in the penitentiary an uncomfortable experience. "They unlock one door and you go into a holding spot," recalls Deenie. "The door locks behind you. Then you wait for another door to open. This happened several times."

They met first with the warden, Charles Lockett, who told them that in his many years in the job, this was the first time victims appeared at a parole hearing. "Everyone else just mails in their statements." Bill Newhall was struck by the warden's reference to them as "victims." "I never wanted what happened at Fraunces Tavern to define me as 'Bill Newhall, bombing victim,'" says Newhall. "Most of my friends, including good ones, don't even know that I was a bombing casualty." Joe reacted, "My father was a victim. He had no chance to fight back. I do."

Lockett escorted them to their seats in the hearing room. A shackled López Rivera was then walked in, wearing owl-round glasses and sporting a bushy white mustache, accompanied by his attorney, Jan Susler. Because attorney status is not recognized at federal parole hearings, Susler's technical capacity at the meeting was as an observer. The two groups sat near each other , across an IKEA table. At one point, facing Joe Connor, Susler exclaimed, "That guy, he just testified against Eric Holder. He's only here for political reasons." Susler argued that the group should be sent out of the room or, at a minimum, not take part in the hearing. "I feel their loss. I regret their loss," Susler said. "They've lived something that's terrible, but they have nothing to offer in the case we are here to talk about today." Her objections were overruled.

Susler spoke first, lauding López Rivera as being a model prisoner and person. She noted his work over his years of incarceration as an artist, teacher, and mentor. Then came López Rivera's turn. As Deenie Ettenson recounts, "He would admit to nothing except that he was a community organizer." To Don Wofford, who had "chased after the guy for years," López Rivera appeared as a "charismatic fanatical maniac and his own worst enemy." Joe Connor described López Rivera's words as "round after round of circular insanity." At one point, a frustrated Tom Connor blurted out to the hearing examiner, "Don't listen to the lies of this pathetic old man."

"He was afforded multiple opportunities to reconcile with the victims and their families," Joe Connor recalls. "Instead, even with his very freedom at stake, he provided nothing more than rambling obfuscations and political diatribes, blaming everyone but himself and offering childish rationalizations for his admitted career in the

FALN and his prison escape attempts. I think we were all hoping for something good in him to come out that we could cling to. Something that would bring us some closure and compel us to forgive. To consent to his release. But there was nothing there."

One by one, Joe, Tom, Deenie, and Bill spoke. Don Wofford remembers "you could have heard a pin drop as they read their accounts." Deenie ended her statement with:

> The argument might be made that López Rivera may not have been present when these random acts of violence occurred. The same argument could be made about Hitler not being present at the concentration camps or that bin Laden wasn't on the plane that hit the World Trade Center. They, like López Rivera, were each a leader of an organization that plotted and extolled the use of terror that destroyed lives. Oscar López Rivera ... is evil and should remain incarcerated.

As his wife spoke, Alan Ettenson observed the beefy guards who lined the room. "Their mouths opened in astonishment as they listened to the story of the FALN and his leadership role in that organization. And his attempts at escape from Leavenworth. It was clear they had no idea about López Rivera's background."

"As I spoke," recalls Bill Newhall, "López sat across from me, yet could not express a shred of regret or empathy for the suffering that I and so many others had gone through. He insisted on characterizing himself as a freedom fighter, but the ideas of his group were bankrupt and they couldn't persuade but a small minority of Puerto Ricans of the rightfulness of their cause. I was prepared to let go my feeling that he deserved continued incarceration, but he didn't allow for that."

López Rivera's lack of contrition or recognition of the seriousness of his crimes may be contrasted with Judith Clark, the former Weather Underground radical who was convicted for her role in the 1981 Brink's robbery. Clark, thirty-one at the time, was the getaway driver and helped plan the heist. Her 75-year-to-life sentence was reduced at year-end 2016 by Governor Andrew Cuomo, although the widow of Nyack Police Sergeant O'Grady publicly complained that Cuomo had not reached out to her, even after her requests to speak with him. Cuomo's action allowed Clark to be eligible for parole. That, however, was denied by the New York State Parole Board in April 2017, which unanimously found her release to be "incompatible with the welfare of society," as she remains "a symbol of violent and terroristic crime." (She is next eligible for parole in 2019.)

Clark had reflected deeply on her criminal activity. "I had spent my entire young adult life wrapped in increasingly isolated, self-contained radical organizations and activities ... While my life is fueled by a hope-filled commitment to repair, I live each day with sorrow, shame and regret for my role in the deaths of Peter Paige,

Edward O'Grady and Waverly Brown … I look at the world differently now. Instead of abstract slogans, I see and am moved by flesh-and-blood people." Joe Connor was struck by Clark's remorse. "It's what I craved to hear from López Rivera but did not get at his parole hearing."

López Rivera's hearing examiner, Mark Tanner, recommended that parole be denied and that López Rivera serve the remainder of his sentence, to be released in June 2023. His recommendation was upheld by the United States Parole Commission, which informed López Rivera that he was "a more serious risk than indicated by the guidelines in that you were one of the recognized leaders of the FALN … The Commission's Chairman noted, "We have to look at whether release would depreciate the seriousness of the offenses or promote disrespect for the law, whether release would jeopardize public safety, and the specific characteristics of the offender." Months later, the Parole Commission reviewed López Rivera's request for reconsideration and denied it.

In his book, López Rivera characterized the parole hearing as an "inquisition," and claimed that Tanner never paid attention to anything he or Susler said. After the hearing, López Rivera wrote to his daughter Clarissa telling her, "I can go to bed every night with a clean conscience because there is no blood on my hands."

# CHAPTER 33
## The Press for Extradition

*The House of Representatives calls for the immediate extradition or rendering to the United States of convicted felon William Morales and all other fugitives from justice who are receiving safe harbor in Cuba in order to escape prosecution or confinement for criminal offenses committed in the United States.*

— House of Representatives Resolution introduced by Peter King (March 2015)

IN 1959, DURING THE initial months after Fidel Castro's revolution succeeded in ousting dictator Fulgencio Batista, the Western press serenaded Castro as Cuba's liberator. Relations with the U.S. appeared promising. New Prime Minister Castro visited the U.S. on a goodwill tour, speaking to large, adulating crowds throughout the Northeast, giving numerous press interviews, and meeting with Vice President Richard Nixon and senior Eisenhower Administration officials as well as various members of Congress.

But all too soon, the honeymoon ended. Castro reneged on his promise to return Cuba to a constitutional democracy and hold an early election, while eliminating rivals and dissenters. The most notorious incident was "The San Juan Hill Massacre," which came eleven days after the triumph of the Revolution. Fidel's brother, Raúl, ordered the execution without trial of seventy-one Batista supporters and members of the armed forces and police. They were lined up in pairs in front of ditches and shot by firing squad. The mass graves were then filled in by bulldozers.

In the summer of 1960, Castro declared America "the enemy of the world," and Cuba nationalized major American-owned businesses without compensation. Among them were refineries needed for the oil that the Soviet Union had agreed to sell Cuba cheaply. Washington responded by prohibiting exports to Cuba except for food and medicine, the first step toward an economic embargo that has existed in varying forms ever since. In January 1961, during his last month in office, President Eisenhower severed diplomatic ties with Cuba. Months later, after the ill-fated Bay of Pigs invasion, Castro declared that the Cuban revolution was socialist, and that he was a Marxist-Leninist. (Traditional Marxism involves the public ownership and control of the means of production. Modern American socialism has morphed into something different, focusing on the redistribution of wealth and income.)

In July 1975, the Internal Security Subcommittee of the Senate Judiciary Committee concluded that "international communism has been using Puerto Rico as a bridgehead to infiltrate, disrupt, and ultimately bring about revolution in the United States. The leading role played by Cuba in these efforts is self-proclaimed and well publicized, because Cuba has been the fountainhead of revolution in Puerto Rico since Castro took over in 1959." During the same month, negotiations led by Secretary of State Henry Kissinger were being held between the U.S. and Cuba on normalizing relations and potentially dismantling the embargo. One of the conditions laid out by the State Department was "restraint in promoting Puerto Rican independence." Those talks broke down after Fidel Castro, while speaking at the United Nations the following month, forcefully called for Puerto Rican independence. Cuba then hosted the "World Peace Council International Conference of Solidarity with the Independence of Puerto Rico," knowing full well this would anger the U.S. Kissinger responded, "A policy of conciliation will not survive Cuban meddling in Puerto Rico or Cuban armed intervention in the affairs of other nations struggling to decide their own fate."

In the 1980s, a two-year FBI investigation of the Wells Fargo robbery in West Hartford by eighteen Los Macheteros members detailed Cuba's backing of the group, including providing forged passports and financing. The *Hartford Courant* reported in a November 1999 story that, "Several FBI and Justice Department officials who were involved in the Wells Fargo case said they have never understood why the extensive evidence of Cuban support for radical Puerto Rican nationalism received only scant attention among policy makers and in the press." The U.S. strengthened its Cuban embargo rules in 1992. In 1996, after Cuba shot down two airplanes operated by Miami-based Cuban exiles, Congress passed the Helms-Burton Act, which codified the embargo into law and extended it to foreign countries trading with Cuba. Under the George W. Bush Administration, existing limits on travel and private remittances to Cuba were tightened. John Bolton, the Undersecretary of State for Arms Control and International Security Affairs, noted, "Havana has long provided safe haven for terrorists, and is known to be harboring terrorists from Colombia, Spain, and fugitives from the United States. We know that Cuba is collaborating with other state sponsors of terror. Castro continues to view terror as a legitimate tactic to further revolutionary objectives." Bolton cited Cuba as one of the nations posing a significant threat to the U.S., and Cuba was added to Washington's list of "axis of evil" countries.

A shift in attitude, however, could be seen during the 2008 presidential campaign. Barack Obama called for an end to the Cuban economic embargo, joined by his opponent, Hillary Clinton, who labelled it an "albatross" on U.S. diplomacy. In 2009, absent the necessary Congressional approval to remove the embargo, the Obama administration lifted restrictions on travel to and cash remittances by family members to Cuba. In January 2011, the administration announced the further easing of restrictions on non-family remittances as well as educational and religious travel to Cuba.

The great leap forward came in December 2014, when President Obama and Cuban President Raul Castro announced the beginning of the normalization of relations between Cuba and the U.S. Three Cuban sleeper agents who had been imprisoned in the U.S. since 1998 were released from U.S. federal prisons and flown home. Simultaneously, Rolando Trujillo, a C.I.A. double agent who had been held in a Cuban prison since 1995 was flown to the U.S., as was Alan Gross, a State Department contractor who was arrested in 2009 for smuggling Internet equipment onto the island for dissident groups.

The Obama administration reasoned that a policy of engagement, rather than one sanctions-based, would "help the Cuban people improve their own lives." But human rights groups alleged that beatings and detention of dissidents soared after the U.S. extended the olive branch. In November 2016, the Cuban Commission for Human Rights and National Reconciliation reported there were at least 9,125 short-term detentions for political reasons during the first 10 months of 2016, higher than annual levels over the past several years.

Left out of the negotiation was a demand by the Administration for the extradition of the multitude of fugitives who've received sanctuary in Cuba. They include those suspected or convicted in the deaths of law enforcement agents, which as Rick Fuentes, former Superintendent of the New Jersey State Police, notes, are "more than murders.

They are attacks on law and order that leave gaping, open wounds to police organizations and society generally."

In addition to William Morales, Assata Shakur, and Victor Gerena, the Los Macheteros member who fled to the island after participating in the Wells Fargo heist and has been on the FBI's most-wanted list for more than thirty years, it's believed there may be hundreds of other criminals who've been welcomed by Cuba. For decades, Cuba was an attractive destination for murderers, scammers, fraudsters, and skyjackers. One is Ishmael Ali LaBeet, convicted along with four others of shooting to death eight tourists and employees in 1972 at a Virgin Islands golf club after yelling, "Kill all the white motherfuckers!" LaBeet later hijacked the American Airlines plane transporting him to a prison. Another is Charlie Hill, who along with two other members of the militant group "Republic of New Afrika" was charged with murdering a New Mexico State Trooper in 1971 during a traffic stop. Hill commandeered a plane to Cuba, where he later declared, "I have never felt guilty about that cop. I never think about that dude." Possibly the most famous person to receive sanctuary in Cuba was Huey Newton, co-founder of the Black Panther Party, who lived in Havana for three years in the mid-1970s before returning to the U.S. to stand trial for murder.

Speaking with Fox News' Stuart Varney, Joe Connor reacted to the Cuban thaw, "They are saying they want reparations from the United States when in fact they owe us eight billion dollars for the seizure of our assets.

Creating a relationship should not be one sided. We have to get something, like bringing Morales back, He's low-hanging fruit in Cuba right now." Former New Jersey Congressman Scott Garrett, who represented Connor's district until 2016, along with two other Republican Congressman asked a House committee to withhold money to restore diplomatic relations with Cuba until the Castro regime returns U.S. fugitives.

The press by Congress for the extradition of outlaws has been bipartisan. Democrat Senator Bob Menendez's parents escaped from Cuba after the Castro revolution. He represents New Jersey, the site of Assata Shakur's most notorious act. Menendez asked, "Why was Shakur's return not part of the deal?" New Jersey Governor Chris Christie, in a letter to President Obama, declared, "Cuba's provision of safe harbor to [Shakur] by providing political asylum to a convicted cop killer ... is an affront to every resident of our state, our country, and in particular, the men and women of the New Jersey State Police." A direct rejoinder to Christie came from none other than Fidel Castro who, speaking through a government functionary, claimed the absolute right to grant asylum to those whom Cuba believes have been persecuted.

In April 2015, Cuba was removed from the State Department's list of state sponsors of terrorism based on the Department's determination that Cuba had not supported terrorism in the last six months and a pledge by Raul Castro that it would not do so in the future. Joe Connor, in an interview on Fox News Latino, pointed out, "We're talking about a Cuba that not only harbors terrorists, but they finance terrorists, they train terrorists, they are bloody with terror." He asked rhetorically, "How can a state that sponsors terrorists be removed from the State Sponsor of Terror list?"

Many others joined the protest, arguing that softening U.S. policy without concrete Cuban reforms only boosts the Castro government, politically and economically, and facilitates the survival of the communist regime. Florida Senator Marco Rubio, the son of Cuban immigrants who later in the year would declare his candidacy for president, urged the president to "make central to the current talks the repatriation of known terrorists and other fugitives from U.S. justice." New York Congressman Peter King introduced in the House a resolution citing William Morales as the "leader and chief bomb-maker for the terrorist organization FALN, [who] committed numerous terrorist attacks on United States soil, including the bombings of Fraunces Tavern in lower Manhattan in 1975 and the Mobil Oil employment office in New York in 1977," and calling for the immediate extradition of Morales and all other fugitives who are receiving safe harbor in Cuba. Law enforcement officials objected en masse as well.

Responding to public pressure, the State Department announced that Cuba had agreed to discuss the status of Morales and Shakur as part of talks on increasing law-enforcement cooperation between the two countries. "We see the reestablishment of diplomatic relations and the reopening of an embassy in Havana as the means by which we'll be able, more effectively, to press the Cuban government on law enforcement issues such as fugitives," said State Department spokesman Jeff Rathke. But the level of U.S. commitment on this issue appeared tepid, and no fugitives were returned during the Obama presidency. In July 2015, the U.S. and Cuba reestablished embassies in their respective capitals. And in February 2016, the two countries signed a memorandum of understanding allowing for the resumption of direct commercial air traffic between the two nations, potentially funneling millions of American tourist dollars into the Castros' pockets. Governor Christie again reacted, in a letter to the Port Authority of New York and New Jersey, which operates Newark Liberty International Airport. "It is unacceptable to me as governor to have any flights between New Jersey and Cuba until and unless convicted cop killer and escaped fugitive [Shakur] is returned to New Jersey to face justice. I will not tolerate rewarding the Cuban government for continuing to harbor a fugitive." Christopher Burgos, president of the State Troopers Fraternal Association of New Jersey, also wrote to the Port Authority, stating, "It appears to me that these fugitive offenders are of no consequence to the White House and business leaders here at home, and that only potential huge profits and the salivating of big revenue by corporate leadership and stockholders is the priority," Joe Connor argued, in an interview with Stuart Varney on Fox News, that "this was not negotiation, but capitulation."

But these words fell on deaf ears. In March 2016, Obama became the first sitting president in almost ninety years to visit Cuba. (Ironically, Joe Connor and his cousin Jean Schlag-Nebbia got word of Obama's planned visit while in Guantánamo Bay observing pretrial hearings for Khalid Sheik Mohammad and the other high-value 9/11 detainees.) Three months earlier, the President had announced that he would travel to Cuba only "if, in fact, I with confidence can say that we're seeing some progress in the liberty and freedom and possibilities of ordinary Cubans. ... If we're going backwards, then there's not much reason for me to be there." Yet, only hours before President Obama landed in Havana, Cuban authorities arrested more than fifty members of the "Ladies in White," formed by wives of political prisoners, who march each Sunday after Mass to demand improved human rights. During Obama's trip, Representative Garrett issued a press release stating, "During President Obama's speech in Havana with Cuban President Castro this afternoon, he talked about a Rolling Stones concert, a Tampa Bay Rays baseball game, and urged Congress to lift the trade embargo against the tyrannical regime. The president did not, however, mention a single word about the extradition of convicted cop-killer Joanne Chesimard or terrorist William Morales ... The president's failure to make this a priority in negotiations between our countries is truly upsetting to those seeking justice."

*

After arriving in Cuba in 1988, Morales earned a master's degree in international relations at the University of Havana. He remarried, and he and his new wife, Rosa, had a son, Rodrigo. Morales has lived what's been described as a "comfortable life" in Cuba, periodically working for a pro-Puerto Rico independence journal and advising visiting revolutionaries when they travel to Cuba. Over the years, he has granted interviews with American reporters. In 1991, speaking of the Fraunces Tavern bombing, Morales told Roberto Santiago of the *Times of the Americas,* while waving his golf putter hand, "Those who died were businessmen who contributed to the debasement of Third World peoples." In 1993, while being questioned by a journalist from *The Cleveland Plain Dealer,* Morales again was asked about Fraunces Tavern. "It may sound heartless," he responded, "but it is hard to fight a war without bystanders getting injured." At dinner with another reporter in Havana in 2001, Morales spoke proudly about life as a Cuban fugitive while eating with a fork wrapped by an elastic band around one of his stumps. A *Washington Post* reporter caught up with Morales the following year when he was "sipping a cappuccino in a chic hotel lobby in Havana."

Morales' most revealing interview came in January 1998 when he spoke with Amy Goodman, host and executive producer of the show, "Democracy Now!" When questioned as to how he had received his serious wounds, Morales responded that he was injured when an "artifact" went off. Asked how he would answer those who label him a terrorist, Morales claimed, "I didn't hurt anybody. The only one hurt was myself." Morales insisted, "If you're fighting for independence, you're not a terrorist." He complained, "The remains of my hands could have been saved, but the cops kidnapped them and just put them in formaldehyde."

In October 2015, Mike Kelly, a columnist for *The Record*, a North Jersey paper, was on assignment in Cuba. Using his sources, Kelly uncovered the address of Morales' apartment building in Havana's Vedado section, near the Plaza de la Revolución, which was the location of the huge assembly held by Pope Francis a month earlier. When Morales refused to answer his doorbell, Kelly dialed a phone number for his apartment that had once been listed in a Havana telephone book. Morales picked up on the first ring. "After I identified myself," Kelly recalls, "he said in Spanish, 'Don't call here anymore. Or I'll call the police.' And then he hung up. I thought it pretty ironic that this criminal was threatening to call the cops on me."

\*

Morales' days as a hero of the global revolutionary movement are long gone, and he may now be viewed by the Cuban government as a liability. Hopes for his return were raised by the election of Donald Trump, who in June 2017, before a crowd of Cuban-Americans in Miami, called on Raul Castro to return the fugitives from American justice.

Fidel Castro's death in November 2016 also may be significant. Professor Antonio de la Cova notes that Fidel had been the one Cuban leader who most maintained the old revolutionary solidarity and fervor. "But that may not mean Cuba returns Morales to the U.S. They may well ship him off to Venezuela."

\*

In 2014, Joe Connor was interviewed by Natalia Guerrero of BBC Mundo about López Rivera. "She asked me several questions about how we were raised after my dad's death, and many about his life. Then she asked if, because I kept fighting to keep him in prison, I was raised with hate. Stunned by the question, when we resumed our conversation, I asked her if she had posed the same question to López Rivera. Of course, she hadn't."

Joe Connor has managed to live his life without hate. "But," he points out, "I don't forget."

# CHAPTER 34
## *Déjà Vu*

*I say to President Obama: Let him out ... And if you do not do this, I will.* Oscar López Rivera's incarceration *violates the principles of justice, democracy, and respect for human rights.*

—Bernie Sanders

IN THE YEARS AFTER Oscar López Rivera's 2011 parole hearing, the push to commute his sentence escalated into a cause célèbre in Puerto Rico and leftist circles globally. A letter to President Obama from nine Swedish politicians, including Sweden's former Justice and Defense Minister members of the Left Party and Green Party, pleaded for the president to "do what is right" for López Rivera, "the longest-held political prisoner from Latin America in U.S. history."

Petitioners relied on Americans' sympathy for the underdog and short memories. Puerto Rico Governor Alejandro Garcia Padilla visited López Rivera in prison and penned a column for Puerto Rico's main daily newspaper, stating, "He hasn't been accused of committing any violent act. He hasn't been connected to any violent act … His sentence, far too excessive, violates the most elemental principles of humanity, sensitivity and justice. Oscar López Rivera owes no debt to society, and if he ever did, he paid it a long time ago." Luis Gutiérrez, born in the same Puerto Rican town as López Rivera, while speaking on the House floor, similarly argued that López Rivera "was not convicted of committing a violent crime, rather he was convicted of … espousing the belief that the Puerto Rican people are capable of, entitled to, and have an inalienable right to self-determination." Even the United Nations weighed in, with its "Special Committee on Decolonization" approving a resolution calling on the President of the United States to release the "Puerto Rican political prisoner Oscar López Rivera without delay." The great irony was that this Committee, which has denounced the U.S. relationship to Puerto Rico as "blatant colonialism," had members from the most repressive regimes on earth, including Venezuela, Syria, Iran, Cuba, and the Congo.

Oscar López Rivera's incarceration became national news in May 2016 when Democratic presidential candidate Bernie Sanders, while campaigning in San Juan, followed the playbook by labeling López Rivera a "political prisoner," and a "respected community activist." In October, Sanders recorded a video with his campaign group, Our Revolution, telling the president that "all over the world, in the United States and in Puerto Rico, thousands and thousands of people are demanding that López Rivera be released from jail."

Joe Connor responded with an op-ed piece in Townhall.com pointing out the myriad reasons why López Rivera is anything but a political prisoner. His article ended with, "To Bernie Sanders and the Clintons, justice is only meant for the criminals and for political points, while the rest of us be damned."

As others have done, Sanders compared López Rivera to Nelson Mandela. Mandela, raised as a Methodist, was a man of faith who prayed regularly. At a religious conference in 1999, he said: "Without the church, without religious institutions, I would never have been here today ... Religion was one of the motivating factors in everything we did." As a political leader, Mandela was not entirely non-violent in the tradition of Mahatma Gandhi or Martin Luther King. But he repudiated terrorism. Mandela observed in his autobiography, *Long Walk to Freedom*, "Terrorism inevitably reflected poorly on those who used it, undermining any public support it might otherwise garner ... Because it did not involve the loss of life, [sabotage] offered the best hope for reconciliation among the races ..." Mandela explained that members of the militant group he headed, the "Umkhonto we Sizwe" ("Spear of the Nation"), were given strict instructions "that we would countenance no loss of life."

New Jersey Democrat Senator Torricelli repudiated the comparison to Mandela during a hearing in 1999.

"I don't know of any political cause that has less merit than that of the FALN. It is not the African National Congress. It is not any legitimate effort at national liberation. The people in Puerto Rico have voted repeatedly to be in voluntary political association with the United States. The day they choose otherwise, they will have their independence ... It is not right and it is not fair to invoke the name of Nelson Mandela in the same breath as the FALN."

The calls for clemency by Sanders and others consistently failed to mention his earlier refusal of an offer of clemency, one of the conditions of which would have required him to renounce violence. They also ignored López Rivera's violent past, his conviction on a number of felonies in addition to seditious conspiracy, and the plots he masterminded to break out of prison which, had they not been prevented by law enforcement, would have resulted in the deaths of prison guards. As stated by former FALN prosecutor Deborah Devaney: "López Rivera was convicted of participating in conspiracies to bomb, kill, and injure. Under the law, he is just as responsible and guilty as if he personally planted the bombs."

Also disregarded in the pleas for his release was López Rivera's long-standing refusal to express any repentance for his actions. In 1998, López Rivera told a reporter from *The Shawnee News-Star*, "The whole thing of contrition, atonement, I have problems with that." During the same year, in an interview with the *Houston Chronicle*, he said, "I have no regrets for serving a noble cause ... Would we be willing to renounce the struggle for Puerto Rico's independence to get out of jail? I will never do that."

The push to grant clemency to López Rivera coincided with the furious debate over the handling of Puerto Rico's debt, which by early 2016 had risen to an unprecedented level of $72 billion. In response, in June 2016, the Puerto Rico Oversight, Management, and Economic Stability Act (PROMESA) was enacted, designed to offer the island some reprieve from debtors and help manage the fiscal crisis. (This action was similar in concept to what the state government in Albany did during the 1970s when New York City came to the edge of bankruptcy.) The statute was controversial for many reasons, chief among them being that it conveyed sweeping power to a seven-member financial-oversight board appointed by the president with no obligation to answer to Puerto Rican officials, raising again the specter of imperialism. New Jersey Democrat Senator Bob Menendez called PROMESA "neo-colonial" and a "Band-Aid" that foregoes long-term solutions such as a route to statehood or a special dispensation that would have allowed Puerto Rico to file for chapter 9 bankruptcy. Bernie Sanders chimed in by labeling the oversight board as having "dictatorial powers that harken back to colonial days."

On a Sunday in May 2016, as the deliberations over PROMESA raged on, thousands of people gathered in San Juan to mark the 35th anniversary of López Rivera's imprisonment. Marchers chanted "Obama, listen to me!

We want Oscar free" and "We don't want this board, we want to be free." Media coverage quoted López Rivera as opposing the financial control board. Legitimate concerns about the structure of the oversight board had become a vehicle to cloak López Rivera as an innocent bystander caught up in the ongoing oppression of Puerto Rico.

A leading supporter of clemency for López Rivera was Puerto Rico-born New York City Council Speaker Melissa Mark-Viverito, the number two elected official in the city. In May 2015, Mark-Viverito organized a march in her East Harlem district—the same district in which Angel Poggi was injured by an FALN bombing in 1974—in support of López Rivera's release. Among the participants was Clarissa López Rivera, who said, "It's hard to be raised by a single mother and far away from your dad." Joe Connor replied in a telephone interview, "I empathize with someone who loses their father. But they should go back and realize why."

In June 2015, Mark-Viverito pushed through a New York City Council resolution calling on President Obama to immediately release López Rivera from prison, "as his continued incarceration is unjust and serves no legitimate purpose." Democrat Councilman Rory Lancman was one of those voting against the resolution. "Millions have peacefully pursued the goal of Puerto Rico's independence within the democratic political process in both Puerto Rico and the United States. Mr. López Rivera chose violence, and we should not honor or dignify that choice." New York State Senator Martin Golden stated, "It is inconceivable that the Council of the City New York, the City that suffered the largest terrorist attack on American soil in history, is looking to release a terrorist from jail because they believe his being in jail 'serves no legitimate purpose.' Each of the New York City Council members who supported this resolution should ponder the severity of the message they have sent all New Yorkers and Americans."

In September 2015, during a visit by Pope Francis to a school in East Harlem, Mark-Viverito presented the Pope with a portrait of him painted by López Rivera, and asked the Pope to pray for a jailed Puerto Rican nationalist. "She is an elected New York official," Joe Connor retorted, "and instead of asking the Pope to help all kinds of needy people in New York, she advocated for someone whose terror group killed New Yorkers."

A year earlier, Mark-Viverito dedicated the city's annual Puerto Rican Day Parade to López Rivera, after the parade board named López Rivera's brother José as grand marshal. At a pre-parade event at Gracie Mansion, Connor introduced himself to Mark-Viverito and explained his disagreement with her support of clemency for López Rivera. When he began to speak of López Rivera's violent past, Mark-Viverito snapped back that "it was a lie" and that he was "only" convicted of a "politically motivated seditious conspiracy charge." Mark-Viverito turned away from Connor after hissing, "This is not the place for this discussion." Later in the evening, Mark-Viverito was joined by López Rivera's brother in advocating to the crowd for his release.

\*

Retired Archbishop Desmond Tutu, winner of the Nobel Peace Prize in 1984, was one of the prominent figures arguing for López Rivera's release "in the spirit of "reconciliation and peace," referring to "the Biblical call of Isaiah: to set free those who are bound." He characterized López Rivera as "a vivid reminder of the ongoing inequality that colonialism and empire building inevitably bring forth," and that he remained imprisoned for seeking "to free his people from the shackles of imperial justice."

In his book, *No Future Without Forgiveness*, the Archbishop speaks of the power of forgiveness and the central role it played in healing South Africa after the end of apartheid. He tackled the question whether amnesty offered to whites who tortured and murdered blacks was given "at the cost of justice being done." Archbishop Tutu wrote, "If the process of forgiveness and healing is to succeed, ultimately acknowledgement by the culprit is indispensable."

In 2008, Deenie Ettenson learned that the Archbishop was to speak at the Cherry Hill High School while on a visit to the Philadelphia area. "I got in touch with the head of the organization in charge of the lecture series that Desmond Tutu was scheduled to participate in, and asked if I could meet with the Archbishop privately. He was uncomfortable with my request, but I told him the reasons why, and that I felt certain the Archbishop would want to meet with me. He got back to me a while later to say yes."

An hour before his lecture was scheduled to begin, Deenie and her husband were led backstage to where the Archbishop and his wife were waiting. "First, he asked that the four of us pray together, which we did. A lovely nondenominational prayer. Then I asked him why he had petitioned for López Rivera's clemency. It quickly became clear that he had lent his name to a petition made by his friend, the Archbishop of Puerto Rico, and knew little himself about López Rivera or the FALN. When we told him of López Rivera's background, he sat with his mouth open. Before we ended the conversation, we all hugged and kissed each other."

Deenie is Jewish, as was Alex Berger. Extending forgiveness is a hallmark of Jewish values, as was stated by no less than Maimonides, the prolific twelfth-century scholar on Jewish law and ethics considered one of history's greatest philosophers. But Maimonides made clear that, "The victim is bidden to grant him forgiveness only once he knows that he repented from his sin and regrets his evil, and not if he has reason to suspect that the offender as yet feels no regret for his crime."

# CHAPTER 35
## *A Second Clemency*

*Sobbing with gratitude here in London. OSCAR LÓPEZ RIVERA IS COMING HOME. THANK YOU, @POTUS.*

—Lin-Manuel Miranda

JANUARY IS A PARTICULARLY painful month for FALN victims and their families. As Deenie Ettenson says, "Every day leading up to the 24th is a knife in the gut, even all these decades later. On that day, the victims' families always exchange messages of consolation."

In January 2017, Barack Obama ended his presidency having granted clemency to 1,927 individuals (1,715 commutations and 212 pardons) convicted of federal crimes, more than any chief executive since Harry Truman. He had received far more requests for clemency than any president, largely as the result of an initiative set up by the Obama administration to shorten prison terms for nonviolent federal inmates convicted of drug crimes.

One commutation grant, made without conditions and days before both the end of his term in office and the anniversary of the Fraunces Tavern bombing, was to Oscar López Rivera, designated to be freed in May 2017. In reaction, López Rivera expressed his happiness at being able to enjoy Puerto Rico and his family. He also mentioned that his organizing work may not be over. "I like to work. I have some skills ... that I want to share with people."

Similar to 1999, no notice or opportunity to comment was given to FALN victims or their families. Deenie Ettenson admitted, "I thought it would happen, but still I was shocked." "In 1999, I was a novice," Joe Connor reflected, "and I took the clemencies more personally. Now I expected the worst from an administration that I knew was not on my side. But it still hurts to once again see that unrepentant criminals are forgiven while the innocent are ignored."

Obama became the third Democratic President in a row to free violent Puerto Rican *independistas*. No explanation was offered by the White House, only a mention by a senior Administration official that López Rivera "had served nearly half of his life in prison and was the only FALN member still in prison." The administration may have reacted to pressure from within the Democrat Party, including members of the Congressional Black and Hispanic Caucuses, as well as the recognition that Puerto Ricans represent an important Democratic voting bloc in key states such as Florida, Illinois, and New York.

President Obama may also have been influenced by statements of support for López Rivera's clemency from prominent figures globally. They included Pope Francis, a proponent of liberation theology, a movement developed by Latin America Catholics that emphasizes liberation from social, political, and economic oppression in anticipation of ultimate salvation. The Pope's behind-the-scenes role on behalf of López Rivera was revealed by Robert González Nieves, the Archbishop of San Juan: "We are grateful to the Holy Father for his support."

López Rivera's clemency grant was the subject of international news coverage, although overshadowed by the clemency given on the same day to Chelsea Manning, the Army analyst convicted of a large-scale intelligence leak that revealed American military and diplomatic activities across the world and made WikiLeaks a household name. The news of López Rivera's impending release was received with jubilation. Luis Gutiérrez thanked President Obama. "We have had our prayers answered." Melissa Mark-Viverito, head of the New York City Council, was "very emotional. I cried." Chicago's Puerto Rican Cultural Center erupted in celebration. Bill Ayers, while on a flight to Havana with his wife, fellow former Weather Underground leader Bernadine Dohrn, tweeted that he was "dancing in the aisles."

Also taking to Twitter to voice his delight was New York City Mayor Bill de Blasio, who chose to ignore the violence that the FALN had wrought in his city. But New York City Councilman Joe Borelli expressed a different perspective. "Commuting his sentence proves that Obama and most liberals are out of touch with reality and willing to sacrifice all norms in the name of progressivism."

One of the most vocal advocates for López Rivera's release was Lin-Manuel Miranda, the creator of the smash Broadway musical hit "Hamilton." Miranda, of Puerto Rican descent and born in the same neighborhood—Washington Heights—as Frank Connor, joyously announced that he would reprise his role of Alexander Hamilton in a special performance for López Rivera. Ironically, Hamilton frequented Fraunces Tavern, and the restaurant is the setting for several of the play's songs.

During the 2016 Tony Awards, which took place hours after a mass killing in an Orlando nightclub, while accepting the award for Best Original Score, Miranda decried "senseless acts of tragedy which remind us that nothing here is promised. Not one day." As Joe Connor pointed out in an op-ed published in the *Wall Street Journal*, "Apparently the FALN's violence did not qualify for such condemnation."

Miranda had penned the famous lecture given by a cast member to Vice-President-Elect Mike Pence in November 2016, at the end of a performance of "Hamilton," that raised the concern that the new Trump administration will not "protect us ... or defend us and uphold our inalienable rights." Connor noted that Miranda "failed to acknowledge that one of the protections and rights that Americans can expect ... is to not be blown to bits while innocently dining in a restaurant."

Within hours of the news breaking, an impromptu celebration was held in a community theater in Humboldt Park. Dozens held Puerto Rican flags and "Free Oscar López Rivera" signs, chanted "Obama finally listened and let Oscar out of prison." The crowd included López Rivera's brother, José, and sister, Zenaida, as well as Edwin Cortes, a former FALN member who called López Rivera's release a "great victory for our movement." In reaction, a *Washington Post* op-ed, entitled, "Forget Chelsea Manning. This is the Obama pardon you should be mad about," asked, "What was Obama thinking when he ordered the release of Oscar López Rivera? ... López Rivera is neither a low-level offender nor a nonviolent one. Nor, crucially, is he repentant."

Anthony Senft, who learned the clemency news via a call from his union boss, felt "disappointed and betrayed by my country." Steven Steinberg, the older brother of Charles Steinberg, penned an article for *The New York Daily News*, in which he stated, "It was with utter disbelief and disgust that I learned President Obama had commuted the sentence of FALN mastermind Oscar López Rivera ... We should never pardon those convicted in connection to murder, whether they actually planted the bombs, obtained the dynamite or simply empowered others through their seditious rhetoric. Sparing these people the death penalty is 'reward' enough." Joe Connor provided commentary on several radio and TV shows. Interviewed by Eric Shawn of Fox News, Connor countered the assertion that López Rivera was a political prisoner. "The United States does not hold political prisoners. These were terrorists. This action does nothing but encourage terrorism by forgiving it."

In the decades after the Fraunces Tavern bombing, Mary Connor Tully would find happiness and achievement, including earning her high school and Associates degrees and graduating from William Paterson University on the same day in May 1986 that her son Tom graduated from Boston College. (The proud mom happily skipped her own graduation ceremony to attend Tom's.) For Mary, López Rivera's release "will not change how I feel about him. He is a cowardly little man who doesn't have the guts to stand up and express sorrow for his part in the terrorist attack that killed my husband, leaving two small boys without a father. One day he will answer to a higher power for his sins, and maybe then he will bow his head, clasp his hands, and ask for forgiveness."

# CHAPTER 36
## *June 11, 2017*

*I firmly reject this being associated with the people of Puerto Rico.*

—Puerto Rico Governor Ricardo Rosselló

IN THE SPRING OF 1958, the inaugural Puerto Rican Day Parade marched up a short stretch of Fifth Avenue, with the island's first elected governor, Luis Muñoz Marín, on hand to participate. The parade, now held on the second Sunday of every June, grew exponentially to become a nationally televised spectacle with dozens of fanciful floats ridden by famous people, hundreds of colorful dancers and fervent musicians, and a sea of Puerto Rican flags that once had been illegal to display on the island. It has become a hallowed New York City tradition, attracting a host of notable celebrities and politicians and tens of thousands of marchers as well as up to two million spectators.

The parade had not shied away from making political statements, including honoring nationalist figures such as Pedro Albizu Campos and Lolita Lebrón. Nor has it escaped controversy. In 2000, dozens of women reported being groped by parade-goers. Some of the assaults were caught on videotape, with the images played repeatedly on news stations throughout the country. In 2010, organizers bestowed upon soap opera star Osvaldo Ríos the title "International Godfather." But because the actor had served three months for beating his girlfriend, corporate sponsors dropped out of the parade, and lawmakers threatened to boycott until Ríos bowed out. And in 2014, the state's attorney general found that a fundraising firm hired by the parade organizers had misappropriated $1 million amid lax oversight, which led to the resignations of half of the parade board's members.

Nothing, however, compared to the firestorm that would surround the 2017 version of the parade. By that year, Puerto Rico was in dire straits financially, and its political and social fabric was eroding. Immigration to the mainland had skyrocketed, hundreds of schools were either closing or facing severe austerity measures, the levels of crime and poverty were high and rising, residents were dealing with a lack of potable water, unemployment had climbed to more than twelve percent, and the cost of living continued to soar. Yet, the organizers of that year's parade, the sixtieth, instead of using its high profile to raise awareness of Puerto Rico's troubles, chose other focuses.

A primary one was Oscar López Rivera. In early February 2017, López Rivera was flown to Puerto Rico, where he finished the final three months of his sentence under "house arrest" in his daughter's home. On his flight to San Juan, López Rivera was accompanied by that city's mayor, Carmen Yulín Cruz, a member of the autonomist Popular Democratic Party, who had claimed before the clemency grant that López Rivera, "didn't steal anything. He didn't bomb anything. He didn't hurt anyone. The sheer injustice of it is so un-American." Later that month, Chicago honored López Rivera by naming three blocks of a city street as "Oscar López Rivera Way."

In May 2017, Puerto Rico, which by then had more than $120 billion in debt to creditors plus liability for unfunded pension obligations, was placed under court protection, in what amounted to the largest-ever U.S. municipal bankruptcy by a wide margin. That same month, López Rivera's clemency took effect, and he was released from house custody. New York City Council Speaker Melissa Mark-Viverito, accompanied by her NYPD security detail, flew to Puerto Rico to greet him. Among López Rivera's first utterances were to thank Cuba and Venezuela for their support over the years. (Venezuela, whose government and military in 2017 effectively were controlled by Cuba, was experiencing the worst economic crisis in its history, with an inflation rate of more than 400 percent and widespread shortages of food, medical care, and necessities. López Rivera spoke by phone with Venezuelan President Nicolás Maduro, widely considered a dictator with blood on his hands, to say he hoped that Maduro and Venezuela "would prevail.") López Rivera then flew to Chicago, where his brother, Jose, and Congressman Luis Gutierrez joined him at a gathering in his honor in Humboldt Park.

Two weeks before López Rivera's release, the Puerto Rican Day parade organizers had announced that the parade would recognize one hundred years of U.S. citizenship for Puerto Ricans, that its theme would be "Un Pueblo, Muchas Voces" (One Nation, Many Voices), intended to "celebrate the creativity and diversity of thought in Puerto Rico and across the diaspora," and that the parade's grand marshal would be salsa musician Gilberto Santa Rosa. Then came the revelation that they had chosen to include Oscar López Rivera among the parade's honorees. Adding fuel to the fire, López Rivera was designated to receive a newly coined title, "Prócer de la Libertad (National Freedom Hero)," and be placed at the head of the procession. Nor was it lost on observers that Mark-Viverito chose to make the announcement regarding López Rivera at the top of the newly opened Freedom Tower, on the very site of the most horrific terrorist attack in the nation's history and where, in August 1977, a threat by the FALN prompted an evacuation of the World Trade Center.

The negative reaction to the honoring of López Rivera was swift, widespread, and furious. It included a wide range of the Puerto Rican community, beginning with Puerto Rico's Governor, Ricardo Rosselló, who decried López Rivera's responsibility for the deaths of innocents and called his honoring "beyond comprehension." NYPD officer Angel Poggi, maimed by an FALN bomb, asked, "How can they praise him after he had a part in the FALN and people dying?" Well-known Nuyorican salsa singer and social activist Willie Colón criticized the parade organizers as having gone too far. Representative of ordinary citizens, fifty-year-old Angi Silva told a reporter, "I'm as Puerto Rican as it gets, but I can't support the parade this year. We should be focusing on helping our island, not honoring a criminal."

By designating López Rivera as the parade's preeminent figure, its organizers effectively sought to compel sponsors and participants to join in glorifying him. But they badly miscalculated, as many prominent New York State political figures backed out of partaking in the parade, including senior Senator Chuck Schumer, Attorney General Eric Schneiderman, and key members of New York City's congressional delegation, mostly Democrats. New York Governor Andrew Cuomo remained silent initially, promoting speculation about his position regarding López Rivera, but then announced that he wouldn't attend. Cuomo eventually explained, "I don't know what they were thinking to invite him and honor him in the first place, but I'm not going to honor a terrorist."

Joe Connor and a group that included several retired FBI agents (including Rick Hahn and Don Wofford), prosecutors (including Deborah Devaney, Tom Engel, and Jeremy Margolis), and FALN and 9/11 victims' family members worked furiously for weeks through social and traditional media to convince public figures and corporate patrons to withhold their support for that year's parade.

The groundswell of opposition via nonparticipation included NYPD Police Commission James O'Neill and Brooklyn DA Eric Gonzalez, the Hispanic Societies for both the Fire Department of New York and the NYPD, the NYPD's Gay Officer Action League, the Patrolmen's Benevolent Association, and the Uniformed Firefighters Association. Every major corporate sponsor of the parade eventually withdrew. The first was Goya Foods, the largest Latino-owned food company in the United States, which had been a sponsor of the Puerto Rican Day Parade since it began. That was followed by JetBlue, AT&T, Coca-Cola, Corona Extra USA, the New York Yankees, Telemundo, Univision, and WNBC. (The *New York Daily News*, another corporate sponsor that dropped out, stated in an op-ed, "López Rivera was never charged in direct connection with a bombing. But it is beyond dispute that he proudly oversaw the unrepentantly violent movement. It is also beyond dispute that he has never expressed remorse or worked with authorities to hold accountable those responsible for unsolved crimes.")

The most prominent politician not declining to participate was Mayor Bill De Blasio, whose former senior advisor, Lorraine Cortes Vazquez, was head of the parade committee. De Blasio, who honeymooned in Cuba and spent a summer working for the Nicaraguan Sandinistas, initially took the view that it was solely up to the parade's leadership to select who was honored, and that he was marching in tribute to the Puerto Rican people. In response, Tony Senft said, "I don't understand how anyone can march with a known terrorist ... I'm Italian, but [late Mafia don] John Gotti doesn't represent me. I wouldn't march down the street with him." As the public outrage grew, de Blasio sought political cover by attempting to put some distance between himself and López Rivera. "I think violence is wrong in all its forms," de Blasio said, "But I am not marching with this individual."

The organizers also attempted damage control by issuing a statement explaining that honoring López Rivera was "a recognition of a man and a nation's struggle for sovereignty" and "not an endorsement of the history that led to his arrest, nor any form of violence." Mark-Viverito, who was not formally on the parade committee but pulled its strings, remained unfazed, publicly speculating that the pushback was being "orchestrated" by "an ultra-right-wing" element that favored Puerto Rican statehood over independence.

On May 22, Mark-Viverito released a letter sent to parade board members commending their decision to honor López Rivera, which concluded with, "We stand in solidarity with Oscar and express our full support for the Board's decision to recognize and uplift the legacy of Oscar López Rivera." Signing the letter along with Mark-Viverito were twenty-nine City Council members and six other elected officials. But many of those Council members later admitted to *The New York Post* that they felt strong-armed by Mark-Viverito, particularly given that budget negotiations were underway at the time, which left the possibility that funding for their districts would get cut. "Most members know that's an important issue to her, so she didn't have to say it," one Council member admitted. "You want to be in line and not make her mad."

On the same day that letter was sent, a twenty-two-year-old British Muslim, Salman Ramadan Abedi, detonated a shrapnel-laden homemade bomb at the exit of an arena in Manchester, England, following a concert by American singer Ariana Grande. Twenty-three adults and children were killed, including Abedi, and more than one hundred were injured, many critically. In the aftermath, many, including Joe Connor, publicly pointed out the stark disconnect of lauding López Rivera during a time in which the world continued to be rocked by terrorism.

On May 30, Connor and Nicole Malliotakis, a member of the state Assembly and a Republican mayoral candidate, stood at the steps of Fraunces Tavern and called for Mayor de Blasio to withdraw from marching in the Puerto Rican Day Parade. "I think it's completely outrageous that we have a mayor and a Council speaker who think it's appropriate to not only attend, but to march alongside the leader of the organization that claimed responsibility for these attacks on our city," said Malliotakis.

Meanwhile, López Rivera was in Berkeley, California, where he was the guest of honor at an event hosted by the

National Lawyers Guild. It took place at a Presbyterian church blocks away from the college campus that was Ground Zero for radicalism in the 1960s. At a reception in a room lined with liberation posters, López Rivera was introduced as "our hero, our patriot." López Rivera then spoke, decrying the "colonialist government that exists in Puerto Rico." At one point, López Rivera held up his hands to show that they were free of blood, declaring he did not have anything to do with the Fraunces Tavern bombing.

On June 1, López Rivera granted an interview with the *Daily News*." In it, he characterized the narrative around the parade as "misinformation about who I am and what I stand for." He backed away from being the focus of the parade, declining to be honored. "I will be on Fifth Avenue not as your honoree but as a humble Puerto Rican and grandfather." Mayor de Blasio's office seized the opportunity to release a statement declaring that López Rivera made the best decision, while calling the controversy around his involvement "needless." De Blasio made it clear that he still would march.

Leading up to June 11, Joe Connor appeared on various TV and radio shows regarding the parade controversy, and was quoted in numerous newspaper articles. He also received hundreds of tweets and emails from Puerto Ricans telling him they were ashamed and disturbed by the honoring of López Rivera. In a television appearance on Fox Business News, Joe was asked by Stuart Varney if he would watch the parade. Joe said he would not, adding that his daughter had a dance recital that day. "That's where I belong," Joe said, "and that's where my dad would want me."

On June 11, led by Mark-Viverito, the parade kicked off around 11:30 a.m., mere blocks away from the Mobil Oil building where Charles Steinberg was murdered. Spectators were noticeably fewer than normal, and the usual number of floats was halved from fifty to twenty-five.

Soon after the parade began, López Rivera, sporting a prim mustache and gray hair tapered at the nape into a small curl, arrived and was whisked to a float blocks away from the head of the parade, where he originally had been invited to march. Wearing a T-shirt bearing a black-and-white image of the Puerto Rican flag, López Rivera waved to the crowd, pumped his fist defiantly in the air, and pounded his chest. Later, Mark-Viverito doubled back to join him. Neither had any contact with the mayor, who remained blocks behind them.

The crowd reaction to López Rivera was mixed. Supporters chanted "Oscar!" and carried signs such as, "Oscar López Rivera is our Mandela." Others booed and cursed at him. Several cops complained to reporters about being assigned to keep safe a terrorist. One said, "I wouldn't be here if I wasn't working. But we gotta do our jobs, man."

\*

Ironically, in Puerto Rico that same day, yet another non-binding referendum on political status, the fifth one in fifty years, was being held, sponsored by the governing, pro-statehood New Progressive Party. The quest to clarify Puerto Rico's status remains at the forefront of the minds of many Puerto Ricans. Illustrative is the fantasy short story, "Searching for January," by W.P. Kinsella, who is noted for his novel "Shoeless Joe," which was adapted into the movie "Field of Dreams." In the story, the author is walking on an empty tropical beach when he meets Roberto Clemente, the great Puerto Rican-born baseball player, who died many years earlier in a crash while flying supplies to earthquake victims in Nicaragua. One of Clemente's first questions is, "Is my home a state yet?"

In February 2015, Pedro Pierluisi, Puerto Rico's Resident Commissioner, introduced in Congress a bill, entitled "The Puerto Rico Statehood Admission Process Act." Modeled after laws enacted by Congress with respect to Alaska and Hawaii, it provided for the first-ever federally sponsored vote in Puerto Rico on the island's admission into the Union, asking one simple question, "Shall Puerto Rico be admitted as a State of the United States?" The bill also set out a clear process to make Puerto Rico a state if the voters once again vote in support of that.

The bill quickly obtained more than a hundred bipartisan Congressional cosponsors but was not acted upon. One reason was the opposition of Puerto Rico's then-Governor, Alejandro García Padilla, who stated, "I do not believe in statehood. That would be disastrous for the economy of Puerto Rico. It would turn Puerto Rico into a ghetto ..." (Presumably Padilla was referring to the increase in federal individual and corporate income tax liability that would result from Puerto Rico becoming a state.)

In January 2017, Padilla was succeeded by Ricardo Rosselló, who tied Puerto Rico's fiscal crisis to its "colonial condition." Rosselló proclaimed, "The United States cannot pretend to be a model of democracy for the world while it discriminates against 3.5 million of its citizens in Puerto Rico, depriving them of their right to political, social and economic equality under the U.S. flag." A proponent of statehood, Rosselló also announced that he would soon hold elections to choose two senators and five representatives to Congress and send them to Washington, a strategy used by Tennessee to join the union in the 18th century.

In the June 11 referendum, voters were asked to choose among becoming the 51st state, establishing an independent nation, or remaining a U.S. territory. Much of the argument for choosing statehood was financially based, including entitlement to increased disability benefits and Medicaid funding as well as the higher federal minimum wage. (Puerto Ricans have access to only certain federal programs, such as a weakened and more restrictive version of Medicaid. They are likewise denied access to Supplemental Security Income despite paying into Social Security.)

The result was an overwhelming vote for statehood, the highest percentage ever. However, voter participation was unusually low due to a boycott by several opposition parties, and the total number of people who voted for statehood was only 500,000 (versus 800,000 statehood supporters in 2012). As was true in the four previous referendums, only a tiny minority voted for independence. Governor Rosselló immediately stated he planned to press Congress to admit Puerto Rico to the Union. "In any democracy, the expressed will of the majority that participates in the electoral processes always prevails," Rosselló said. That same day, White House Press Secretary Sean Spicer acknowledged the vote as a first step, saying "now that the people have spoken in Puerto Rico, this is something that Congress has to address." Congress, however, is not bound by any aspect of the referendum vote, and whether it will act is uncertain, particularly given the low voter turnout in Puerto Rico. Commentators rate the chance of the island becoming a state as a long shot.

But, yet again, and on the day that López Rivera was put on public display and lauded by many, the truth was revealed that the vast majority of Puerto Ricans do not share the FALN's stated independence goal or its "colonialism" narrative.

# POSTSCRIPT

*I will use the past to write my future, and only then can I
hope to live the beautiful and full life that the man in the
picture deserved.*

—Kathleen Connor

IN FRAUNCES TAVERN TODAY is a plaque quoting Virgil's
"Aeneid": *"Tu ne cede malis, sed contra audentior ito,"* which
translates to, "Do not give in to evil, but proceed ever
more boldly against it." It preserves the memory of the
callous murder of civilians committed without warning. But public consciousness of the Fraunces Tavern
bombing has largely been lost. Bill Newhall tells of the
time, decades later, when he was given as a Christmas
present by his younger daughter a walking tour of lower
Manhattan, knowing her father was a self-admitted history nerd. "We started out at Bowling Green, toured
the Customs House, and then our group was brought to
Fraunces Tavern. Our young guide told us there was a
bombing in the restaurant years ago, but 'the nice thing
about that was no one was hurt.' I piped up to correct

her in some detail. The guide responded, 'How do you know all this?' I responded, 'Because I was there.'"

*

During the summer of 2016, Donald Trump hired David Bossie, the president of Citizens United, as his deputy campaign manager. Bossie took a leave of absence from Citizens United to join the Trump campaign, and was widely perceived as instrumental in Trump's upset election victory.

That same summer, at the Democratic convention in Philadelphia, Bernie Sanders focused on the *Citizens United* decision. "Brothers and sisters, this election is about overturning *Citizens United*. [It] is one of the worst Supreme Court decisions in the history of our country." Only days before the start of the convention, Hillary Clinton announced, "In my first thirty days as President, I will propose a constitutional amendment to overturn *Citizens United* and give the American people—all of us—the chance to reclaim our democracy." With Clinton's defeat, the impetus to overturn *Citizens United* faded.

*

In September 2017, Hurricane Maria devastated Puerto Rico, killing dozens, causing tens of billions of dollars in property damage, and leaving a large majority of residents for weeks without access to food and essential services such as electricity, water, sanitation, medical care, communications, and fuel. Speculation followed that many of the island's residents would move to the American mainland. Such an exodus would accelerate an ongoing migration trend, which has left the island with far fewer residents (3.5 million) than the number of Puerto Ricans in the States.

There were calls for the Trump administration to mount a Marshall Plan-style economic rehabilitation program for Puerto Rico along the lines of what the U.S. successfully adopted for Europe after World War II. Polling that followed to determine the level of support for providing significant financial aid to Puerto Rico revealed that a majority of Americans don't know that Puerto Rico is a U.S. territory and that Puerto Ricans are American citizens.

\*

The push to restore the Morales-Shakur Center lives on, intertwined with other radical causes, fanned by periodic rallies, supported by articles in select media sites, and touted on web sites and Facebook. Always, the past is ignored, facts are twisted, and a concept of "social justice" is hyped, one focusing on ensuring that the aggrieved, no matter their actions, contributions, or character, receive what is their "due" from society. In the case of the Morales-Shakur Center, an "ends justify the means" mentality elevates monsters and crucifies the innocent.

\*

One night soon after 9/11, Joe dreamt about his cousin Steve. "I asked him, 'So now that you're dead, what do you do all day?' Steve smirked and said he works from 5:00 a.m. till 8:00 p.m. 'You work that much? I didn't know you had to work in H ...' My voice trailed off, and he could tell what I was thinking, to which he laughed that ridiculous Schlag laugh, "No, I'm not in Hell. I'm in Heaven.'"

Steve Schlag's remains, including his wedding ring and altimeter watch, were identified the week before Christmas 2001. "At least he had been found," thought Joe. "God bless your soul, Steven. You will always be in our hearts." Tomoko honored her husband's wish to be cremated, with a return of his ashes to the earth. In 2005, she fulfilled the plan that she and Steve had crafted years earlier by moving to Park City, Utah, where her family had taken their last vacation before 9/11. Their son Garrett, now a writer and actor, believes that his father, "an outdoors man, would be honored by my pursuit of happiness in wild places."

\*

For Jean Schlag-Nebbia, 9/11 began a torment that haunts her to this day—the image of her brother Steve's suffering during the 102 minutes between when the North Tower was struck by Flight 11 and when it fell. Jean believes those who came before us and have died remain with us to guide and protect, and even interpret our acts for the greater being. In a conversation with her cousin Joe Connor weeks after 9/11, she lamented that she had not been visited in dreams by Steve as others had. "She wondered sadly," recounts Connor, "if Steve still was around her. She laughed when I asked her if she was sure she wanted him around her all the time."

In February 2016, Jean and Joe traveled from Joint Base Andrews to Gitmo's Camp Justice by invitation to observe several pre-trial sessions. Camp Justice is the informal name granted to the complex where

*Joe Connor at Camp Justice, February 2016*

Guantánamo detainees face charges before military commissions. Set up on a temporary basis and consisting of a series of hardstand tents and living trailers set atop asphalt in a desert-like space, Camp Justice has existed for more than a decade and a half.

Six other 9/11 victims' family members joined Joe and Jean, including the parents of Jeremy Glick, a passenger aboard United Airlines Flight 93, which crashed in Pennsylvania. Glick was one of the men who banded together in an attempt to take control back from the hijackers. "The first night on our 9/11 family bus at Gitmo," Connor recounts, "I explained what it would be like walking into the courtroom and facing someone like KSM, by relating what it felt like sitting across from López Rivera in 2011, and advised that we would need to be outwardly tough, even stoic, while in the terrorists' presence."

Certain of the family members suggested holding hands in solidarity as they walked into the gallery. Others wanted to turn their backs or heads. The eight finally decided simply to walk in confidently and with a "steely determination, giving the terrorists nothing they could gain any satisfaction from." They were seated mere feet away from the defendants, who were attired either in traditional Muslim dress or U.S. military-style camouflage jackets and represented by an expert defense team comprised of lawyers, paralegals, linguists, and security analysts advocating on their behalf.

The Military Commission operates under its own set of rules, which doesn't include the right to a speedy trial.

"From the very best defense attorneys to acquiescence to various personal requests," Joe Connor observed, "including ones for Middle Eastern food, these terrorists are being allowed to drag the process on indefinitely. Through burying the prosecution team in legal minutiae and keeping them from their families for months at a time, it is the terrorists who are torturing our earnest public servants."

Among the means by which the Gitmo detainees—who have their own portable DVD players, wireless headphones, and access to satellite TV and PlayStation—have sidetracked the hearings include complaints of strange noises and vibrations in their cells, allegations of being subject to physical and psychological torture, threats to fire their attorneys, and their refusal to be escorted by female guards. The defendants are allowed to bring prayer mats into the courtroom, where the direction of Mecca is marked on a wall, and proceedings stop to allow them to engage in prayer.

The lifestyle of the Gitmo internees compares starkly with the conditions in Cuba's own maximum-security prison located on the Cuban side of Guantánamo, where inmates are stuffed into dark tiny cells, denied sunlight or medical treatment, beaten, and tortured. As described by José Daniel Ferrer, a Cuban dissident who was incarcerated there, the American Gitmo is a "kindergarten" next to its Cuban sibling.

One morning, two observers of the proceedings sitting in the gallery at the invitation of defense counsel were a male interpreter whom the KSM defense team was attempting to have granted the necessary security clearance, and Sharlette Holdman, a prominent death sentence mitigation strategist. Standing in the gallery before the day's proceedings began, the two bowed and gave a military-style salute to and traded other friendly hand gestures with KSM. Later, when the youngest members of the 9/11 families, aged nineteen and twenty-two, were alone in the gallery, Holdman audibly referred to KSM as her "buddy" and "pal." KSM, while turning to acknowledge her, tauntingly smiled and smirked at the two young adults, whose fathers had been murdered at his direction. The 9/11 observers reported the matter and had Holdman and the interpreter removed from the room. Jean felt this incident was calculated and manipulative. As Connor recounted, "We witnessed pure evil in the courtroom that morning."

During the press briefing with Gitmo media that occurs at the end of each week of hearings, 9/11 family members recounted the event. They observed that defense counsel appeared to relish stringing along the proceedings, showing off, and upsetting the prosecutor and the observer families. "I'd like to see more forceful decision-making in the courtroom," one said.

The twenty-two-year-old at whom KSM had smirked is the daughter of a man who died in the North Tower. She confided to Joe Connor that "she felt guilty she didn't hate the terrorists." Connor responded, "Like the FALN, they are not worth our hatred, not deserving of it. What matters is our families' lives, our lives, and justice."

# Postscript

On the day that President Obama assumed office in 2009, there were 242 detainees in the U.S. military prison at Guantánamo Bay. On the day he left office, forty-one inmates remained. Regarding Gitmo, President Trump stated, "We are keeping it open ... and we're gonna load it up with some bad dudes, believe me, we're gonna load it up." Trump plans to keep Camp Justice open as well.

*

Numerous attempts over the decades to have Assata Shakur extradited, including a Congressional resolution, all have proven unsuccessful. In the fall of 1998, the FBI drew up a proposal to trade five captured Cuban spies for Shakur, but Cuban authorities refused to discuss the deal. In 2013, on the fortieth anniversary of Officer Foerster's death, the FBI designated Shakur the first woman to appear on the bureau's most wanted terrorists list, with a combined FBI and New Jersey State award of $2 million for her capture.

During the final week of the Obama administration, the White House announced an agreement on law enforcement cooperation with Cuba, including sharing information on international criminal activity such as human trafficking and terrorism. Various Congressmen cried foul over the deal, because of objections to sharing sensitive information with the Castro regime and that it did not require the island nation to extradite high-profile U.S. fugitives it has been harboring. New Jersey State Police head Rick Fuentes declared, "Their omission from this agreement and from the negotiations-at-large is so glaring as to signal a clear intent by the Obama administration to ignore these fugitives. By burning the last bridge to this administration's opportunity to gain their negotiated return, families who have long suffered the consequences of their terrorist acts and law enforcement everywhere in this country have been shown the back of the hand."

Many government officials, including President Trump, continue to expressly call for Shakur's return. In response, senior Cuban officials have consistently made it clear that extradition is off the table as an issue for consideration.

Shakur remains living openly in Cuba. She has written an autobiography, been featured in a documentary, and become a cult figure. The godmother of slain rapper Tupac Shakur, Shakur is lauded in a rap song called "A Song for Assata." Its lyrics include the following, "Shot twice wit her hands up, Police questioned but shot before she answered, One Panther lost his life, the other ran for his, Scandalous the police were as they kicked and beat her." The unseemliness of the plaudits for Shakur is encapsulated by an oft-repeated sentiment of Dominick Dunne, the former best-selling author and television personality, whose daughter was murdered by an ex-boyfriend. "I'm sick of being asked to weep for killers. We've lost our sense of outrage."

\*

William Morales also remains in Cuba to this day, free to enjoy visits by his son, a father-son bonding that Joe and Tom Connor, as well as Adrian Berger, have been robbed of. At the end of an op-ed penned by Joe Connor and published by *The Wall Street Journal* in January 2017, days after the second clemency for Oscar López Rivera was announced, Connor refers to William Morales' continued grant of political asylum by Cuba. "Perhaps those who have lauded the clemency for López Rivera will find it in the interest of justice to speak out for Morales' extradition to the U.S. Nothing will bring my father back, but justice is something I still believe in."

The vigil for Morales' extradition wears on Mary Connor Tully. "I just want to live long enough to see Morales returned."

*

Most of the Nationalist Party and FALN members were Catholic. In the Catechism of the Catholic Church is the admonition that sin is a personal act, and "we have a responsibility for the sins committed by others when we cooperate in them." But there also is the Lord's Prayer, which, on March 1, 1954, the four Nationalists recited before firing on the House of Representatives. Joe Connor continues to ponder the meaning of the fifth petition of The Lord's Prayer, which reads, "And forgive us our trespasses, as we forgive them that trespass against us." Those words reflect the principle that we cannot ask for forgiveness for ourselves unless we also are willing to extend it to others. The prayer also teaches that, while we must decide which behaviors we can and cannot personally accept, we must leave the judging to God in order that we may live our lives at peace. As a practicing Catholic, Connor admits that "my lack of forgiveness has bothered me." Connor has spoken to his priests about the petition's admonition. "They've assured me that I am under no obligation to forgive those who do not seek forgiveness. This has made me again question why so often those who perpetrate the crimes are viewed by many as angels, entitled to forgiveness, while those who push for justice are demonized."

\*

Deenie and her second husband, Alan Ettenson, were blessed in March 1981 with a daughter, Hilary, who joined Adrian as a part of their family. Joséf and Cilly Berger remained close with Deenie, Adrian, and the entire Ettenson family. The Bergers never recovered from the loss of their only child. When Joséf was eulogized in November 1984, his rabbi declared that he was finally at peace, because a part of him had died nine years earlier. Adrian would become a chemical engineer, work for the same company his father did, and mourn for a man he never had the opportunity to know.

Cilly, now in her mid-90s, is in fading health. When the news of Oscar López Rivera's second clemency became public, Deenie chose not to relay it to her. Days later, on January 23, 2017, Deenie received a call from her mother-in-law. "Her short-term memory is quite poor. And she has to be told of basic things like putting on a coat to go out in the winter. But she called to remind me to say *Yahrzeit* (the memorial prayer for the dead) the next day. The memory of her son's death is burned in her brain."

\*

When López Rivera's sentence was commuted by President Obama, the Cuban Communist Party expressed its delight that "the imprisoned independence fighter, whose unjust sentence was reduced after 35 years and eight months in U.S. penitentiaries, was transferred to his native country." President Raul Castro proclaimed, "Please accept our fraternal congratulations on behalf of the Party, government and people, who share the joy of your liberation. We await you in Cuba, with all the honors and affection you deserve, whenever it may be possible for you."

In November 2017, Oscar López Rivera visited Cuba for the first time, receiving the "Order of Solidarity" at a ceremony at the José Marti Memorial in Havana. There was speculation that López Rivera met with William Morales. If that happened, it would have been a reunification of two men in the spiritual birthplace of the organization they had led. One that cost each of them, and so many others, dearly.

# ACKNOWLEDGMENTS

ANY BOOK, PARTICULARLY an historical one, is far from the product of only its authors.

Many thanks to Buddy Howe, Tom Mullany, and Joe Quinn for their recollections of Frank Connor as a youth, young adult and father, and of Washington Heights and suburban New Jersey in the 1950s, '60s and '70s. Their ability to vividly recreate the "old days" was phenomenal.

The recounting of the Fraunces Tavern bombing was enabled by three remarkable men—Dave Erskine, Charlie Murray, and Bill Newhall—each of whom sat at the table closest to the bomb yet miraculously survived. They provided vital and discerning information with great eloquence about that day and its aftermath. Bill and Charlie also furnished insights on work life at Morgan Guaranty Trust, and Bill assisted in bringing to life the parole hearing for Oscar López Rivera. Despite suffering severe injuries, each would carry on his life with fortitude and courage. We also wish to acknowledge the help of John Harrison and Richard Shadick in recounting the Fraunces Tavern bombing.

Our thanks to Michael Boos for the education he provided us regarding the *Citizens United* decision and its vast implications, to Tim Redman for background on Judge Leighton, to Colonel Rick Fuentes, former New Jersey State Police Superintendent, for his insights on law enforcement and its quest to have Morales and other fugitives returned to the U.S., and to Sergey Kadinsky for helping us to tell the story of the Morales-Shakur Center. Reporters and columnists understand so much, and we benefited from the smarts and knowledge of Mike Kelly and Phil Messing. Moreover, many facets of the book, including the discussion of the clemencies, the ongoing battle against terrorism, and the underpinnings of fundamental concepts such as forgiveness and justice, profited greatly from the insights and wisdom of Debra Burlingame, Ed Smith, and Rabbi Aryeh Spero. And thanks to Richard Curtis for his generous assistance in helping to restructure the book to make it a better one, to Harry Hamburg for his recollections of taking photos in the aftermath of the Fraunces Tavern bombing, and to Dave Buckmaster for reading the draft and providing invaluable feedback.

The review of the rise and fall of the FALN, including the investigations, arrests, and prosecutions of its members, would not have been possible without the enormous and generous assistance given us by Rick Hahn (who also provided drafts of his two comprehensive and scholarly books on the FALN), Deborah Devaney, Tom Engel, Jeremy Margolis, and Don Wofford (who was extremely generous of his time over the course of several interviews). We are thankful to help preserve the memory of how they and many others acted with great courage, fortitude, and wisdom in fighting the war against the FALN. Many thanks also to Professor Antonio de la Cova for conveying his deep knowledge of and intuitions about the workings and structure of the FALN and the possible identity of the person who planted the bomb in Fraunces Tavern.

Our deep appreciation and respect goes out to Tony Senft and Don Sadowy, heroic Bomb Squad officers who helped us to recount the horrific 1982 New Year's Eve bombings and describe the inner workings of the NYPD Bomb Squad. We also wish to note that Tony and his wife Carol started The Police Self-Support Group, of which Tony is president. It provides comfort for officers who have been wounded physically or have experienced emotional trauma. Contributions to this worthy organization can be sent to Tony at 299 Pond Road, Bohemia, NY 11716-3410.

Family members of the victims were critical to our ability to offer a complete story of the shattering consequences of the Fraunces Tavern and Mobil Oil bombings, which resonate to this day. One is Bruce Steinberg, through whom we were able to tell of the wonderful person that his murdered brother Charles was. Another is Kelley Murray, who provided us with a remarkably poignant and honest summary of the impact of the Fraunces Tavern bombing on her father, herself, and the entire Murray family.

We are especially grateful to Deenie Berger Ettenson, who not only sensitively and honestly recounted the life of Alex Berger and the impact of his death on his family but, also, gave us a treasure trove of original documents about the FALN and Fraunces Tavern bombing. Deenie's persistence over the years in maintaining the memory of her husband and seeking justice for him is extraordinary.

Of course, the book could not have been written without the assistance and cooperation of the Connor and Schlag families. We are deeply appreciative to Tom Connor, Donald Schlag, Jean Schlag-Nebbia, and Tomoko Schlag for their remembrances. And, of course, to Joe's wife Danielle, son Frank, and daughter Kathleen, stepfather Gerry, and mom Mary, who continues to have great clarity of recollection and was able to provide much color and detail, both orally and through her beautiful writings, in addition to support and encouragement. Mary remains an inspiration and role model to her family.

Joe notes that his intent in writing this story was to provide a reminder that long before the Twin Towers bombing of 1993 and the Oklahoma City bombing in 1995, there were other heinous terrorist attacks on US soil, including the one at Fraunces Tavern that took the lives of four remarkable men. He also wants Americans never to forget the infamous clemencies by President Clinton. The fight that he and a few other private citizens waged against the clemencies provided many low and high points in his life.

# Acknowledgments

Ironically, Joe finally began to write his story on September 10, 2001 on the commute home from Manhattan, exactly two years to the day after the FALN clemencies. He started with these words:

> There is likely no event in a man's life as monumental as the birth of his children; particularly his first child. Being a second child, I feel justified in making that statement. Please my Kathleen, do not hold this against me. You and your brother Frank are by far the greatest things your mother and I have ever been associated with. Joy intertwined with the overwhelming sense of responsibility for a new life and the feeling that you will forever be connected with that of another softens the hardest of men.
>
> Perhaps equally monumental would be the loss of a child. Luckily, I have not had to experience such pain, but my mother and grandmother have not been so fortunate.

Finally, Joe wishes to note that this story would never have been told without Jeff and his wife, Linda. Jeff, until 2016 a stranger, immersed himself into our family with both compassion and discipline, creating this account of our lives. He showed us that justice is not "Just Us," which we had begun to feel, but that others care. The Connor family is forever in Jeff and Linda's debt.

Jeff would like to express the admiration that he and so many others have for Joe. Joe has been unyielding in his efforts over the decades to preserve the memory of his father and demand justice for him, as well as to point out the continuous threat that terrorism poses. And he has done this in the face of opposition, indifference, and difficult odds, and at great personal cost.

Jeff thanks his wife, Linda, deeply for her invaluable insights, edits, and suggestions. Nothing of significance that he has ever written has been done without her integral support.

At the heart of the book is the story of Frank Connor. Joe remains thankful every day for the time, all too brief, that he spent with his father, and the love between the two of them, which time cannot erase.

# BIBLIOGRAPHY

Ali Soufan, *The Black Banners: The Inside Story of 9/11 and the War Against al-Qaeda* (W.W. Norton & Company, 2011)

Barbara Olson, *The Final Days: The Last, Desperate Abuses of Power by the Clinton White House* (Regnery Publishing, 2001)

Bill Gertz, *Breakdown: How America's Intelligence Failure Led to September 11,* (Regnery Publishing, 2002)

*Boricuas: Influential Puerto Rican Writings—An Anthology* (edited by Roberto Santiago, One World, 1995)

Bryan Burrough, *Days of Rage: America's Radical Underground, the FBI, and the Forgotten Age of Revolutionary Violence* (Penguin Books, 2016)

Candice DeLong & Elisa Petrini, *Special Agent: My Life on the Front Lines as a Woman in the FBI* (Hyperion, 2001)

Cesar Ayala & Rafael Bernabe, *Puerto Rico in the American Century: A History Since 1898* (The University of North Carolina Press, 2007)

Congressional Research Services, *Cuba: Issues for the 114th Congress* (Mark Sullivan, Specialist in Latin American Affairs, November 2016)

David Bossie, *Intelligence Failure: How Clinton's National Security Policy Set the Stage for 9/11* (WorldNetDaily Books 2004)

David Klaidman, *Kill or Capture: The War on Terror and the Soul of the Obama Presidency* (Mariner Books, 2013)

Desmond Tutu, *No Future Without Forgiveness* (Doubleday, 1999)

Dick Morris, *Rewriting History* (Regan Books, 2004)

Federico Tovar, *Albizu Campos: Puerto Rican Revolutionary* (Plus Ultra Educational Publishers, 1971)

Fraunces Tavern Museum, *54 Pearl Street: If These Walls Could Talk ...* (2006)

Gordon Cucullu, *Inside Gitmo: The True Story Behind the Myths of Guantánamo Bay* (HarperLuxe, 2009)

Harry Truman, *Where the Buck Stops: The Personal and Private Writings of Harry S. Truman* (edited by Margaret Truman, New Word City, 2015)

Howard Zehr, *The Little Book of Restorative Justice* (Good Books, 2014)

James Traub, *City on a Hill: Testing the American Dream at City College* (Addison-Wesley Publishing, 1994)

# Bibliography

J.E. Fishman, *Dynamite: A Concise History of the NYPD Bomb Squad* (Verbitrage, 2014)

Jeff Ingber, *Resurrecting the Street: Overcoming the Greatest Operational Crisis in History* (2012)

Jeffery Crouch, *The Presidential Pardon Power* (University Press of Kansas, 2009)

Jeffery Crouch, *The President's Power to Commute: Is It Still Relevant?*, 9 U. St. Thomas L.J. 681 (2012).

Jim O'Neil & Mel Fazzino, *A Cop's Tale: NYPD The Violent Years* (Barricade Books, 2009)

John Fund & Hans von Spakovsky, *Obama's Enforcer: Eric Holder's Justice Department* (Broadside Books, 2014)

John Marshall, *The Life of George Washington* (1807)

Karl Rogers, *Citizens United* (2016)

Lawrence Wright, *The Looming Tower: Al-Qaeda and the Road to 9/11* (Vintage Books, 2007)

*Latinos and Citizenship: The Dilemma of Belonging* (edited by Suzanne Oboler, Palgrave Macmillan, 2006)

Louis Mizell, Jr. *Target U.S.A.: The Inside Story of the New Terrorist War* (John Wiley & Sons, Inc., 1998)

Louis Perez, *Cuba and the United States: Ties of Singular Intimacy* (The University of Georgia Press, 2003)

Louise Richardson, *What Terrorists Want: Understanding the Enemy, Containing the Threat* (Random House, 2007)

M.E. Brandon, *Economic, Political and Social History of Puerto Rico: From 1898 to 1990* (2012)

Marc Aronson & Marina Budhos, *Sugar Changed the World: A Story of Magic, Spice, Slavery, Freedom, and Science* (Clarion Books, 2010)

Margaret Power, *From Freedom Fighters to Patriots: The Successful Campaign to Release the FALN Political Prisoners, 1980–1999* (Centro Journal, Spring 2013)

Mario Murillo, *Islands of Resistance: Puerto Rico, Vieques, and U.S. Policy* (Seven Stories Press, 2001)

Mark Owen, *No Easy Day: The Firsthand Account of the Mission That Killed Osama bin Laden* (New American Library, 2014)

Mark Rudd, *Underground: My Life with SDS and the Weathermen,* (HarperCollins, 2009)

National Parks of New York Harbor, *George Washington's New York: How England's Treasured Colony Became the Capital of a New Nation* (Official Walking Tour)

Nelson Denis, *War Against All Puerto Ricans: Revolution and Terror in America's Colony* (Nation Books, 2015)

Nelson Mandela, *Long Walk to Freedom* (Little, Brown and Company, 1994)

Oscar López Rivera, *Oscar López Rivera: Between Torture and Resistance* (PM Press, 2013)

Pedro Albizu Campos, *Free Puerto Rico* (Prism Key Press, 2013)

## Bibliography

Peggy Noonan, *The Case Against Hillary Clinton* (Regan Books, 2000)

Pete Earley, *The Hot House: Life Inside Leavenworth Prison* (Bantam Books, 1992)

Rafael Cancel Miranda, *Puerto Rico Independence is a Necessity: On the Fight against U.S. Colonial Rule* (Pathfinder Press, 1998)

Richard English, *Terrorism: How to Respond* (Oxford University Press, 2009)

Richard Esposito & Ted Gerstein, *Bomb Squad: A Year Inside the Nation's Most Exclusive Police Unit* (Hyperion, 2007)

Richard Hahn, *American Terrorists: The True Story of the FALN, America's Most Prolific Terrorist Group* (2011)

Richard Hahn, *Terror's Dawn: The History of the FALN and the Beginning of Terrorism in America* (2007)

Robert "Buzz" Patterson, *Dereliction of Duty: The Eyewitness Account of How Bill Clinton Compromised America's National Security* (Regnery Publishing, 2003)

Ronald Fernandez, The *Disenchanted Island: Puerto Rico and the United States in the Twentieth Century* (Praeger, 1996)

Ronald Fernandez, *Los Macheteros: The Wells Fargo Robbery and the Violent Struggle for Puerto Rican Independence* (Prentice Hall Press, 1987)

Roberta Belli, *Effects and effectiveness of law enforcement intelligence measures to counter homegrown terrorism: A case study on the Fuerzas Armadas de Liberación Nacional (FALN)* (Final Report to the Science & Technology Directorate, U.S. Department of Homeland Security, August 2012)

Rosemary Palermo, *Samuel Fraunces: The Life and Times of a Revolutionary War Hero, Spy, and Man of Color* (2015)

Rudolph Adams Van Middledyk, *The History of Puerto Rico From the Spanish Discovery to the American Occupation* (1903)

Sonia Sotomayor, *My Beloved World* (Vintage Books, 2013)

Stephen Bowman, *When the Eagle Screams: America's Vulnerability to Terrorism* (Birch Lane Press, 1994)

Susan Herman, *Parallel Justice for Victims of Crime* (The National Center for Victims of Crime, 2010)

Susan Miller, *After the Crime: The Power of Restorative Justice Dialogues Between Victims and Violent Offenders* (New York University Press, 2011)

Stephen Hunter & John Bainbridge, Jr., *American Gunfight: The Plot to Kill President Truman and The Shoot-out That Stopped It* (Simon & Schuster, 2005)

Tad Szulc, *Fidel: A Critical Portrait* (1986)

*The 9/11 Commission Report: Final Report of the National Commission on Terrorist Attacks Upon the United States* (W.W. Norton & Company, Inc., 2004)

# Bibliography

*The Puerto Rican Movement: Voices from the Diaspora* (edited by Andrés Torres & José Velazquez, Temple University Press, 1998)

Vicente Fox, *Revolution of Hope: The Life, Faith, and Dreams of a Mexican President* (Penguin Group, 2007)

*Violence, Terrorism, and Justice* (edited by R. G. Frey & Christopher Morris, Cambridge University Press, 1991)

Vionette Negretti, *Times of Upheaval* (2012)

William LeoGrande & Peter Kornbluh, *Back Channel to Cuba: The Hidden History of Negotiations Between Washington and Havana* (The University of North Carolina Press, 2014)

William Slater, *Puerto Rican Terrorists: A Possible Threat to U.S. Energy Installations?* (A Rand Note, 1981)

# ABOUT THE AUTHORS

Jeff Ingber is a former financial industry executive who now
consults on anti-money-laun-
dering and other regulatory
compliance matters. His writings include numerous novels,
screenplays, short stories, and
articles. (Please visit Jeff's web-
site at www.jeffingber.com for

more information.) A graduate of Queens College and
NYU Law School, Jeff lives in Jersey City with his wife.

*

Joe Connor is a recognized spokesman and advocate on anti-terrorism and national security matters. His articles have appeared in numerous publications, and he is a regular guest on various well-known local and nationally syndicated TV and radio programs. Joe  conceived of and co-authored the novel, *The New Founders*, which brings the Founding Fathers alive in 21st Century America. A 1988 graduate of Villanova University, Joe is married and lives in the New York metropolitan area with his wife and two college-age children. He works in the financial services industry.

# INDEX

**Y**
Young Lords, 78–79, 81, 291
Yulín Cruz, Carmen, 359

**Z**
Zehr, Howard, 320–321

Made in the USA
Middletown, DE
02 February 2023

23255631R00236